Every Trail Has A Story

EVERY TRAIL HAS A STORY

Heritage Travel In Canada

BOB HENDERSON

Foreword by James Raffan

NATURAL HERITAGE BOOKS
TORONTO

Published by Natural Heritage/Natural History Inc.
P.O. Box 95, Station O, Toronto, Ontario M4A 2M8
www.naturalheritagebooks.com

All visuals unless otherwise indicated are courtesy of the author.
Original maps by Mark J. Smith.

Design by Blanche Hamill, Norton Hamill Design
Edited by Jane Gibson
Printed and bound in Canada by Hignell Book Printing, Winnipeg, Manitoba

The text in this book was set in a typeface named Simoncini Garamond

Library and Archives Canada Cataloguing in Publication

Henderson, Bob, 1956-
    Every trail has a story : heritage travel in Canada / Bob Henderson ; foreword by James Raffan.

Includes bibliographical references and index.
ISBN 1-896219-97-7

    1. Canada—Historical geography. 2. Canada—History. 3. Canada—Description and travel. 4. Trails—Canada. 5. Water trails—Canada. I. Title.

FC76.H45 2005   971   C2004-907326-5

Canada Council   Conseil des Arts
for the Arts   du Canada

Canadä

ONTARIO ARTS COUNCIL
CONSEIL DES ARTS DE L'ONTARIO

Natural Heritage/Natural History Inc. acknowledges the financial support of the Canada Council for the Arts and the Ontario Arts Council for our publishing program. We acknowledge the support of the Government of Ontario through the Ontario Media Development Corporation's Ontario Book Initiative. We also acknowledge the financial support of the Government of Canada through the Book Publishing Industry Development Program (BPIDP) and the Association for the Export of Canadian Books.

This book is dedicated to C.S. (Stuart) Mackinnon.
Stu was an important teacher for me in my early days of graduate
school in 1979–80. Stu encouraged me to follow my own path as a
budding historian/storyteller. There is no one for whom I would have
been more pleased to first deliver a copy of this book. Sadly, Stu passed
away just before I had planned to send him an early draft.

Contents

PART THREE – PEOPLE

List of Maps

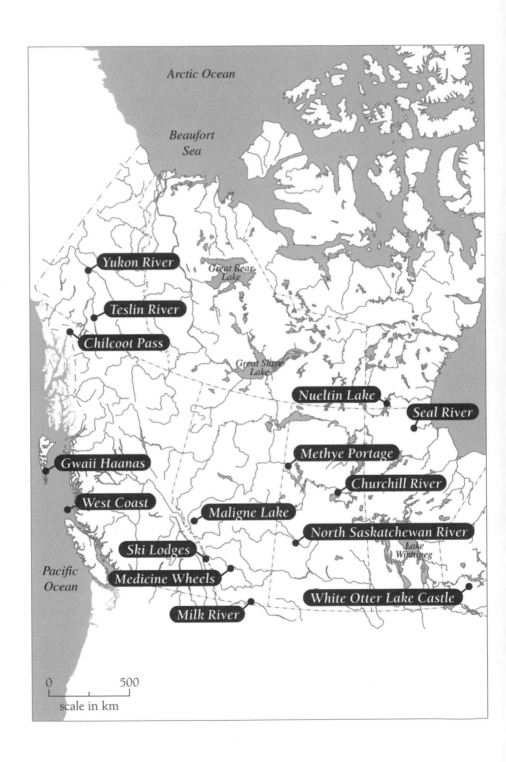

Arctic Ocean

Beaufort Sea

Great Bear Lake

Great Slave Lake

Yukon River

Teslin River

Chilcoot Pass

Nueltin Lake

Seal River

Gwaii Haanas

Methye Portage

Churchill River

West Coast

Maligne Lake

North Saskatchewan River

Lake Winnipeg

Ski Lodges

Pacific Ocean

Medicine Wheels

White Otter Lake Castle

Milk River

0   500

scale in km

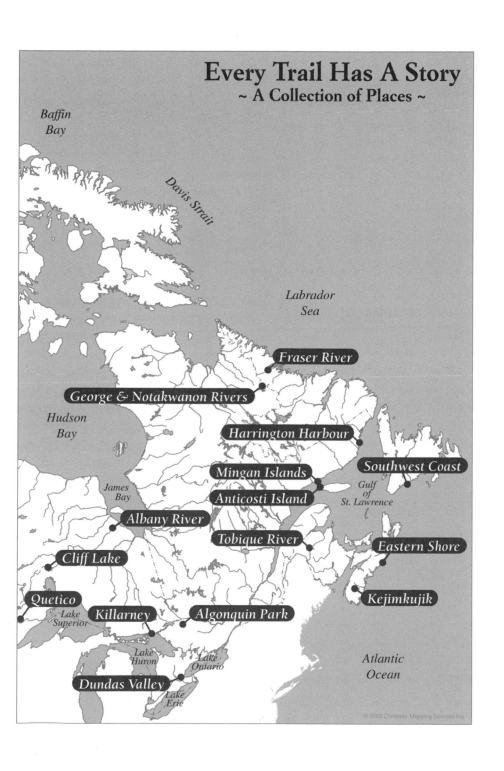

Foreword

Bob Henderson was known to me long before we actually met. I began teaching outdoor education in the 1970s and learned of a chap at McMaster University who was doing interesting things in the outdoors with university students. It wasn't really physical education although that, apparently, was his department. And it wasn't formal history he was teaching, although people said that he had a passion for the past. And neither was pedagogy his discipline, although the term "outdoor education" was often used to describe what it was that this enigmatic young lecturer did with his students.

It was his approach to teaching that piqued my interest. It was never enough for him to engage students in a scholarly discussion about the connections between land and people. No. Apparently, most of his courses involved some kind of experience in the out-of-doors. To get an "A" you had to travel into the lands you'd been discussing in class. You had to strap on a pack and wade through muck. You had to pick up a paddle and bend into the wind. You had to burn socks by a roaring fire. You had to hear the stories punctuated by owl song or the crack of winter ice. That was Bob Henderson's way, or so I heard.

We eventually did meet. It may have been in the Beluga Motel in Churchill, Manitoba, way back when. Bob was with a group on their way home from somewhere north of sixty. Me, the same. As parsimonious canoeists (possibly redundant), we had both found the cheapest hot showers (and saggiest beds) on Hudson Bay. I remember thinking that he seemed younger than the image in my mind. And he seemed a damn sight fitter and more angular than your typical fat-cat university professor. But even then the names and stories from literature rolled off his tongue with disquieting ease.

After that, we began to communicate more regularly. He wrote the most entertaining reference letters for students who would move from his program to mine. These would always be written in his almost unintelligible scrawl and usually on the back of a piece of already used paper, with parenthetical insertions stuffed between lines and up the margins. Obscure citations. Anecdotes. Ecophilosophy. Trip notes. Poems. Song lyrics. Whatever came to mind.

And we'd cross paths at conferences. At one of these, around a campfire one Bark Lake Saturday night, I got a glimmer of the enigmatic and colourful character behind the scrawl. One minute he was serenely strumming his guitar, chatting between songs about lyrics and wilderness. But in the wee hours, he morphed into a red-eye Rolling Stone, complete with Mick Jagger hip thrusts, Keith Richards guitar riffs – the whole rock-and-roll Magilla.

On the strength of these connections, I invited him to speak to one of my classes about his take on outdoor and environmental education. Expecting him to show pictures and tell stories of times on the trail with his students, I set up a screen and slide projector – that never got used. He turned up with a tape player, a stack of audio tapes and wailed on for a couple of hours about how musicians were the vanguard of new environmental thinking. It was a pretty off-the-wall approach to teaching and learning that was, in the end, totally refreshing. That is Bob.

But whatever the topic, be it history, historical travel, ecophilosophy, enviromusic, paddling, bannock baking, outdoor education, his message always returns sooner or later to the same heuristic: if you want to learn anything about anything, you need to immerse yourself in it, you need to experience your subject fully, deeply and preferably with food cooked over an open fire. And, if what you're wanting to learn happens to be environmentalism or Canadian history, you need to read and listen broadly and to get out on the land, preferably under your own steam and certainly, though not always, away from urbanity.

Until now (with the possible exception of his doctoral dissertation which, like all theses, should be approached by casual readers with extreme caution) the Hendersonian view has always been presented piecemeal, in presentations, chapters in books, articles, columns, but never as one cohesive whole. And that's why the publication of this book, his first, is so exciting. For years I presumed that the only way to get full measure of Bob Henderson's unique and eclectic approach to life and living would be his student and go on a trip with him. For most of us, that will never happen. This book, I'm happy to say, is the next best thing. It's the world according to Bob.

Every Trail Has A Story is a generative blend of wilderness places, practices and people, and it's like nothing else I've encountered. It takes readers to places from Methye Portage, Maguse River and the Mingan Islands to Nellie Lake, Running Rock, Jane's Hill and the Committee's Punch Bowl. You'll explore practices from snowshoeing to rock painting and making "cougar milk" by the light of the silvery moon. You'll meet people from A.Y. Jackson, J.B. Tyrrell, P.G. Downes and R.M. Rilke to Robert Pirsig, Michael Bliss and Bertrand Russell with cameo appearances from Yi Fu Tuan, Krishnamurti, Timberline Jim, Esther Keyser, Ian Tamblyn, Mark Twain, Samuel Hearne, Hugh Brody and some 17th century Japanese poet called Matsuo Bashō. Phew!

This book is vintage Henderson. He's got the map of Canada in his head, an eclectic canon of sources at his fingertips and the wilderness in his bones. And binding it all is a narrative thread that eventually stitches ideas into meaning. There's lots here to keep you warm, plenty to chew on and stories to engender a dream. It's funny. It's challenging. It's quixotic and occasionally obtuse. But there is no doubt in my mind that those of us who follow Bob's trail through these pages will become actors in making the world a better place. It's just the thing for a long winter's night or a lingering read by campfire light.

— JAMES RAFFAN

Preface

*My subject is history as a pleasure, as an agreeable and profitable
way of spending such leisure as an exacting world may permit. I am
not a professional historian, but I have read much history
as an amateur. My purpose is to try to say what I have derived
from history, and what many others, I am convinced, could derive,
without aiming at becoming specialists.*
— BERTRAND RUSSELL[1]

That's perfect! That's what I'm all about. Bertrand Russell provides a
concise epigram to capture my personal view as an author for the forth-
coming pages. I can only add that beyond the reading of history for
leisure is the quest here to render the historical text as felt experience.
Exploration in the library and exploration on the land go hand in hand,
text in one hand and paddle/ski pole/reins in the other. This book
could possibly be called "Local histories I have come to know." While
that doesn't sound right, it is an accurate description of much of the
text to follow. Over a twenty-year period, *Kanawa, Explore, Nastawgan* and others, all Canadian outdoor travel magazines, have provided
me with an outlet for sharing local histories with an attention to both
the then and now. My trips never seem that exciting when compared
to the places, peoples and historical practices in question of my historical precursors. Indeed I've often had the same feeling Sigurd Olson
describes when completing a 1950s trip down the Churchill River. To
close his classic *The Lonely Land*, he wrote:

> We tried to satisfy them all [newspaper reporters] but somehow our
> answers sounded flat and innocuous. There was really nothing we had

done that was exciting or that would make a good story, no hairbreadth escapes or great dangers, nothing but a daily succession of adventures of the spirit, the sort of thing that could not make headlines. Our newspaper friends, I know, were disappointed. They had expected something sensational, but nothing we gave them sounded good.[2]

There is an adventure of the spirit I am hoping to convey in these pages. Every trail does have a story and I am an avocation historian in the storytelling tradition. And connecting to these stories broadens and deepens one's personal perspective of life. And this propels an adventure of the spirit with time and space. The wise geographer, J. Wreford Watson, once wrote, "the geography of any place results from how we see it, as much as from what may be."[3]

Every trail has a story has been a defining axiom that begins the experience of planning each new trip year in, year out. It is a good way to go. In Canada, it is a way still open to us and this is, while not totally unique in the world, a special quality of enormous potential for Canadian outdoor travel. It is my hope that together we can tap this potential for places in pockets of Canada I have touched down on as a visitor, for modes of travel I have "tried" or often practised, and for people I have met imaginatively or met in the flesh along the way. And by the way, while I have done my best to get my resources complete, please accept my apologies for those that are missing.

Absolutely central to this reading of history as a leisure pleasure and as a personally felt experience, is the ability to imagine. From the poet, Wallace Stevens comes, "Imagination, we have it, because we don't have enough without it."[4]

Acknowledgements

I'm one of those people who, with each new book, turns first to the acknowledgements. Those that are involved or influence a writing project provide that all-important initial insight. Hey, perhaps I'll know someone. I do the same for new records, (oops CDs). The musicians or producers involved can tell you a lot about the upcoming music. Certain musicians and producers, to my mind, seem to ensure quality.

That said, I'm anxious about writing acknowledgements for this book. When your writing project is about travel throughout Canada east to west, and your claim to any historical expertise rests on an avocational "check in" to local histories you have come to explore, you have all-too-many people to thank. Against my own enjoyment of starting with acknowledgements as a reader and for fear of leaving too many people out, I will opt for the general category and mass grouping approach.

In the reading of a landscape and a text there is first, and foremost I think, reading as a story. Telling the stories of the place is a sharing activity, and one I have enjoyed with so many. There are students, fellow guides and tripping partners, coffee break friends and teachers all along my trail. Folks that stand out as storytellers and listeners on my trail include Stu Mackinnon, Harvey Scott, David Taylor, Linda Leckie, Don Standfield, Bruce Murphy, Margot Peck, Jeff Cameron, Gord Henderson, James Cottrell, Steve Terhljan and Zabe MacEachren.

There is also the reading of a landscape and/or text as interpretation. Here you, the reader or listener, produce context. You build themes to landscape/text. You begin to see the invisible and unsaid. I have many friends with whom stories are shared more centrally in this vein. They include John Doormar, Chris Blythe, Mike Beedell and Craig Macdonald. In this company I am usually a student.

Finally, there is reading as criticism. This story-based book does bring into play some reading of what is omitted or suppressed along with what is strongly asserted. Within these pages Ian MacLaren is well represented in helping me read beyond the written text. Others such as Joss Haiblen and Herb Pohl over decades have helped me read beyond the landscape as straight text. Herb has served in the valuable role as a first reader of the draft manuscript, promising me that he would help by offering the curmudgeon role of a thoughtful evaluation. Thanks goes to Lynda Holland for her suggestions made to Chapter 5, Part 1, "Filling Cabins with Stories."

Also, I must acknowledge the important role that American author (Canadian traveller) Sigurd Olson has had in the general thinking behind this book. This influence will become obvious as one reads these pages. Sigurd, Sig as I like to call him, was my first true serious inroad to northern literature, the mystique of the land, and to the gaining of intimacy that comes with learning the history of a place. I must thank a camp counsellor, David Lang, for this introduction back in 1972.

To my family, Kathleen, Ceilidh, Meghan and Quinn, I owe thanks for allowing me to indulge in reading one more historic passage on the water when all they were interested in was the continued tale of *The Paper Bag Princess* or *The Toilet Paper Tigers*. I am also fully aware of the freedom allowed to me to wander off from family-trip campsite duties to explore for artifacts and the like. Not to mention the freedom and support of time to write (to wander off yet again) during a busy household life. There is inspiration for me in the energy they each bring to life.

I must especially thank Greer Gordon. Greer has been, for me, a most dynamic typist of my archaic pencil-and-paper style. Greer has been a partner in the initial messy job of editing and computer work. Greer has been that first "that's great," "that's crap" friend of the text. I've learned that every writer needs a Greer. You'll be lucky if you find Greer Gordon.

Finally, thanks to all the folks at Natural Heritage Books for believing in this project and all their support along the way.

While I am most appreciative of all the support provided by so many, the final responsibility for accuracy is mine. Any errors brought to the attention of the author and the publisher will be rectified in subsequent editions.

Introduction

You'll sometimes see it in travel articles, or hear it from travel clients, out-door education students and worse still – from outdoor travel guides; I've said it once or twice myself! "We could be the first person to ever stand on this spot." It is a statement steeped in ignorance but understandably well-suited to the Canadian North as Canada and Canadians have evolved. The North, an oscillating concept for Canadians, inspires such a dreamy sentiment of delusions and grandeur of an untouched pristine land. I've learned to distrust this dreamy sentiment. What's more, I fear it.

In reality, someone has been there: a timber cruiser plotting a future logging cut; a Haida craftsman seeking a choice tree for a future dugout canoe; an explorer as "discoverer," a fur trader; a surveyor lost or en route; a Chipewyan (Dene) family hunting caribou; a shipwreck sur-vivor. Canada is an "echoing" land, ringing with stories of human life over centuries. It is not, even in its now remote reaches, an empty place. The ringing may be faint, demanding much of the imagination. It may be pounding, dominating one's perspective and experience. I hope this book can serve to awaken the echoing land so that on your trips by canoe, car, or dog team, the ringing of heritage stories is a steady sound in your ears. It is a good ringing. Think of it as a song, a rhythm. Given this metaphor, what I am doing is sharing my "greatest hits" here.

The ringing may be connected to First Peoples, literally, as with rock formations on the prairies 5,000 years old. The Majorville rock forma-tion (a central boulder pile with radiating rock spokes) dated at 5,000 years, is older than Britain's Stonehenge and speaks to a time when peo-ples on both sides of the Atlantic created artistic rock expressions to celebrate their experience on the land. The ringing may be connected to more contemporary times, as with rock art images painted on cliff surfaces, noted vision quest sites, teepee rings and camps left in April as the snow recedes to be returned to the next season, snowshoes still hanging on tent frames. The ringing may be connected to artists' sketching sites, explorers blazing a trail, gold-rush seekers, settlers' homesteads, early recreationalists, or the ringing may be connected to preserving self-propelled ways of travel best suited to the particular conditions the land presents: canoe, kayak, ski, snowshoe, horseback, dogsledding, walking. The echo may be felt connected more to one place than another. This rendering of the past as a felt experience is a personal thing: experiencing people, practices and places; listening, imagining; being in both the then and now. There is evidence of this storybook landscape, both the obscure and the obvious, on the physical land that is able to be explored from the perspective of both the past and the present.

Perhaps you hear this echoing landscape as song as I have suggested. Australian Aborigines understood the landscape as "songlines" that describe a connected pattern of features and song to be experienced in a walkabout.[1] Perhaps, as Sigurd Olson wrote of the "ancient rhythms" of the earth and as a Montagnais hunter finds his endurance with the beat of the drum, a trance-like rhythm can be heard that…well…makes sense as if you were part of a universal human-to-earth language, part of a greater enterprise of life beyond your mind and body in the realm of spirit and soul. Perhaps this echoing historic presence to the land can be seen as a mirage, a shimmering other world; another world but it is still within this one. One must stretch one's notions of time for a larger participatory consciousness. Perhaps there is nothing mystical at all guiding your perspective. Rather, you are intrigued by the practical material culture of another time. How they fashioned draglines for a toboggan's steep downhill run? How sails were rigged on voyageur canoes? What would be the logical winter route between "A" and "B"? Perhaps you ask concrete but difficult human questions. How did David Thompson prevent mutiny over the Athabasca Pass? How did Isabel Gunn hide her female identity from fellow "male" fur trade labourers?

There is a literature, historical and anthropological, that both informs and enhances today's travel experience. There are travel literature, historical fiction, local histories and biographies. There are people to talk with who remember, who were there. The working task here is to awaken the reader to this echoing land, to negate the notion of the all too readily imagined empty landscape. Indeed, every trail has a story! And because many of these trails by land and water, have, in some cases, remarkably held on to their natural rhythms, there is an imaginative possibility for human rhythms. The wild, the bush, the pristine, the "song of the paddle," the north; choose whichever you like. The Canadian landscape still largely maintains its authentic qualities of wildness, less mediated by modern human technological constructs. Yes, in much of Canada, the snowshoe trail of the winter packeteers and explorers, traders and trappers, and hunting trails can still have us actively camping and travelling in traditional self-propelled ways. It still makes sense, to walk, to paddle, to ride with an animal. But again, happily there is more beyond the activity. There is a literature. Every trail has a story: a story, usually recorded in a book, an old tattered issue of *The Beaver,* an explorer's journal, a collection of Native legends, etc. Such stories, in print, become good friends, comforting and informing. For me, this sentiment is best captured in a 14th-century Japanese text:

> The pleasantest of all diversions is to sit alone under the lamp, a book spread out before you, and to make friends with people of a distant past you have never known.[2]

The trail may be a local one. The story lives under your feet amidst daily patterns of life. My own home of Dundas, the valley town at the head of Lake Ontario, had a canoe portage used by LaSalle, Jolliet and others to avoid Niagara Falls between lakes Ontario and Erie. It was part of an extensive pre-contract Native Peoples' walking trail system. My runs in the Dundas Valley woodlot at times cross or follow the elusive old footpath. I've seen it. I can pause and think of Louis Jolliet (1645–1700) our first Canadian-born internationally known explorer, who followed a route down the Mississippi River hoping it would drain out at the Sea of California. On his return from this trip, after running over forty rapids, his canoe dumped at the final rapid of the 2,500-mile venture. His party met disaster at the Lachine Rapids. Jolliet lost his maps and journals, and lost three companions with whom he had travelled for over four months. Epic stories and travellers connected to a local jogging trail. Just imagine! Supported by such stories, I pick up the jogging pace a little.

When living in Edmonton, near the banks of the North Saskatchewan River, I felt a heightened connection to the fur trade. The river connects so many stories of sweeping geographical proportion. The city, once and still a gateway to the North, served as a gathering spot for western adventures for the likes of the artist Paul Kane, Arctic wanderer John Hornby and the pride of Lakefield, Ontario, explorer George Douglas. It was an imagined fort-like frontier scene in a recent best-selling fiction, Guy Vanderhaeghe's *The Last Crossing*. Often the place gave me the shivers, opening many directions for travel and the many doors to so many more stories. Edmonton, on the banks of the North Saskatchewan – worthy of a pause and gaze back through time.

The trail may be familiar or exotic. Each year I return to a particular canoe route at the same time of year. This standard Canadian Shield route has become a touchstone for me to revisit for its now much-loved stories. On this one five-day route, north of Sudbury, Ontario, there were a murder mystery, a flamboyant pictograph (Native rock art), logging relics, old lodges and an abandoned mining camp – just another "any old place" in the Near North Canadian Shield. Now with over thirty years of familiarity with this route, I have my own stories to tell of life events and life highlights with too many fellow trippers to remember. But, as one may envision the earlier Native and trapper presence on this landscape, one can also bring personal meaning to every familiar campsite, every bend on the shore, every swimming hole and every portage put-in – a collection of memories punctuating a familiar landscape.

The exotic trail is different. All is curious and exciting for its unfamiliarity. As a lad from Ontario, I just had to experience the Mississippi watershed Milk River in southern Alberta with the extensive Writing-On-Stone rock art and associate Sweetgrass Hills. Once the idea took shape, no other trip would do. Petroglyphs, North West Mounted Police stations to stave off whisky runners from America, ancient eroding landforms, long-billed curlews and long-eared owls, and the bizarre possibility of Ogam script etched on certain soft rock dating back thousands of years. You can't just know of such things, you have to go there. Curiosity fuelled by imagination rules! Canada is just packed with such intriguing places for travel.

I remember combing over the maps of Labrador with travel buddy, James Cottrell, and seeing the strange inland fiord of Harp Lake. Would we find a history here? Yes, of course, but it didn't matter, Labrador's Harp Lake was a storied place in the macro way. That was enough for us. This long lake (60 kilometres or about 38 miles) with its river trip out to the coast was a taste of all this area's past, and a spot on a map too exotic not to see. The echo ringing for the Milk River/Sweetgrass

Writing-On-Stone petroglyph site in the Milk River Valley, with the associated Sweetgrass Hills of Montana in the distance, is a long-standing spiritual destination for many Plains Peoples.

Hills was specific and intense as a place far from the familiar. The echo ringing for Labrador's Harp Lake and the Adlatok River was of a generic kind, connecting us to the broad sweep of the overall region and history – faint and mysterious.

But, Harp Lake, Labrador, brings up another point. We did find a few axe marks on a tree or two and a broken snow machine part. We learned of no early settlers in the area or travel-through route. Not much immediate heritage. But it didn't matter, not just because we were in *the* Labrador and felt some of the weight of its collective history simply by being there, but because of the land itself. Beautiful and real, haunting – a comforting thought at times, a landscape rich with "ancient rhythms." As canoe tripper Stewart Coffin has said of Labrador, but I think he would permit me to generalize to the north – the Canadian North; "there is a riddle in the spruce trees."[3] There is a powerful complexity, a relational buzz of authenticity for a more-than-human presence of being in relationship with nature. I assert we do not just want a relationship with the non-human, with nature we need such relational contact. I believe it brings an organic authenticity to life. Perhaps a Norwegian axiom captures this energy of the spirit I struggle to put to language. Norwegian outdoor educators (*friluftsliv* guides) might sum up this energy of the captivating relationship between human beings and the land accordingly – "nature is the true home of culture." Think long and hard on this one. The land is the centre. The heritage is the powerful derivative of the land. Together, they, the land and the heritage, shape the pages that follow.

Once we have a grounding in the place of travel as acquired through a sense of the land, its ancient rhythms and a curiosity for its human traditions, we awaken in us a spirit of being of a place, or at least, glimpsing into it. We move along a continuum from traveller to dweller. We may start to see things as a whole or at least, less fragmented and detached. We learn first to see and hear. Then we learn to care and bear responsibility. Grey Owl, the famous Native impostor and brilliant conservation writer in the 1930s, once wrote in *The Men of the Last Frontier* of the feeling of connection to the trail:

> Each succeeding generation takes up the work of those who pass along leaving behind them a tradition and standard of achievement that must be lived up to by those who would claim a membership in the Brotherhood [and Sisterhood] of the Keepers of the Trail.

To be a "Keeper of the Trail" is to have a spirit of belonging, to have an intelligence, a native or natural intelligence, intelligence not for abstract ideas, but for a place, for places – a big place like Canada. Novelist David James Duncan captures native intelligence in his absorbing novel *The River Why*:

> A native is a man [human] or creature or plant indigenous to a limited geographical area – a space boundaried and defined by mountains, rivers or coastline (not by latitudes, longitudes or state and county lines), with its own peculiar mixture of weeds, trees, bugs, birds, flowers, streams, hills, rocks and critters (including people), its own nuances of rain, wind and seasonal change. Native intelligence develops through an unspoken or soft-spoken relationship with these interwoven things; it evolves as the native involves himself in his region. A non-native awakes in the morning in a body in a bed in a room in a building on a street in a county in a state in a nation. A native awakes in the center of a little cosmos – or a big one, if his intelligence is vast – and he wears this cosmos like a robe, senses the barely perceptible shiftings, migrations, moods and the machinations of its creatures, its growing green things, its earth and sky. ...I don't think you get native intelligence just by wanting it. But maybe through long intimacy with an intelligent native, or with

your native world, you begin to catch it kind of like you catch a cold. It's a cold worth catching.[4]

There is something worth catching "out there" in "the country way back in," or just a little way in. Perhaps these "then and now" stories that follow, will help us all find a native/dwelling intelligence inspired by being part of a tradition on the land and if this connection inspires us to be "keepers" of the trails, of *our* trails, then we should do good work and live well in our places.

The places selected for this book are mostly, relatively speaking, accessible Canada. With family activities and work and whatever else to consider, we usually set our trips to be of the five to two week variety. One doesn't head to Baker Lake in the Arctic with only ten days available. While many places mentioned within are quite remote, many others are possible offshoot short treks from a summer driving trip across Canada east to west or west to east, or north, with lots of gear along or a healthy list of local area outfitters. I use to joke with a friend, Joss Haiblen, about all those experts out there who visited a place once and wrote an "experts" book on the place. We called this phenomena, "90 Minutes over Baker Lake." Given the breadth of the subject matter here, the best I can ever hope to be is a "good visitor" with lofty aspirations. No expert. No pretence. Just a year in/year out set of questions: okay, what now, where to go, what people, place and/or practice are just right now for study and a visit? How should this place be met?

This book is divided into three section headings: Places, Practices and People. These three sections denote organizational themes that inevitably overlap greatly. There are special *places* both in the "out there" and in the "in here" – the exotic and familiar. Some places seem universally energizing or calming. Other places are special for how they impact only you, individually. Several places have helped me attempt to bridge the distance of time and culture and to explore Native Peoples' ceremonial sites. Grand stories such as the Chilkoot Gold Rush of 1897 forever energizes the Yukon landscape. The big horizons of Nueltin Lake, Manitoba and Labrador's Fraser River Valley hold calming, comforting qualities for me in a personal manner.

Likewise, there are special *people* both in the "out there" and "in here." Louis Jolliet is one who for me is close to home. Artist, canoe guide, Tom Thomson in Algonquin is another. Members of the Group of Seven have always been intriguing. Then there are the explorers. Certain explorers and fur traders have grabbed my attention. What personalities! And those earning the label of "Hermit." What personalities indeed! Certain accounts of women on the land have also stood out for the lessons they teach, for the inspiration they offer, and for plain amazement at their incredible stories.

Practices involves the ways of travel that best suit the lands and waters through time. Travel modes evolve but we would be wise to keep an eye on the past. While I mostly live in cities and spend more time travelling by car, bus, plane and train, our travelling precursors were by definition dogsledders, canoemen, horse-packing outfitters, walkers, not hikers, *not* canoeists, but walkers and canoemen or canoe workers. One would be wise to keep close to mind how these travellers carried a load over a portage, made decisions about the wind and rapids, or how they related to the land and other cultures. There are lessons to be learned, do's and don'ts that are both informing and contemplative. I have attempted to move beyond my standard modes of travel to take up the practice that, given heritage insights, best suit the particular terrain for self-propelled (or assisted) travel.

As Russell wrote in his essay, "How to Read and Understand History":

> Our bodily life is confined to a small portion of time and space, but our mental life need not be thus limited…It is a help toward sanity and calm judgement to acquire the habit of seeing contemporary events in their historical setting, and of imagining them as they will appear when they are in the past…We live in the present and in the present we must act; but life is not all action, and action is best when it proceeds from a wide survey in which the present loses the sharpness of its emotional insistence.[5]

A sharing of the present with the past puts the present into a wiser perspective, providing a humbler stance and a broadened vision. I hope this book is an aid towards a richer mental life, a calmer judgment and a greater awareness of Canadian Trails and Waterways.

PART ONE

PLACES

*Geography…is finally knowledge that calls up some-
thing in the land we recognize and respond to. It gives
us a sense of place and a sense of community.*
— BARRY LOPEZ[1]

All self-propelled travellers have places that stick in their minds. They
come to places slowly. A fact: all self-propelled travellers "come to places
slowly." These are places that linger poetically in one's mind years later
and come to the forefront of long distance gazes and imaginative day-
dreams. One might inadvertently ponder at the oddest times, "I wonder
what it is like at 'X' now. This might help explain those "blank looks"
not uncommon to otherwise urban dwellers who are also travellers in
Canada's wild lands.

The Canadian bush, also referred to by Robert Service as the land
"back of beyond," or described by Labrador traveller, Elliott Merrick,
as the "country way back in," is perhaps too immense to be grasped as
a whole, but it is a good exercise of the mind to try. Rather, we connect
with places; places that allow us to extend our thoughts to the whole of
the "beyond" and "way back in." Each such particular place can be
informing to one's spirit or soul. The necessary "time out" must be taken
to consider spiritual meanings and mysteries linked to the place. I have
always loved the idea of the German visionary Goethe, that truth and
mystery were dancing partners.[2] A favourite campsite, a once-visited lake,
a hilltop winter view from snowshoes, a particular waterfall, that one
portage: these areas are all possible "Xs" that inform. Likely they are
places where we have settled, quietly and serenely, allowing the setting
to wrap around us. We all have such places that we have internalized at
the gut level where the relationship between the beholder and the beheld
epitomizes adventure, beauty, truth and mystery. The first three of these
constitute "civilized virtues" for philosopher Alfred North Whitehead.[3]

Nueltin Lake straddling the Manitoba/Nunavut border is such a
place for me. I associate the lake with the best of a 40-plus-day canoe
trip in 1983. I also associate the lake of 225 kilometres (140 miles) in
length with people, although it is relatively without people now.

Labrador casts a spell on the mind. It is beautiful and haunting at the same time. Its stories are harsh and rough. Its travellers go to the extremes though I have found my trips there mostly calm and gentle. One can connect its particular heritage stories to the whole of its landscapes.[4]

The Yukon is a vast sweeping-view country. The place is dominated by the mighty Yukon River, which, in turn, is forever connected with the Gold Rush of 1897–99. My chance discovery of a seasonal Native Peoples' walking migration route from the coast to the interior serves as a constant reminder though, that what the Klondikers perceived as "wilderness" and/or "the frontier" of the North is also a place called "Home" to particular First Nations' groups.

The excursion model of life is well and good and I, like many Canadians, have developed seasonal life patterns based on travel outings near and far – the so-called weekend warrior (I'd rather think of it as wanderer) and the extended tripper. But while one may aspire towards a feeling of home in, say, the boreal forest, we might settle elsewhere. And that elsewhere should not be neglected for the exploration and stories it can offer. I worry that the traveller tends to neglect, or at worst negate, the settled home as a site of inquiry and meaning. We should especially make *places* out of where we live, preferably with a similar level of passion brought to the next exotic destination.

There are sacred and special places out there. You will know it when you are there. It might be so because you have been so told or you might discover one place peculiarly special to just you and a particular time and space. Sacred can mean public – a cultural place – or private, meaning a personal place. Most often the public or cultural ones have layer upon layer of culture significance or sacredness. The private ones just hit you – wow – and stay with you. Both themes of place, the cultural and the personal, can be set apart in our minds and hallowed for the qualities they inspire in us. I have been particularly fascinated with prominent rock sites and ceremonial initiation sites along the transcontinental voyageur canoe routes.

In the general study of Literature, Geography and Outdoor/Environmental Education there is a unifying label now called "place-based" studies. This label points to one of among many signs of an emerging rethinking, focusing us back towards the earth. Eminent Canadian scientist Stan Rowe captures this hope of a return to what we have never left:

Now we are struggling to understand what it might mean to become compliant co-operators with Earth's Ecosystems, hitherto insensitively appropriated as *our* resources and *our* heritage. What monumental conceit![5]

Now we are rediscovering "our place" and the notion of a place both as home and as worthy of our time, and rediscovering the need to dedicate time for "place-based" studies linked to our well-being. Again, Stan Rowe, in writing about Grey Owl, said, "For him...the spiritual dimension of wilderness experience [and our local home environments] was foremost – the antidote to humanity's preoccupation with itself."[6] I do believe we are slowly moving away from a monumental conceit towards a humbler engagement with place.

1

SPECIAL INVISIBLE PLACES

It is precisely what is invisible in the land...that makes
what is merely empty space to one person, a place to another.
— BARRY LOPEZ[1]

EARLE BIRNEY HAS A PASSAGE in the poem "Can.Lit." – "It's only by our lack of ghosts/we're haunted."[2] Honestly I don't get it. I feel the presence of ghosts all over the place in the Canadian bush and in our cities.

John Hornby, a wanderer of the tundra, still haunts my visits to the streets of Strathcona in Edmonton. The Cree and Ojibwe Windigos, men turned cannibalistic monsters, can cause an "on-edge" feeling during a solo trip's evening campfire sit. The great explorer/mapmaker David Thompson is with me on morning paddles on Smoke Lake, Algonquin Park. It is 1837. He is old now, 67 years, and searching for a height of land portage between the Muskoka River and Madawaska River systems. I remember walking on the Newfoundland interior on Jane's Hill at the end of White Bear Bay with William Epps Cormack's 1822 march across the interior east to west much on my mind. Haunted yes – by a lively larger reality than the present.

Mostly the presence of ghosts is connected with special places: places with a particularly rich story or the presence, through time, of multiple human associations reflected in many stories. I also do not concur with the passage from a speech presented in the legislative assembly by soon-to-be Father of Confederation, Thomas D'Arcy McGee. He said, on February 9, 1865:

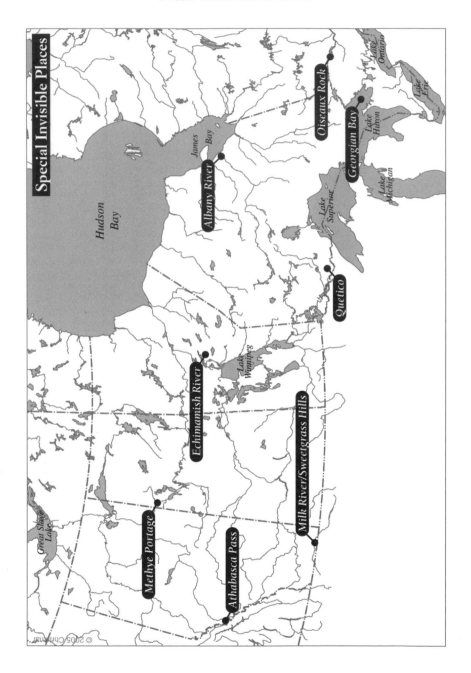

We have here no traditions and ancient venerable institutions;…here, every man is the first settler of the land;…here, we have none of those old popular legends and stories which in other countries have exercised a powerful share in the government…This is a new land![3]

To be truthful, I somewhat get this one. He was, like so many Euro-Canadians of his day, in a strange state of denial and/or oblivion to the presence of indigenous peoples on the land and their rich associations with their special places. There was also ignorance of Canadian geography, an ignorance of the sites and people who explored and settled here, performing daunting tasks that most of us have yet to truly understand today. This ignorance was Birney's problem too it seems. Birney clearly suggests that generations of pre-and post-contact dwelling and immigrant presence has produced hardly a haunting mood. Meanwhile, for those folks who generally live by the creed of the Haiku by the seventeenth century Japanese poet, Matsuo Bashō, "If you want to know the pine, go to the pine,"[4] then ghosts and places in Canada can be omnipresence. If you want to know special places, go to the special places. That is where you will find your Canadian ghosts. Ghosts like Hornby, Windigos, David Thompson and Cormack (hunting in 1822

Climbing Jane's Hill. Newfoundland provided an opportunity to imagine William Epps Cormack's 1822 walk across the island from east to west.

for the lost recently extinct Beothuk tribe, not to mention the Beothuk themselves as ghosts of the Canadian bush) can be real enough to shape a fertile larger-than-life presence. Rather than poet Birney, on this matter of associations with the past, I'd favour the words of the poet Dorothy Livesay who wrote in the poem "Artifacts" – "The map leaps up from namelessness to history, each place made ceremonial when named and its name peopled! events shouted!"

Trips can be organized to visit special places: be they car travel[5] or canoe, day trips or extended outings. It seemed reasonable to divide special places for outdoor travellers into two categories: pre-contact indigenous places/stories and post-contact discoveries, explorers' and settlers' places/stories. Then again, I suppose there is that third category... places made special by our own gathering of experiences. I'll share a few of my favourite special places. There is an overwhelming wealth of ghosts by which we can be haunted, but I'll focus my comment on the general themes of rock sites and ceremonial baptism sites.

ROCK SITES

In the late 1980s, canoe-tripping friend Gordon Hommes and I stopped at the *Mamatowassini* (Wonderful Stone). This unusual glacial erratic sits in the open width of the 500-metre (547-yard)-wide Albany River, near the river's mouth in the James Bay Lowlands and the town of Fort Albany. While hardly ordinary in appearance, it is easily missed without prior knowledge of its significance in the area. To see this rock on day 18 of our trip and to have visited the Cliff Lake pictographs (north of Lake Nipigon) on day three helped tie this Northwestern Ontario trip together thematically. We were in country long inhabited by First Nations peoples with a spirit world elegantly tied to the land. Would the *Maymaygwayshi* (rock men living in shoreline cliff crevices) help or hinder our passage? It behove us to be attentive to their possible presence.

Our knowledge of the Wonderful Stone came from a 1969 article in *The Beaver* and from talking with local Cree peoples along the river. The unusual boulder was well-known and well-storied with a spirit presence associated with the stone's surface shape.

The peculiarity of the Wonderful Stone, translated from the Cree words *Mamata* (wonderful or strange) and *Assini* (stone), is its colour and texture compared to all other boulders in a radius of 338 kilometres (200 miles). This is a green boulder. Greenstone is a dark green, compact, metamorphic rock formed by the alteration of igneous rock. It is created by lava that comes to the surface of an ocean bed. This condition does not occur in the James Bay Lowlands. The solo boulder must have been broken off by glaciers, scoured for at least 200 miles by glacier activity, and left here as an oddity for the river to reveal eventually after years of erosion. All is not just simple facts for the geologist, however. Beyond this knowledge, controversy still surrounds the origin of this rock millions of years before it was plucked up by the ice. Perhaps a spiritual force might still provoke plausible interpretations today.

The *Mamatowassini* seemed to be known to most local people. Asking around in Fort Albany following our trip and questioning the odd river guide from fishing camps upstream, we learned that the rock emotes mixed sentiments today. One fellow in Fort Albany remembered his father taking him to the rock as a young boy for his first major cruise upstream. Another river traveller told us, "If you shoot at it, you're going to get it, not right away, but some day." We heard no formal legends associated with the rock, but it became obvious to us that the boulder was known and revered in some way to most. The common local interpretation today is, "Oh, you mean that meteorite upstream."

Early Fort Albany journal entries first recorded the Wonderful Stone in the 1760s as if it were simply a local landmark. Another mention of the stone by Hudson's Bay men referred to it as the Indian Stone. George Thorman, researching the stone in the early 1960s, learned from a Native elder at the time that "the Mamatowassini is the only magic rock in James Bay area that all the Indians know about." The stories continue, claiming that while the spirits in the rock have no names, two spirits made comfortable, grooved resting places in the rock, which then served as portholes into its core. These resting places, which are clearly identifiable today, once were used by shamans (spiritual leaders) to gain power through inspiration and connection with the spirit world. Undoubtedly the rock held some spiritual significance at one point and most reports past and present suggest the spirits in the rock must be treated with great care and respect.

With most of this information in hand we approached the mysterious stone with great excitement. We lay on the rock's natural resting places, surprised at the comfortable and choice sunning spot they offered. We sat and talked of its role in a culture steeped in spirit and land relationships. Then true to our western culture we measured its size, examined its texture and hardness, then carried on downriver concerned with substance more than relationship: quite removed from the shaman's "knowing" of this sacred spot. A wiser traveller might have elected not to lie in the spirits' resting places. Today I would stay in my canoe to admire the stone.

Running Rock, Warrior's Hill and Warrior's Rock are all labels in use to describe a smooth-surfaced, steeply terraced mass of pre-Cambrian granite that graces the shoreline of Lac La Croix in Quetico Provincial Park. The vertically impressive rock band has that classical alluring quality: a spot to stretch out tired knees, the ideal spot to climb for a view down the lake, a choice "feel on top of the world" lunch site, or, as the late canoeist and educator Bill Peruniak had described it to me, "a place for the simple passion of lying on cool granite."

Warrior's Rock is easily all of these, but it is also much more for many a heritage-steeped canoeist. The rising rock, for decades to white travellers and perhaps centuries to the area's Ojibwe people, is a noted site to challenge strength and endurance and the power of one's personal guardian spirit. The task is a simple one: run up and down from the water's edge to the hilltop and back. Over the years I've heard instructions of bare feet and no hands added to the task. I've also been told of the challenge diminished by achieving success in simply making it to the top. The specifics of the challenge seem to be lost to obscurity, although likely specifics were never important in the first place. None of this detail is critical. No matter what your fitness level, no matter what rules you prescribe, the *run* up Warrior's Rock is a test.

I was 15 years old when I first visited the site. Then it was yet another example of the rich heritage of the Native Peoples in the Quetico/Superior area. Like the spectacular pictographs just to the north visited earlier, I was caught by a vague pre-conceptual sensual sort of awareness of all this Native culture significance, new to my canoe-tripping experience. It captured an imagination, but there was a lack of focus. The bush that day seemed full of ghosts judging my worthiness as a traveller. These ghosts – a rock art artist and an Ojibwe boy my age but more worldly than I – were not scary, but they commanded a regular and lengthy daydream muse.

At this time, I was introduced to the traditional notion of puberty rites, guardian spirits and living spirits of both animate and inanimate worlds by my camp counsellor, David Lang. The secret world of my imagination was reeling in confusion. For cartoon fans, I was a Calvin without a Hobbes – a boy without a proper imaginary friend. Attaining the top without hands (but with spotters for the most vertical section which was run obliquely for safety and sanity) quickly became of great, but vague importance to the physical youth such as I was.

I did it. Rather I did it as the challenge was laid out to me. I could never have run down. I remember methodically plotting my route, lunging for foot plants on mini ledges and cracks with cramping legs near the top, and pumping with my arms. Most of all I remember being on top, hunched over and continually spitting up with a strange new taste of what I took to be blood. Enough histrionics. But that's what I remember; it was over 30 years ago now. It was not a hollow victory, but then again it was not really a victory. It was a connecting experience that helped set me on a path to focus that vague sensual imagination from a pre-conceptual knowing towards a clearer sense of who these Ojibwe runners, whose foot plants I struggled for, really were.

Years later in Sigurd Olson's *The Singing Wilderness*, I discovered the only written reference I have ever read of Warrior's Rock. It reads:

> We paddled out to the mouth of the bay, from which we could see the open reaches of the lake. The great surfaces of Running Rock were alive with movement, glittering with thousands of rivulets that spread fan-like over the granite slopes, caught the light, and lost it when they ran over the mosses and lichens and into the crevices. In the old days, so say the Chippewas, young braves stared at the water's edge, raced clear to the top 1,000 yards or more away, turned there, and ran back to their canoes.[6]

This passage has likely served as the lone source or spark that has sent many a modern runner on his own rites of passage. Then again, this "great surface" of smooth granite can just be a place to stretch tired knees or pass by with a fleeting sidelong glance. Is it irreverent to explore such cultural practices of another culture? At age 15 this question didn't enter my thinking. Now I think it is a matter of *how* the cultural practice is approached by the outsider.

Not easily recognized as part of New Brunswick, Mount Carleton represents the northern end of the Appalachian Range and, I think, likely a vision quest location.

Vision quest locations are another pre-(and post-) contact rock-based special set of places for my particular study of Canada. I have visited many, but certainly have unknowingly passed by many more. Well-known ones include: Dreamer Rock on the southern tip of the La Cloche Peninsula to the west of Killarney Park, Ontario; the smooth rock bands stretching out into Lake Kejimkujik in Nova Scotia, and the conical dynamic Sweetgrass Hills in Montana looking north into the Milk River Valley in southern Alberta. Here hills and petroglyphs (rock art etchings) and visions are in close association.

When standing atop Mount Carleton in New Brunswick between the Tobique and Nepisquit rivers and when overlooking a large part of Ontario's Temagami from Maple Mountain, I've had a tingling sense that vision quests were a common practice there as well. Was my much-loved hometown Dundas Peak once a site to seek vision? One can feel the benevolent presence of ghosts urging one on as if they were say-ing, "keep asking these questions, and keep this past in your present. We will reveal it to you only in bits and then only if you are worthy." At vision quest sites, noted or assumed, I remember a line from an e.e. cummings poem, "always the more beautiful answers, who ask the more difficult questions."

As for Dreamer Rock, once local permission is received, the hike up to the 60-metre high quartz rock prominence affords a view that makes a vision quest seem readily plausible to my non-native secular, disconnected world view. At Dreamer Rock we passed an historical plaque that described a vision quest.

The facts of this quest can be explained. It is a puberty rite of adolescent male youth, which involves several days and nights of fasting alone in anticipation of a vision. The vision would come usually in an animal form, which thereafter remains with the individual as a source of strength and identity. Known as a guardian spirit, this benevolent force aids the individual in his spiritual needs. All objects and phenomena, animate and inanimate, were believed to have a spirit, so one's guardian spirit served to help interpret all life. Using language as a source for explanation, Minnesota writer Louise Erdrich describes the word *Andopawatchigan* meaning "seek your dream":

It means that first you have to find and identify your dream, often through fasting, and then that you also must carry out exactly what your dream tells you to do in each detail. And then the philosophy comes in, for by doing this repeatedly you will gradually come into a balanced relationship with all of life.[7]

While the initiation vision quest was an integral transition in the maturation of the male, judged as a gift for those who were ready in the view of the spirits, females were not compelled to seek a guardian spirit. A woman was complete in herself due to her link with the spirit women from Ojibwe mythology, who first gave birth to humanity.

One fact that does excite me is the Ojibwe First Nation's strong spiritual link with nature, which in itself is a mystery to our western culture. Unquestionably, it is this unity that makes the vision quest possible and my quest, or visit really, problematic. Can a spiritual association of humanity in sync with nature be revitalized as a life force through study and association with such places?

We spent our time on Dreamer Rock absorbing the view, watching the complexity of nature in action with a sensitivity we rarely take the time to summon of ourselves. Our solitude was a joy – a break for sore muscles, a chance to reflect on past and future life direction, and a time to simply look out on the landscape. We headed quietly down at dusk, content with our reflection and alertness. My Jasper, Alberta, friend, Leona Amann, was thrilled with her introduction to the Canadian Shield.

I, however, had a reluctant acceptance of my detachment from nature tainting my mood.

For the Native youth, personal identity with nature might be established on this rock. He would gain an insight, or direction for his life in nature. Cultural anthropologist Paul Shepard has called this, "receiving the full weight of the cosmos in your head."[8] The Native youth would be a conscious participant in nature. Could I claim this? Perhaps I didn't try hard enough? Perhaps there is nothing to try? Maybe if I came back for a week of fasting and solitude I could learn to know that which is deep within myself?

The question remains: were we enlightened? And my response – spending a quiet afternoon on Georgian Bay's Dreamer Rock, content to let one's mind wander, might not offer a vision of a guardian spirit, but it certainly can't hurt either. No discovery! Just a satisfying search which led me a little closer to *seeing* nature from the inside-out rather than *looking* at nature from the outside in.

The experience of Kejimkujik and the Sweetgrass Hills is strongly influenced by the adjacent petroglyphs. The Mi'kmaw experienced these inland lakes of Kejimkujik as sites for vision and revelation. The Blackfoot, Shoshoni and others had similar intentions for a vision-seeking site on the Sweetgrass Hills overlooking the open prairie with the Milk River Valley to the north. In Kejimkujik Park, rightly so, only certain petroglyph sites on the soft chalk-like rock bands are allowed to be visited now, given the deterioration of the images over time. Today, guides accompany bare-footed visitors and provide local histories connecting rock, visions and art.[9] "On the open plains of northern Montana, soil scientist and archeologist John Dormaar led me up, and up and up, West Butte to the plateau top at 2,130 metres (6,984 feet). But wait, I thought we were in the Prairies! West Butte is the highest of the three isolated "mountains" in the area. They all rise at least 1,000 metres (3,000 feet) above the surrounding prairie land and cover about 52 square kilometres (20 square miles). Geologically speaking, the buttes are igneous bulged stock emerging over sedimentary rock layers. In terms of climate, the hills are peculiar as well. The summits receive about 18 millimetres (7 inches) more precipitation annually than the lower country. In terms of an outdoor activity, the hike is a steady strenuous walk and, as the hills stand lonely overlooking the plain, I was glad John had joined me rather than simply providing me with a map. For me this was

John Dormaar's head is visible, looking eastwards to the next prominent Sweet-grass Butte. Note the cedar tree blocking clear vision, evidence of a very old vision quest site.

an eerie place – remote, exciting and easily connected imaginatively to the once waves of buffalo – just right for a vision quest site.

On top of West Butte there are a number of loose rock wall formations. These are mostly three-sided horseshoe-shaped structures that are waist height. Usually they look to the east and the rising sun. At one such site close to the mountain's edge, John had drilled a wood core sample years earlier from a cedar that by now had awkwardly grown in such a way as to obscure a clear view of the east. The tree was well over one hundred years old. One can easily surmise therefore, that the site is not a recent one, however, it has been much modified in recent years. There were recently left prayer flags similar to ones I have seen atop ridges in Temagami, Ontario, where there are excellent lookouts and signs of rocks having been moved to build and enhance cairns and other shelter features. Certainly this site has seen regular use over centuries and is to be respected as an active vision site today.

Standing atop West Butte is an exciting place to be, truly quite the "igneous bulged stock." Actually, I remember saying, "What a rock!" John, who has written a distinguished book on the natural and cultural history of the Sweetgrass Hills, referred to certain walled resting places as "waiting for a vision sites."[10] Other sites might have been eagle-catching pits. While there we examined unique flora and fauna and the rugged indigenous trees. Mostly though, I was in awe of the whole big picture of the place and its significance in the spiritual life of the Blackfoot in whose language these hills are considered animate – full of life. That's it!! This place really does feel alive. There is a force to the prairie here like no other and the view is like no other. Long experienced as a watchtower over the prairie for hunting buffalo and raiding tribes, and as a vision questing site, the hilltops would have been a familiar spot. Often these activities would be subsequently recorded on the soft rock forming the Milk River Valley. Today, the staff of Writing-on-Stone Provincial Park (Alberta) are bent on preserving and showing these extensive and remarkable petroglyphs on equally remarkable dikes (rock walls) and hoo-doo pillars in the main river valley and branching coulee systems. Both the park site and the Sweetgrass Hills are connected as a sacred animate place, a place alive with history and alive through time as an extraordinary energy on the prairie. A special place indeed!

The petroglyphs themselves comprise a variety of carved human figure shield bearers, stick figures, animal shapes (predominantly horse figures), a battle scene with over one hundred figures, Cree syllabics (an alphabet created by Methodist missionary James Evans in the 1840s to convert the oral Cree language into written form);[11] and the *remote possibility* of inscription of Ogam, a European/Mediterranean (Celtic/Iberian) alphabet form that dates back thousands of years.[12]

The Native petroglyphs date back certainly to the 1600s, and likely before, with the Blackfoot First Nation being the principal artists/storytellers of the 1700s. The horse, a dominant figure, is believed to have been introduced to this area by 1730. The Shoshoni from the south, Sioux from the east and Nez Perce from the west were among other tribal groups who lived or travelled through the area, using the sheltered coulees as travel ways and camps. Much of the rock art is along the cliffs that form these coulees. The rich variety of drawing styles, which helps set the Milk River petroglyphs apart from Canadian Shield petroglyphs and pictographs (paintings), is explained by the variety of tribal groups using the area over time. In the fall of 1866, according to a Peigan account, all the coulees between the Sweetgrass Hills and the Milk River were full of lodges. Wherever there was water flowing, there was a camp of lodges.

Atop Rock Coulee in the park stands the odd table rock platform, another "waiting for a vision" site. Upon leaving this lofty perch, young men would return to the river valley of Writing-on-Stone to carve their personal vision into the ongoing spiritual record of people in this sacred valley. As with other etchings/drawings in Canada, it was often claimed that the rock art was the work of the spirits themselves, perhaps travelling out of the sky or down from the animate Sweetgrass Hills. What helps make this geographical complex of 1000-metre rock mountain upthrusts, coulees and river valley special, is that this "specialness" is recorded in the rock itself.

CEREMONIAL BAPTISM SITES

In his book, *Listening Point*, Sigurd Olson wrote, "Everyone has a listening point somewhere…some place of quiet where the universe can be contemplated with awe." Special, "now mostly invisible," rock sites have been such listening points for me. However, also in this listening point category are the four major baptism ceremony points along the voyageur transcontinental canoe route from Montreal to the Pacific. Marked by the sheer brilliance of Canadian geography as a continuous waterway link, and by the grandeur of these special sites where canocmen voyageurs and their bosses shared a rite of initiation important to an early east to west Canadian psyche, this route is peppered with story, ceremony and meaning. Today's invisibility of it all adds significantly to the intrigue.

The baptism is about maintaining a ritual through time, acknowledging a special quality to a particular moment or location. The voyageurs seemed to borrow from both Native and French Roman Catholic traditions in creating their own ceremonies. In 1793, John Macdonell, a clerk with the North West Company recorded his crossing of the height of land portage between South and North Lake, heading from Grand Portage on Lake Superior into the western interior:

> I was instituted a North man by Batême performed by sprinkling water in my face with a small cedar Bow dipped in a ditch of water and accepting certain conditions such as not to let any new hand pass by that road without experiencing the same ceremony which stipulates

particularly never to kiss a voyageur's wife against her own free will, the whole being accompanied by a dozen of gun shots fired one after another in an Indian manner. The intention of this Batême being only to claim a glass, I complied with the custom and gave the men...a two gallon keg as my worthy Bourgeois Mr. Cuthburt Grant directed me.[13]

This journal entry is packed with curiosities. How could the lowly voyageur enforce such a practice on all others, significantly their bosses? (There are references to superiors paying their way out of a full immersion dunking baptism with extra monies and extra rum.) Why is becoming a North Man significant to the fur trade life and why would one ask the voyageur's wife her permission for that kiss? A nice touch for sure but it seems unusual here.

The voyageur's custom shows that for brief moments in key locations, the "servant" could turn the master/servant relationship upside-down. As Canadian fur trade historian, Carolyn Podruchny, put it, "The ritual baptism reminded the bourgeois and clerks of their obligations to their indentured servants, and for voyageurs it signified the admission into a new state of occupation and manhood."[14] So the baptism represents a good reminder for the bosses of the reciprocal nature of master/servant and a heightened rite of passage status moment for a canoeman as he travels across the country time and time again over the length of his career. From east to west, from Montreal to the Continental Divide of the Pacific and Arctic watersheds, voyageurs had their own personal mapping of the terrain based on gained prestige. Like so many settings in male culture, their status was clearly delineated. Along the route four ceremonial places separated out the Montreal-based canoemen by status as determined by western and northern progress.

Finally, seeking permission from a voyageur's wife (not the voyageur) for a kiss bespeaks the importance of Native women in the fur trade, particularly as the trade moved west. Native Peoples made the entire fur trade process possible. Men who stayed in the interior often formed kinship ties with Native families. Clearly this ritual of permission acknowledges new social and sexual arrangements in the western interior that John Macdonell and so many others entered for the first time. It is significant to note that there were an estimated 3,000 hired canoemen in 1821 at the time of the Hudson's Bay Company takeover of the North West Company.

Left, John Cockburn at Oiseaux Rock cliff, reading about various fur trade baptisms. As he looks up from this location, he is looking into the now much forested rock prominence that gives Oiseaux Rock its name. *Above,* A short swim with snorkel in front of the former Fort William fur trade post (Quebec shore of the Ottawa River) allowed a few clay pipe artifacts to surface.

All travelling fur trade "novices" were baptized at specific locations. In essence there is a cultural map that can be overlaid on the conventional waterways map that delineates the transcontinental fur trade canoe route and trading posts. The first in-the-wilds baptism was the Ottawa River site at Oiseaux Rock and Pointe aux Baptêmes. For the greenhorn travelling west, this was the initial exposure of major cliff formations of Canadian Shield rock to appear along the waterway. The Rocher Fendu rock and rapids complex just downstream was avoided by the voyageurs who preferred the Muskrat Lake and Creek offshoot along the north shore of the Ottawa River. This is the place, by the way, where the so-called Champlain's astrolabe was found. Interestingly, this claim is now being revisited and there is some ongoing solid questioning as to the actual owner of the Cobden Astrolabe. More evidence points to it being in the possesion of a Jesuit missionary.[15] I visited the much graffitied cliff face hoping to conduct a mock baptism at the adjacent beach in an attempt to be part of a great Canadian tradition. The cliff and adjacent Oiseaux Rock are an impressive entry to the Canadian Shield, however, the beach is now off limits, being part of the Chalk River Nuclear Power Station. Friend John Cockburn and I combined this exciting paddle on the Ottawa with another of the region's fur trade sites. At Fort William (Quebec), the lesser Fort William, we hunted with snorkel and mask for clay pipes from the fur trade era in the shallow water in front of the old post (a small stone-walled structure still remains from the post of the 1800s).

The second site as one moves west is the North/South Lake height of land signifying the separation of the Great Lakes/St. Lawrence waters and Hudson Bay waters. The 13.6-kilometre (8.5-mile) Grand Portage is downstream on the Pigeon River. The rise from Lake Superior to this gateway to the western interior is...300 metres (1000 feet). Here Macdonell became a "North Man," (*hommes du nord*) no longer a "Pork-eater," (*mangeurs de lard*), while only travelling the Montreal to Lake Superior leg of the larger route. As a summer camp canoe trip-per, I passed by from the west to east along the Quetico/Superior American/Canadian border route four times. Each time my companions and I were sincere in recreating some semblance of a mock rite of initiation. It was late in our 30-plus day trip and some form of initiation before the long Grand Portage was certainly deserving. Sigurd Olson's sense of "listening point" worked for me here at the North/South Lake portage. As a kid, this spot was a clear touchstone to the voyageur era. And it has always seemed so strange that at this point, it is a short, level trail, a massive separation of watersheds. The next two heights of land would increase in portaging difficulty.

At the Methye Portage, also known as La Loche Portage, at the head of the Churchill River in Saskatchewan, the traveller becomes an "Athabasca Man," now a true veteran of fur trade travel. Once over the 19-kilometre (12-mile) portage with a steep 180-metre (550-foot) drop to the Clearwater River, one enters Arctic water and, as British scientist and surveyor, John Henry Lefroy, commented here, "...the very mosquitoes do or ought to respect him."[16] These men rarely met the *mangeurs de lard* and *hommes du nord* men. They wintered over at interior posts for multiple years and travelled north to a mind-boggling extent from the Montreal canoemen's perspective. There was a mystique and reputation that they won the privilege to hold. Imagine the spirited canoe race with the "Athabasca" men's reputation on the line when on August 18, 1794, a challenge was posed with a *hommes du nord* brigade when both brigades found themselves travelling Lake Winnipeg. Both groups reached the north end of the lake together after forty-eight hours of straight paddling. A tie (imagine a tie after forty-eight hours) preserved the reputation of both. This reputation also made these Athabasca voyageurs choice canoemen for Arctic-based exploration. Despite their

The Methye Portage height of land lookout was an exciting history-rich destination for these 1981 University of Alberta students. *Courtesy of Darcy Desyshyn.*

skills and long association in the country, they were anxious to uphold this image of superiority. Mackenzie and certainly others were able to quell a mutiny by reminding these men of "the honour of conquering disasters and the disgrace that would attend them on their return home, without having attained the object of the expedition."[17] These same Athabasca Men would eventually take Mackenzie to the Pacific in 1793.

I travelled the Methye Portage in the winter with fellow students from the Department of Physical Education at the University of Alberta. My listening point along this height of land, a rite of initiation spot, was not the final drop to Arctic waters, but the winter quiet of Rendezvous Lake along the portage. Here I removed myself from our merry band and lay out on the frozen lake considering all who had passed and their circumstances. Here, as a special place, "events shouted," as the poet Livesay suggested. Here "the map leaps up." Here is a rendezvous site for centuries of long-distance tribal and later fur trade connections. Here "…each place made ceremonial when named and its name peopled."

The Portage La Loche is a who's-who in Western and Arctic exploration history. From Alexander Mackenzie's first description in print (1778) to the accounts in the 1870s, the overland passage is well-recorded and often exaggerated as being 300-plus metres (over 1,000 feet) high. Many, who usually were not inclined to wax poetic, given the business of travel, were so moved at the portage viewpoint. (Perhaps they had more time or were "so moved" during the dispensing of rum). John Rae is one such example. He wrote in an 1848 letter to George Simpson, governor of the Hudson's Bay Company:

> Not having crossed to the west end of the portage until this morning, I was much struck with the splendid view down the valley of the Clearwater River. The beautiful effect of light and shade on the variously colored foliage, the undulations of the sides of the valley and the pure water showing itself here and there over and between the branches of the trees, looking like sheets of polished silver produced a scene which I have seldom or never seen surpassed.[18]

Northern traveller Sir William Francis Butler, writing in 1873, is certainly correct to say, "this long portage…is not a bad position from whence to take a bird's-eye view of the Great North."[19] I wonder if Butler stopped for a shot of rum to commemorate the recently past heydays of the fur trade? Historically, coming from the west to east via the western mountains, the portage view was hardly mentioned. Coming from the east on the prairies and low-lying lakes of the Upper Churchill River, the expansive view is exhilarating and a much venerated spot well-recorded in travellers' journals.

The Methye lookout over the Clearwater River is still remote today, still a significant geographical feature but a quieter place now. And it is still a place where extra rations of rum and a baptism is deserving.[20]

The third height of land site, though fourth baptism site to be discussed, was visited by smaller numbers in the far-flung reaches of the later trade. At the Committee's Punch Bowl at the top of the Athabasca Pass, one would have an extra dram or three before departing the Whirlpool River of Athabasca waters to Arctic waters for the Pacific watershed. Here, out of the small punch bowl mountain lake, waters run in both directions, both east and north and west and south. Now we are talking about a mountain pass on a canoe trip, a far cry from the North/South Lake level trail along the Canadian/USA border near Lake Superior and a long way from Oiseaux Rock on the Ottawa River.

It was here at the Punch Bowl that Ross Cox commented on May 31, 1817, "One of our rough-spun unsophisticated Canadians, after gazing upwards for some time in silent wonder, exclaimed with much vehemence, 'I'll take my oath, my dear friends, that God Almighty never made such a place!' "[21] Certainly this fellow was deserving of an extra shot of rum to calm his spirits if nothing else. George Simpson in 1825 set off his toast at the Punch Bowl with the following words, "At 6:00 a.m. got to the Committee's Punch Bowl where the people had a glass of rum each and ourselves a little wine & water which was drunk to the health of their Honors with three cheers." All told, it is a remarkable thought to consider the voyageur who experienced his fair share of rum and initiations at each of these four locations while crossing the country during a career in the fur trade. Too bad, we only know our history from the clerks' and bourgeois' perspective, those who wrote up their accounts because they could, or by necessity as part of the job. We do not read the words of the proud servant canoemen who either couldn't or didn't have to write.

My own arrival to the Committee's Punch Bowl, a summit lake on the pass, was thwarted by an accident while leading a ten-day winter trip – a dislocated elbow within sight of the summit plateau means today I have a future trip in waiting. And I'll never play volleyball again – can't straighten one arm fully.

Once at the Committee's Punch Bowl, I had planned to read the following two passages by the explorer David Thompson:

Many reflections came to my mind; a new world was in a manner before me, and my object was to be at the Pacific Ocean before the month of August.

And to continue:

[The Pass] was to me a most exhilarating sight, but the scene of desolation before us was dreadful, and I knew it. A heavy gale of wind, much more a mountain storm, would have buried us beneath it. My men were not at their ease, yet when night came they admired the brilliancy of the stars, and as one of them said, he thought he could almost touch them with his hand.

Of the first quote, one can easily ponder what might have been Thompson's reflections. Now this is a height of land worth pondering. It was *all* of what is now British Columbia that he were entering. Later, on the Columbia River, after wintering over near the pass at Boat Encampment (now under water due to the damming of the Columbia River), he posted a note claiming possession of the land for King George III. Of the second quote, one can imagine his feeling of good fortune to camp in idyllic conditions that December night. Five men had already mutineered and descended back to familiar country.

Though it was a clear March night back in 1981, I saw no stars and shared no Punch Bowl reading either. I was delirious with an arm swelling to proportions I'd thought unimaginable. I was helicoptered out. Indeed, I have to return to the Athabasca Pass with a flask of rum and Thompson's journals along.

There is one other ceremonial height of land destination that deserves attention here. Though it was not part of the Montreal-based canoe route to the Pacific, it was a significant fur trade canoe route involving a height of land emanating from the Hayes River of Hudson Bay to the Lake Winnipeg waterway. And emanate it does! At the Echimamish Creek, the flow is both ways, (*echimamish* is Cree for "river that flows both ways") to the east into the Hayes River to Hudson Bay and to the west to the Nelson River in such a way that the Nelson and Hayes' tributary is shared. At the place of reversing flow is the Painted Stone ceremonial site. The significant geographical phenomena was not missed by Native Peoples travelling downstream to the major fur trade post, York Factory, or earlier out to Hudson Bay to hunt. David Thompson recorded in 1786, "On the short carrying place by which we crossed this ridge [a portage around a shallow rapid on the Echimamish], the Indians, time out of mind, had placed a Manitou stone…painted red with ochre, to which they make some trifling offerings."

He also noted, "…but the Stone and offerings were all kicked about by our tolerant people." Thompson regularly used sarcasm when referring to general matters of the trade and labour force. It seems that as the Hudson's Bay men became more familiar with the interior they correspondingly became more impatient with Native practices that slowed progress. The Native worshipping place might deserve extra rum, but not the day or half day of worship reported here in the early days of the Hudson's Bay Company charter. It appears the Painted Stone/Echimamish site (later called "the Gates" by fur traders) wasn't a height of land deemed worthy of continued ceremony. Only thirty-three years after Thompson's journal entry, John Franklin in 1819 en route to an ill-fated Arctic trip, recorded:

> It is said that there was formerly a stone placed near the centre of this portage on which figures were annually traced, and offerings deposited by the Indians; but the stone has been removed many years, and the spot has ceased to be held in veneration.[22]

A sad story I think. The Painted Stone site was at first acknowledged as a gift of geography. Later, and perhaps still, it is largely passed by unnoticed. A symbolic reconstruction of the Painted Stone was erected by Robert Newbury and friends in 1973. I hope to travel there some-day and add some offering to this ceremonial height of land site.

No ghosts, no traditions, no venerable institution in Canada – *no way*! Listening points for ghosts and traditions abound. These may be largely invisible, without historic plaques, buildings, footpaths, food concession stands or brochures; but in Canada there are "places" galore to *feel* a place alive with spirit and spirits, with First Nations and later with exploration and fur trade history – all connected to self-propelled travel. My take-home message here is simple and quick; get out on the land with a bit of knowledge and a big curiosity. I have considered here two of my favourite themes for special invisible places. They are: rock sites (these make sense given the dominant role of the Canadian Shield over three-quarters of this country)[23] and baptism or rite of initiation sites, which makes sense given the importance of the transcontinental canoe route to the shaping of Canada. As Matsuo's Haiku informs, "If you want to know the pine, go to the pine." Go to the venerated rock or rock outcrop or vision quest rock prominence or rock initiation site or baptism site. Seek vision. Seek approval with the spirits. Seek newly deserved prestige. Seek a shot of rum or perhaps chocolate. Seek those invisible telling places on the land and water that turn empty space into an echoing place, reverberating with our past.

2

THE LABRADOR

*He's discovered that time is like sound – that the past doesn't
vanish, but encircles us in layers like a continuous series of voices,
with the closest, most recent voice drowning out those that have gone
before. And just as it's possible to sit on a bench in a city reading a
book, oblivious to the complex racket all around, then to withdraw
from the page and pick out from the cascade of noises the voice of
one street vendor two blocks away, so for Cartwright it's possible
at times to tune in a detail from either the past or the ongoing
course of time and by concentrating on it, become witness
to some event in the affairs of the dead or the living.*
– JOHN STEFFLER, writing on the ghost of the 18th century
Labrador trader/adventurer, George Cartwright.[1]

LABRADOR, NO, *The* Labrador, had long been a personal canoe-tripping destination. It is wild and hard, open and beautiful. This I
had gathered from reviewing maps with friends who had left
firewood by stone fire rings I might visit, and from a well-storied past.
Mostly, Labrador, as a destination where the more-than-human world
of wild nature so dominates, is a place of ambivalence to visiting travellers. The land is both charmed with wild beauty and haunted with
wild terror. The traveller likely goes there awash in this simultaneous
working of the mind. Two incompatible ideas (or perhaps not) work
on the mind; one is, "Show me what you've got, Labrador. Place me
in those stories of your harshness." Another is, "Spare me all this gloom
and doom and show me what you've got. Show me your wild beauty
and mind-expanding landscape." Labrador, *The* Labrador, has lots of
personality.

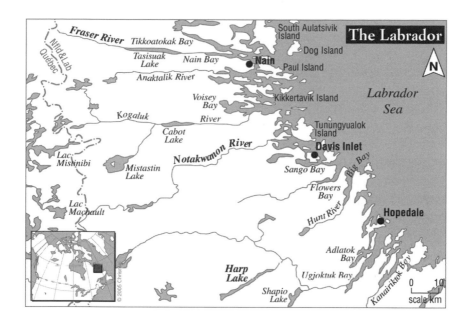

Explorer/adventurer H. Hesketh Prichard noted, at the turn of the last century, that it was not just Labrador, not just another place on the planet, but *The* Labrador, the "menacing wilderness," the land of the "dreary prospect." It was from books that I had read, including Prichard's *Through Trackless Labrador* (1911); William Brooks Cabot's, *In Northern Labrador* (1911); Elliott Merrick's classic *True North* (1933); George Cartwright's, *A Journal of Transactions and Events…*(1792) and John Steffler's historical fiction treatment, *The Afterlife of George Cartwright* (1992), that I received images of a grand distinctiveness, mostly of the "dreary prospect" flavour to things. How did John McLean in his 1820s' crossing of Ungava into the Labrador Plateau put it? "…The eye turns away in disgust from the cheerless prospect which the desolate flats present."[2] But along with all this, "the most God-fearing land," "land that God gave Cain" stuff, all writers were drawn to a charm – perhaps more like a spell – a quality that seemed a mystery before departing, and builds even more so following their time in Labrador. I had also read all the varied accounts of the Hubbards' story: Leonidas Hubbard's starvation, the ill-fated trip in 1903 and the Mina Hubbard/George Elson more thoughtful 1905 follow-up. Then there are the Herman Koehler trips in the late 1920s, early 1930s – not the stuff of children's bedtime stories.[3] All these stories

Herman Koehler, with son Hans on his right and John Michelin on his left, during their trip to the interior of Labrador in the 1920s. Koehler would die on the Labrador Plateau, a victim of his poor judgment. Michelin would go on to a long life of trapping and guiding. He warned others not to travel with Koehler. *Courtesy of Them Day Archives, John Michelin Collection, Goose Bay, Labrador.*

within all these pages filled me up with the notion of *The* Labrador, as Prichard claimed it was called. The distinctiveness most deserved perhaps because through the 20th century, Labrador was among the last *terra incognita* left on the ice cap free part of the planet. In *Through Trackless Laborador*, Prichard writes:

> These vast spaces, containing an area of many thousand square miles, lie within 2,000 miles (about eighteen days of sea travel then) off Britain and it seemed to us a pity that such a terra incognita should continue to exist under the British flag.

Just a reminder, that this *terra* unknown was, and still is, well-known to the peoples who call the Ungava/Labrador Plateau, *Nitassinan*, meaning "Homeland." Admittedly though, on my first of three trips to date in Labrador, I felt more akin to the foreigner Prichard than to the indigenous peoples and settlers. With time I hoped (and still hope) to feel more at home there. Today Labrador is still a vast space, though less populated in its interior now than it was for surveyor A.P. Low, Prichard and others. Innu peoples (formerly called Naskapi), once inland caribou hunters, now live mainly in coastal communities. But this is not abandoned land. Along the trails I travelled were many signs of active travel (mostly spring snowmobile-based camps).

There were friends too, canoe-tripping associates though countable on one hand, who could talk wisely about Labrador from among their own assorted canoe travel experiences. Herb Pohl, Bob Davis and George Luste, all seemed to switch gears when asked about Labrador trips as compared to, say...anywhere else. Premier Labrador canoe tripper Herb Pohl writing generously in *Nastawgan: The Quarterly Jour-*

Warren Trimble enjoying a bit of Labrador's vast spaces on the Lower Notakwanon.

Journal of the Wilderness Canoe Association has lit many a warming fire in this land. For me, he has fuelled many a directional beacon fire towards Labrador. "The dramatic and beautiful canyon lake of Harp seems to hold secret mysteries." That one liner of Herb's proved to be an alluring enticement for a first visit.[4] Once after a long portage around a tough part of the Notakwanon River, I noted a neat pile of wood stacked besides a small campsite. "It had to be one of Herb's fires from 1984," I thought. This was a small inspiration on one of those less charmed dreary days.

It was clear to me that the distinctiveness of *The* Labrador has remained through time. Whatever the mysterious spell of beauty and dreariness, it had to be experienced firsthand. And ideally, its northern variety had to be experienced: its plateau lakes on rocky plains of dwarf spruce and glacial erratic boulders, its sweeping river valleys, its fiord-like lakes with cascading waterfalls off vertical shorelines, its coastal waters – a mix of bare rock, convoluted shoreline and island prominences. All this is *The* Labrador – a place with a lot of personality.

James Cottrell and I had circled Harp Lake to the coast as a route that had it all. Then we had two years to daydream before we were to discover the reality of Labrador. The route was distinctively Labradorian, but then again, there are so many such routes. Harp Lake and the Adlatok River to Hopedale were first: lake, river and coastal paddling seemed like a sound initiation. Two more trips would follow and two more routes are still in the long-term game plan.

While I've never felt a strong need to retrace specific exploration

Day one – exploring Harp Lake in early June before the bugs.
Courtesy of David Taylor.

routes in Labrador, I do feel a pull to directly link my trip to some historical story with other parts of Canada. There are two reasons for this. Firstly, most of the routes north of the Churchill River (Grand River historically) were certainly travel ways for Naskapi interior caribou-hunting peoples. These people would follow interior Labrador waterways to the coast in summer. Coastal European and mixed blood "settlers" and the Inuit Peoples would follow Labrador waterways inland from the coast as well to hunt. The human presence in river valleys and along river ridgelines, despite the remote setting, is a strong one. Secondly, like Cartwright's ghost, it is possible in Labrador, I feel, to tune in a detail from the ongoing course of time for the region as a whole rather than in its specific linear lines of travel. The Hubbards, Herman Koehler, the settler families of Michelin, Goudie and Blake, 20th century adventurers W.B. Cabot and H.H. Prichard and the writer of a winter traveller's "bible" of sorts, Elliott Merrick, come to mind. All feel close wherever you are on the overall plateau or in certain river valleys. There are voices in the winds in Labrador. Learn the stories and you can hear them echo on the land. The past doesn't vanish, but can encircle you in a swirl of storied chaotic meaning.

For the Harp Lake trip, it was enough to simply be on the Labrador Plateau and one of its rivers. There was a focus then on the whole story of Labrador. Resembling a land-locked fiord in mountainous surroundings, Harp Lake is 65 kilometres long, roughly 1.5 kilometres wide and 260 to 350 metres below the plateau landscape. Canoeing partner James

Cottrell described Harp as paddling down a long crack that flushes you onto the Adlatok River. Upon arrival there by floatplane, it seemed more tomb-like, or like a serenity chamber at a spa. The lake was dead calm. There was one lone seagull. There was an eerie quiet. We took it as welcoming. Jacques Cartier in 1534 only saw the Labrador coast, not the interior. He called it, "a land of stones and rocks, frightful and ill-shaped...the land God gave to Cain."[5] He never saw Harp Lake on a calm day. Labrador welcomed us with beautiful shapes. The dreary, frightful storm days would always be a change of pace from the welcoming splendour of *The* Labrador's spell. That first day was monumental. Thankfully, our first low level flying NATO jet from Goose Bay didn't zoom by until day three. Strange to realize, but we'd arrived on a holiday weekend. At 1,100 km/hour, when these babies fly by on manoeuvres you notice. We figured Harp Lake was a tempting spot to drop extra close to ground level, to fly below the ridgelines.

The next year was the Notakwanon River trip from Lake Machault on the Quebec side of the height of land to the coast. Relative to other rivers in Labrador, the Notakwanon is a steady flow whitewater paddler's river, not a pool and drop variety. And for this reason, it is also not a main historical waterway. Herman Koehler in 1931 was hoping to use it as an access to the coast from the plateau at Indian House Lake, east over the height of land. He was advised not to use this route because of its difficulties. The Native Peoples rarely used the waterway and when they did they skirted much of the steady drop of whitewater with a long

The Notakwanon – not a pool and drop river. This section of water visible here took us all morning to negotiate with portaging, ferrying and running all in bits.

inland portage cutting out a huge bend in the river. Difficulty was a big part of the appeal to Koehler. Lesser fame was to be had on better-trodden routes like the main Native summer migration route, the Mistinibi-Kogaluk route, one river to the north. Koehler never made it to the Notakwanon headwaters. He and his American partner died in the open barrens within gunshot sound of Naskapi hunters. The two bodies were found in separate camps five kilometres apart.

The third, the guide's body, young Jim Martin from Cartwright in Labrador, was never found, nor were Koehler's journal, axe or gun. This story, only now tangentially connected to the Notakwanon, is as compelling as the 1903 Hubbard story. We know just enough to recognize that there is much more to the story. We do know from elders who remember their passing, that they had broken up their canoe and fashioned it into a toboggan to deal with the newly fallen snow, only to have the snow melt. Bummer! We also know that with the passing of time, Martin's body was never found. I speculate that Martin survived but as the guide, though under Koehler's notorious dictatorial leadership, he was not able to return home for fear of shame or a murder charge. A guide returning without his people was not a viable option back then for Martin. Perhaps he took what he needed to survive, mainly the axe and gun, and headed back towards Indian House Lake. But, of course, I'm only playing with the story here. From John Michelin, a guide for Koehler on an earlier trip, we do know that Koehler was a difficult man as a travel partner. Michelin reported Koehler once took a knife to his son's throat merely because he was inclined to go a bit "strange" during a full moon. Michelin had travelled with Koehler two years earlier and had advised Jim Martin not to take the job.

With ABS and Kevlar boats, reliable topographic maps and farmer-john wetsuits, we felt well prepared for the Notakwanon, but still had an awkward canoe dump in the last rapid before a right-angled 22-metre (72-feet) high waterfall. On the ensuing long portage while watching the continuous whitewater, I shared some pensive moments of doubt with companion David Taylor. I wonder what the cavalier Koehler's paddle in this rapids might have brought us by way of a story had he made it this far. Like Leonidas Hubbard, no book to garner sure fame was to be written by Herman Koehler.[6] Though my ambitions in Labrador pale in comparison to these early adventure tourists/explorers, and are tame compared to the experiences of Herb Pohl and others,

The mouth of the Fraser River looks down to the fiord and out to sea. The Parisians who arrived by float plane were camping to our left.

having these fellows along in story form adds a quality of "tuning in a detail" and becoming witness to both the greatness and hubris of human endeavour.

A third trip, third summer in a row, involved paddling out the back door of Nain, Labrador's northernmost community for a classic northern fiord trip. If this were Norway, we might expect to see a luxury cruise ship in this dynamic terrain. As it was, we saw no other paddling groups, only three men from Paris, France, accumulating their needed flying hours for their float plane license – a license not available in France because they have no places to land such planes. Hmmm, perhaps their adventure is Hubbardian/Koehleresque with a modern techno-twist. They wished to score a first and to be exceedingly different. We were neither of these, but our book buddies brought along for inspiration were certainly both. In another techno-twisted historical retracing confusion, these Parisians showed us the upper Fraser Canyon we would not get to on their camcorder. From their birds-eye view we saw our next day upriver paddling. What would Hubbard and Prichard have made of this? It was a weird moment of disconnect.

Paddling from the coast into the Fraser River involves following the route, in part, of Englishman H. Hesketh Prichard, his partner G.M. Gathorne-Hardy, and Newfoundlander Robert Porter. In 1910, from a European standpoint, Labrador was one of the world's last great expanses of unknown. Prichard had recently returned from Patagonia, located at the southern tip of South America. He was no stranger to exploration, but one gets the notion that in Labrador Prichard may have lost the appetite for more. He, with associates, would canoe up the Fraser River until upriver progress was impeded, and then make the 1500-foot climb out of the canyon (at Bear Ravine – you guessed it, so named by them because of a bear hampering their progress) to traverse the Labrador Plateau to the infamous George River. Here they would meet the Naskapi (Innu) peoples, a people shrouded in mystery at that time. Even the Naskapi themselves were not common travellers on the Fraser. The Kogaluk River to the south was their preferred corridor between the George River (the main caribou lands) and the coast (the place of trade). It was an ambitious plan, no less ambitious than Leonidas Hubbard's ill-fated trip for its departure into the unknown from the North West River. Certainly the knowledge of this earlier exploration (1903), where the party became lost early on and Hubbard himself died on the retreat back to the coast once the plans had been abandoned, was a constant source of reflection for Prichard, who himself credits "good luck" as much as anything else for his successful trip. Indeed, Prichard writes in the preface to his 1911 classic *Through Trackless Labrador*, "Luck was with us as it was against him [Hubbard], and in wilderness travel it is a truism to say that luck decides the issue." It must be added here that William Cabot knew more about the Native travel routes to the coast, and his book *In Northern Labrador* does not refer to the land as "trackless." There were many Native travel ways.

Luck was with us too, on our trip into the fiord in 1994. We, six friends, enjoyed good weather, predictable winds that, when severe, always found us camping or close to take-out spots (there are very few along the canyon-like shore). Luck for us also meant spotting a whale while paddling, enjoying clear skies for planned and unplanned windbound hiking excursions, and finding some of Prichard's spots of interest so many years later. Luck for us also came easy, compared to Prichard's party. We had never planned to climb out of the valley via his Bear Ravine, nor walk the Labrador Plateau, caching our canoe at the top of the ravine! We also knew what would be in store for us with such a challenge. Prichard was in the dark, and this certainly influences one's perspective. For example, we took a day to climb out of the valley to gaze out over the plateau; Prichard and company carried a canoe and supplies up the ravine walls only to discover with their first gaze that there would be no wood for fuel, little to offer directional aid and not enough water to make carrying the canoe worthwhile. He knew he needed luck – a caribou for food at just the point of a weakened state due to hunger would make all the difference to their "predatory life." On the other hand, although reflective of Prichard's circumstance, we felt free from worries, even without a camcorder.

Yes! Luck was with us on our trip. We were greeted to the friendly and quiet town of Nain and a travel experience that felt remote and free of human intervention. Remember that Prichard, Hubbard and others of the day were on a quest to meet people. Wilderness – we are inclined to think of it as pristine, remote, without people. This sense of remoteness is reflected in what Labrador settlers called the interior – "the country way back in." 1994 was a good year to be on the Fraser for a sense of capturing some of the same spirit Prichard had felt, of being "way back in."

After the summer of this 1994 trip, Diamond Field Resources found the richest known copper/nickel/cobalt deposit at Voisey Bay just south of Nain. By 1997 over 245,000 mining claims had been staked there, covering 21% of Labrador; all of this is complicated with the Innu (Naskapi) Nation land claims. An Innu leader, Peter Penashue, stated at that time, "We will not tolerate the hit-and-run antics…as aboriginal leaders, we need to remember that the decisions we make today will affect not only us but our children and their children."[7] Notice, he did not say he was opposed to mining, only to the greed of the maximum profit margins in an exploitive ethos of progress. In short, exploration drilling has begun in earnest in Labrador. My travel partner, David Taylor, pointed out that our folksy low-key welcoming time in Nain can now be considered archival, and Prichard's Labrador has likely changed forever. I haven't yet been back to compare. But I fear that when I do, certainly now ten years later, I will feel something of this valuable epigram delivered by Margaret Atwood at a University of Waterloo commencement in the early 1980s, "Nature used to surround us, now we surround nature and the change hasn't necessarily been for the better."

Lucky is how I now feel when I think of our travels that commenced before the Voisey Bay mining development. Prichard's sense of luck was quite different; his was a luck of survival, ours was, in fact, a luck of timing. But back to Prichard's Labrador. As for the 1910 group's departure from Nain, "For a long time until we rounded the point, the Eskimo remained watching us, and as we turned north one or two waved their hands to us. I think they believed we had already earned failure." Quite a send-off thought.

While they experienced hardships early on, mainly in response to the omnipotent bug life, they also experienced moments of intense beauty and good luck, as Prichard was so keen to acknowledge. Where we, in 1994, experienced an intense orange sunset and a dead calm morning with the big lake of the valley before us, Prichard reports:

> We reached the big lake of which we had been told. Our first view of it was intensely typical of Labrador beauty. The mountain tops which surrounded it on every side were not clear of mist and the waters shaded to a dark and peaty blue before the sun rising over the hills turned them to turquoise...We were extremely lucky to get two days of easterly winds at this time of the year.

It is likely that we were at the same camping spot where beauty and good luck graced both our experiences. Prichard and company were pleasing travel companions for us, often filling the role of interpretive local guides.

We delighted in finding the obvious Poungassé Gap in the southern cliff shoreline where, Prichard tells us, the coastal "Eskimo" [now Inuit], "haul their Komatiks [sleds] when on the spring deer hunt, and thus attain the great central plateau." We were wind-bound across from Poungassé both going into the river and coming back. Without the historical travel literature, the significance of this gap would have been missed.

On our own climbs, "for fun," out of the valley to access the plateau, we had reason to marvel at the 1910 party's "portage" out of the valley. Prichard's honest writing captures what might be among the most difficult portage carries in Canadian history. All things considered, I think his following passage is quite understated:

> Difficult as portaging the canoe would have been in any circumstances, it was rendered doubly so by the fact that a wind sprang up, which continually caught and overbalanced it. It is not an easy

matter for one man to portage a canoe over really bad ground, but for two men, especially if there be a marked difference in their heights, it becomes almost an impossibility. And, in fact, there was little that I could do, beyond shout to Porter to stand firm and to seize the end of the canoe in my hand, in order to prevent it swinging round whenever a gust struck it.

In this way we climbed the defile, cutting a path with the axe through the alders, until, as we rose, the vegetation became more and more scanty and the incline steeper and steeper. The whole distance was between 3 to 4 miles, the gradient becoming gradually sharper as we mounted; but much the worst spot was beside the second waterfall of the torrent, for here the chaos of rock had only recently fallen from the cliff above, and had not yet settled. More than once these great fragments slipped and overbalanced as Porter only just stepped clear with the canoe. First and last it was the nastiest bit of walking any of us had ever done, and we were glad enough when late in the afternoon we left the defile behind us, and laid down the canoe in a little mosquito-haunted glen, from which the gradient to the level of the plateau was easy. Interested as we were to see the tableland we did not make any attempt to do so that evening. Truth to tell, the climb up Bear Ravine with packs and the continual vigilance necessary when walking over the rock had strained us to the limit of endurance. Our faces, too, were streaming with blood from the bites of mosquitoes and black flies, which had preyed upon us to their hearts' content as we balanced ourselves upon the boulders. Indeed, we were most thoroughly tired, when by evening, carrying the bear meat, we once more threw ourselves down in a camp on the banks of the Fraser.

Prichard's mixed emotions about his explorations may appear a tad confusing. Mixed emotions here bespeak a wavering perspective, a fear/joy response wrapped up into one sublime feeling for this land. Such a response to the Labrador Plateau was one we could easily understand. Travellers from then and now share this gaze out over an excitingly unfamiliar and disorienting landscape. You can both revere it and be loathsome of it. It cares nothing for you. You can feel all of this simultaneously at a gut level. Exciting feelings.

Prichard had luck; so did we. Now it is left to wonder whether luck for this land is running out. From a canoeist's perspective, that is a new unknown; but also, from the Innu view and the animals' view, there is a new sense of unknown now associated with Labrador. There is a new sense of disorientation, different in kind, different in its implications. One exceptional discovery of minerals in 1994 and the sublime unknown of the Labrador interior has become, while as yet mostly visually untouched, a staked-out place of promise – promise not for caribou or travel ways of old or new. Not a place of, "first views of intensely typical Labrador beauty" and vigorous portages of achievement, but a promise of temporary base camps and jobs (not temporary) it is hoped, helicopters, all-terrain vehicles and mining tailings. How will all this affect these new resource-based human dwellers gazing over the "elemental spirit"? The canoeist hopes the meaningful relationship will not be ravaged. *The* Labrador simply has too much personality to lose its distinctive wildness – a wild harshness and wild beauty. Perhaps in 1534, for Jacques Cartier it was "the land God gave to Cain," but now, getting close to 500 years later, it seems more the land God gave to humanity and other animals to celebrate for its enduring wildness. George Cartwright's ghost (and there are other ghosts here) is a part of this "personality." Other possible ghosts that add detail and personality to which one can regularly tune in, are in both the hubris category of the Leonidas Hubbard and Koehler tradition, and in the greatness of the John Michelin, Prichard/Gathorne-Hardy/Porter and Mina Hubbard/Elson/Blake tradition of inspired travel. I wonder what they would all make of mining claims, low-level flying and us modern-day canoeists.

3

THE YUKON: A BIG SPACE
TURNED BIG PLACE

We are attached to place and long for freedom.
What begins as undifferentiated space becomes place
as we get to know it and endow it with value.
— YI-FU TUAN[1]

WITH A POPULATION of approximately 25,000 in a territory that covers about 482,515 square kilometres (186,300 square miles); the Yukon is by any world standard, a big space. And for an outdoor traveller of any description – hiker, hunter, canoeist, climber and fisher – it is a space that defies knowledge as a "place"…perhaps. It would constitute travel upon quite a list of rivers, lakes, mountain ranges, plains, even a coastline, to explore what today fits the bill as wild space. "Making" a place of the Yukon that one can come to know, seems beyond reason for all travelling visitors.

How to start? That part's easy – easy to start, that is. To come to know the Yukon as a place I'd suggest you start at the obvious historical entry points and work your way into the interior. In the Yukon, you can follow the history inland from the Pacific and from the mighty Mackenzie River to the east. In both cases you travel over a mountain range into the Yukon River basin. Native Peoples' migration routes for trade and seasonal hunting, gold seekers, North West Mounted Police, patrollers – all travelled into the Yukon interior from entry points that paradoxically may have been, relatively speaking, bustling ports-of-call. Learning the stories from entry points into the Yukon interior is a good step in coming to know the Yukon as a space turned place. Perhaps most of the travellers, then and now, who turn their sights into the

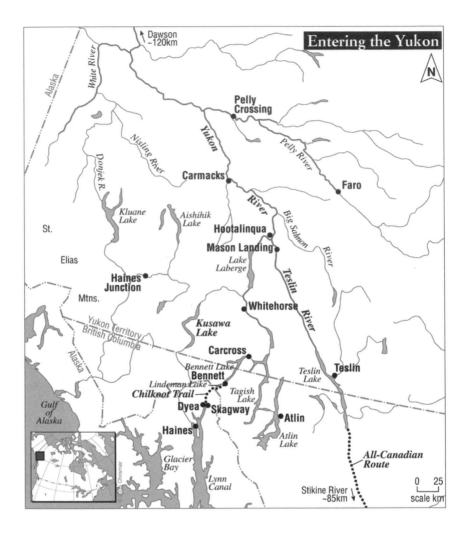

Yukon interior share the sensations so well recorded by Barbara Hodgson's fictional traveller "Hippolyte Webb":

> He loved this point in travel, the very beginning, the moment when the decision to go hit his heart and his gut, when the whirl of topography careening through his brain burned his feet, when the fine lines of maps tangled themselves around him like a net and drew him up and away, when his mind travelled the world before he even walked out the door.[2]

The "whirl of topography" is generally understood by the visiting traveller as the "tracing of one thin line" by linear routes explored through the country. Here are a few such thin lines.[3]

In 1990, on a two-family camping outing at the remote south end of Kusawa Lake, fellow father, Tony Gonda, and I had an afternoon hike in mind. We would simply climb the significant hill behind our campsite. Walk up, walk down and use the lake as a landmark reference. We took maps to be safe. Soon we reached a bench – a natural levelling on the slope – to cross on our continual climb. The forest was quite open. The going was good. We'd be up and down before dinner. But on this bench, we discovered a trail. There were blazes (axe-cut notches hacked out on both sides of the trees) though only a few. There was a faint path following along the bench. Curious, we walked it to confirm that this really was a trail. It was a trail, a human trail, but why here? There seemed to be no logic to a trail in this remote corner of this big lake, wild river-dominated landscape. A trail climbing this hill from the obvious beach campsite would be odd as well but would confirm recreational usage at least. Also, this was an old faint trail and, with time to hike that day, we would learn it was obscured in swampy land and by new, dense vegetation. We soon abandoned the hill climb for the mysterious qualities of the unknown trail. We'd lose the trail and pick it up again. We'd get into gnarly woods but resurface with a trail again. At one point we were rewarded with a stunning open view

Hiking from our campsite on Kusawa Lake, Tony Gonda and I found an ancient migration route following this river valley into the interior.

to the east up a river valley. Reviewing maps later, we figured this river would join Tagish Lake to the southeast and from there onto the 3,000-kilometre (1,864-mile) plus long Yukon River. At the big open view we stopped and returned. What was this faint trail all about? Puzzled, we reviewed our maps. The outing was an inspired one. Later we would confirm our speculation with a Yukon Parks Canada staff member.

We had stumbled onto an old migration route for the Tlingit, Tagish or Tutchone peoples moving between the Pacific coast and the interior Yukon River. Only with a big view of the land does any travel route in this area make sense. The Chilkat Pass is off to the southwest with access to plentiful marine life. The link to the interior meant fur-bearing animals and big game. The lakes are huge and the river fast flowing. It is not water travel country, though it took this discovered route to really make me understand this. Naively, I'd thought the Parks Canada people would be as excited about our discovery as we were to underscore our discovery; we were told matter-of-factly, "walking migration routes are all over this country, no big deal." But this in no way diminished my personal excitement. Returning again to Hippolyte Webb, we shared the understanding that there was a hidden wisdom to be had in our little discovery:

> "Through his reading, he amassed proof that the earth could still hide parts of itself from the prying eyes that seemed to be everywhere these days; aerial and satellite photography, geographical positioning systems, radar, electronic mapping devices, all the instruments that intimately and thoroughly inspected the world's secret features, its dimples, crevices, and pockmarks. What was once seen from a vantage point on the surface, the summit of a mountain, for instance, and measured by eye, by hand, by pacing, was now diminished by accuracy and certainty. Press a button on a hand-held whatever and know instantly where you are, especially relative to where you've been, where you want to go. Whatever happened to just being in a place and knowing it for what it is?"[4]

No button press, "presto" knowledge: this discovery was tied to quiet curious walking on an ancient land. Not a portage, but rather a hunting/trading/migration route though the centuries, I felt we had "snapped the thread of linear time"[5] tracing this one thin line.

The rock protruding into the river channel to the left likely was the culprit that caused Klondike-bound Stampeder John Mattes' ultimate death. He is not buried at the Bennett Lake Cemetery because he committed suicide after losing two sets of supplies bound for Dawson City.

Tony and I had discovered a quality of the Yukon that reinforced the Native Peoples' presence on this land. We could reach down with roots to the past and know this hidden place for what it is. And we could more easily wander at will and lose ourselves with each new big view and map-reading gaze. A bit of the puzzling Yukon was revealed that day. Simply put – people walked!

There is another quality of the Yukon central to understanding the place – the Klondike Gold Rush of 1898–99. Mark Twain once wrote of his tourist travels in Palestine, "How wearing to have to read one hundred pages of history every three or four miles." I remember first reading this passage and wondering, "Wow, where could you do this in the wilds of Canada?" The answer lies along the Klondike Gold Rush Trail in the Yukon. Two families, the Hendersons and the Webers, totalling four adults and five children, (we typically don't recommend a ratio of more children than adults) headed Yukon-bound in the summer of 1999 for our own commemorative travels on parts of the famous Gold Rush Trail. Our choice was to paddle the Teslin River, part of the all-Canadian route, to the Dawson City/Bonanza Creek gold fields and to hike the Chilkoot Stampeder Gold Rush Trail of 1898–99 to the Yukon River headwaters at lakes Lindeman and Bennett.

Earlier, in 1986, my wife Kathleen and I had hiked the Chilkoot and paddled the Big Salmon River to the Yukon River. The 1999 trip was all about returning to a favourite region and showing the kids some of "big country" Canada.

Mostly we were eyes-wide keeners, checking out every prospectors'/trappers' cabin along the Teslin shores and examining relics along the hiking trail. Cheeckako, or newcomers, they would have called us back in the 1890s. Tourists, we are today, in a strange place by conventional tourist standards, where the tourist highlights are not conveniently just off the roadways, but rather on rugged hiking trails and waterways that demand multi-day trips. Twain resented the fact he was a burdened "tourist." We embraced the Yukon way of rugged tourism. Still, I can concur with Mark Twain; at times, there was the burden of so much history, so many stories.

It is a rare feeling in the Canadian wilds to feel overwhelmed by a combined big picture of the wealth of individual stories of men wandering up the lesser rivers of the Yukon River system, and the one massive sea of humanity story that is the stampede of prospectors, 30,000 in all between 1897–99, heading over the mountain passes and down the Yukon River. Imagine 800 boats departed on *one day,* May 29, 1898, from Bennett Lake to the gold fields. Imagine the Boswell brothers from Peterborough, Ontario, quietly exploring waterways for gold, for close to twenty years before the '98 rush. One brother, Thomas, lost a leg to a grizzly bear in 1891, but was still active in the '98 Klondike rush. Imagine John Mattes, hiking over the Chilkoot with his mandatory requirement of a ton of supplies, only to dump them in the rapids between lakes Lindeman and Bennett, still very much at the river's headwaters. Undaunted, he returned to the Pacific coast at Skagway to resupply, to hike over the pass again, only to dump all in the same rapids months later. Standing beside his gravestone while looking over the river to the rapids of his demise was a moving experience. He committed suicide at this spot, right after the second loss of gear. Imagine the very first four Victorian Order of Nurses, whom former Prime Minister Sir Charles Tupper called "female quacks," joining a North West Mounted Police march and paddle on the all-Canadian Teslin route to the gold fields. What a first assignment!

Well, you get the picture. Twain is right. Such a well-storied landscape can eventually prove wearing at the time. On the Teslin there are so many abandoned historic cabins that a normally "must-see" historic landing from the turn of the century can become, "oh not another set

Sailing on the mighty Yukon River – as if one needs extra help on this fast flowing river.

of cool sod-roofed 1900–30s cabins, let's keep going" or, "yet another lonely gravestone of a dejected prospector, we won't bother hunting for this one." The burden of so much history is not common to the Canadian wilds. At the time it was a strange sensation of saturation.

Only a few stories will suffice here. First, our own. The allure of the "big view" – the sweeping expanse of the Yukon and its rivers – easily captured our family tripping group. We selected the Teslin River, which flows from its Teslin Lake headwaters on the British Columbia/Yukon border for 184 kilometres to the Yukon River. We would then shift from the more intimate Teslin to the expansive Yukon River at the dramatic Hootalinqua River junction settlement for a 176-kilometre (109-mile) paddle to our take-out at the town of Carmacks.

This is a standard Yukon trip. The scenery is stunning, heritage sites abound, the logistics are easy and the trip overall relatively inexpensive. You should allow eight to twelve days for paddling the route giving time for the many heritage sites. Because of certain travel itinerary circumstances, our timing was tight. We paddled the route in seven days, certainly doable, but compromising in terms of time to fish for the elusive grayling. We played endless rounds of kids' card games such as Cheat, Speed and Uno, even in the canoe, and we had time to stop at most heritage landmarks along the way. Doing the math of this tells you we averaged over 50 kilometres (31miles) per day. In fact, on the Yukon River we had two 70 kilometres plus (40 miles plus) days. While this sounds like a "push" trip, it really wasn't, that is, until the last few days. Remembering that the current on the Yukon River rolls along at anywhere between five and ten kilometres per hour meant that we had time to explore the many shoreline stops while at times paddling into the midnight sun. The Teslin current is speedy as well, though you can really "make a mile" if you have to, once on the Yukon. Paddling leisurely, stopping often, and covering 50 kilometres (31 miles) per day is certainly an exciting feature to Yukon paddling.

Having to rush a bit at the end of our trip seemed oddly suited to the river's history. Here you are with a grand vista, an obstacle-free route of fast current and long days of sunlight, (typically, we happily pulled into camp between 7:00 and 9:00 p.m.) and yet there is a pervasive push on to round the next bend, then the next. The current propels more than the canoe. It affects the psyche. You want to go and the going is easy. Most Klondikers were rushing to stake a mining claim before the next guy. And, admittedly, we rushed a bit at the end so to squeeze in another Yukon trip in limited time. If we'd planned to rush more, we might have added a few days to push on to Dawson, over 400 kilometres downstream. "Only another five days," you catch yourself saying. All the while, these rivers flow along as if smugly aware of Winnie-the-Pooh's ponderous observation, "Rivers know this: There is no hurry. We shall get there some day."

From Carmacks, we returned to our base camp, Whitehorse, our base camp with its two Tim Horton's on the main street, before heading for a Chilkoot Gold Rush hiking trail. Doing both trips together seems critical for a full sense of the overall Yukon gold rush story. It is a story involving both the hiking/mountain pass experience and river travel of epic proportion, and not just to Dawson City but later down river further to Nome, Alaska. There are also travels on the Teslin to the lesser-known Livingstone Creek gold discoveries, just east of the Teslin via the Swift and Boswell rivers and overland routes.

One little-known story involves the North West Mounted Police "All-Canadian Route" to the gold fields in 1898–1900. The route involved rafting up the Stikine River to a 250-kilometre hike over the Teslin Trail – a questionable label – where the water route on the Teslin system leads to the gold field. Known as the Yukon Field Force, the two hundred men volunteering for the trip for double wages, departed from Ontario by train. The party also included the first of the Victorian Order of Nurses. Another first should also be noted. These NWMP troops were basically peacekeepers for the 30,000 plus population burgeoning in the Yukon interior. They were the first garrison in Canada's Subarctic. Mostly they were there to show a determined display of Canadian sovereignty of the North. Approximately eighty percent of the Yukon population in 1898 were American. Historian Ian McCulloch states, "the Field Force may well have played a greater role in the evolution of Canada than the record would indicate."[6] The Yukon, as had the territory of Oregon fifty years earlier, could have easily shifted allegiance to the United States.

The North West Mounted Police established Fort Selkirk upriver from Dawson City and were a determined presence there in the hectic early days. Law and order would rule in the Canadian frontier. A few quick comments should provide a sense of the travel experience endured on this "alternate route." Sixty tons of supplies were carried over the Teslin Trail; mules carried 200 pounds (about 91 kilograms) each and men carried 50 pounds (about 23 kilograms) each. One soldier composed the following favourite song/chant for the trail:

> *Damn the journey, damn the track.*
> *Damn the distance there and back.*
> *Damn the sunshine, damn the weather.*
> *Damn the goldfields altogether.*[7]

Mutiny was threatened. The more difficult route via the Teslin would easily become shrouded in resentment, given that the added drudgery for the men was endured because Canadian officials wished to avoid asking permission to march Canadian troops over American soil (the first half of the Chilkoot Trail). One last detail, not a minor one to many of my paddling friends, their two-year supply of coffee was lost on the Stikine in the early goings. The lime juice for scurvy prevention was not however. The trail was never much of an open visible or viable route, though two groups recently have travelled its twisted tangled way. Larry Pynn, in 1997, and Ian and Sally Wilson, in 1998, both set their sights for the Teslin River over this trail. Both wrote a book of their adventures. Given their experiences on the trail, their time on the easygoing Teslin River was a dream come true for them. For us, we all marvelled at our floating speed as we watched the river bottom cobblestone speed by. This is a powerful lasting memory.

Most of the intriguing Yukon stories are small individual personal tales that can be compiled to form a collective consciousness. It is this "back of beyond," "law of the Yukon," "strange things done in the midnight sun," consciousness that was the source of inspiration for poet Robert Service and author Jack London. One such Teslin story captured my imagination.

Jonas Hagstrom was found dead at his Teslin cabin in 1941 at age 70. In 1906, at the age of 35, he departed from his family farm in Sweden, likely lured to the Canadian North by the stories of fortunes had and riches aplenty. Today we might call these accounts, "urban legends." Jonas (John) like so many before him, sought out that one big strike in many Yukon locations, before, at age 60, settling for good up the Teslin, near the Swift River for his final ten years. From his humble Teslin cabin, he hunted, trapped and served as a machinist to those in need. He also received a government pension of $20.00 per month. In the early years, presumably he had intended to make a fortune and send for his family or return home. He did send letters home, occasionally with poetic verse. One poem, written back to Sweden in 1930, had the following lines that clearly capture the character and echoes of remote Yukon living:

> ...for you know, 'tis constant dripping
> Wears away the hardest stone.
> Never slack sublime endeavour,
> Nor midst cheerless toil despair;
> If you'd rise above your fellows,
> Remember, you must "Win and Wear.[8]

In 1940, at age 69, John received a letter and ticket for his return to Sweden from his daughter Elsa. Now 35 years in Canada, ten years on the Teslin, but having written home of longing to see his native land and family, he responded to the encouraging invitation in a strangely dispassionate tone:

> ...the news are very scarce, but very welcome indeed. Perhaps if you had to go to Stockholm for your mail, crossing mountains, swamps and glaciers, and no sign of a road or a house for 300 kilometers,

and the thermometer sometimes falling to 90 degrees (fah.) below zero; you would not likely hitch up a couple of dogs and go and get your mail everyday….On account of the war in Europe the travelling facilities are dangerous and uncertain, and I hope the tickets are good for some time…

John Hagstrom, along with the remains of his cabin, rests quietly, like many others along the Teslin. Did he "really" want to return to Sweden, and was it for only a visit? I suspect the Yukon had gotten under his skin. Perhaps he missed the chance to return a decade earlier. John's story along the Teslin is special, not so much for its contents, but because we can know something of it – thanks to Yukon traveller/guide/researcher Gus Karpes. Along the river that day I felt an excitement to be directly in the midst of such stories, stories about people who truly did, "Never slack sublime endeavour," or tried to live that virtue. John's story, as best as I can know it, seems both sombre and noble at the same time. His story and those of others along the Teslin help make the river feel like a place more than a space.

Jonas Hagstrom, 1939, one of a countless number of gold rush seekers who never returned home. *Photo taken from A.C. (Gus) Karpes, The Teslin River.*

Just downstream from "John's place" there are stories about travellers on the Swift and Boswell river tributaries, stories from Teslin Crossing and Mason Landing, a place which once boasted a roadhouse, stable, telegraph station and trading post. Although the Teslin and Yukon rivers can become "wearing" with their wealth of individual stories, it is, however, a worthy endeavour to compile the stories as you travel downstream. There really were strange and wonderful things done in the "land of the midnight sun." Organizational theorist Harrison Owen uses the expression, "How big is your now? This eloquently pertains to the Yukon travel corridors. As the stories accumulate, your "now" grows and grows. The space shrinks but the place expands. You may feel saturated by the *big* history. But this is a good "big!"

Central to so many of the Pacific entry-point stories of the Yukon, be they one of Native seasonal migrations or gold seekers, is the "long portage" – the Chilkoot Trail, now a National Park.

Above towered storm-beaten Chilkoot. Up its gaunt ragged front crawled a slender string of men. But it was an endless string. It came out of the last fringe of dwarfed shrub below, drew a black line across a dazzling stretch of ice…Even as she looked, Chilkoot was wrapped in rolling mist and whirling cloud, and a storm of sleet and wind roared down upon the toiling pigmies. The light was swept out of the day, and a deep gloom prevailed.

This is famed Yukon storyteller Jack London's best description of the infamous "Golden Stairs" – the final assault of the Chilkoot Gold Rush Trail that became the symbol of hardship for the 600-mile trip to the Yukon goldfields. He describes the pass in his story, "A Daughter of the Snows," during its peak season of winter in 1898 when over thirty thousand made the climb. In winter, snow steps were easily cut in the thirty-degree or greater steepness with an estimated 12,000 steps needed to complete the climb. Today, most hikers travel on the rocky ankle-bending terrain of summer. Based on all reports and our own experience of two crossings there, the weather of the pass has remained a constant for the one hundred years since London's description. A ranger's report at the last designated camp before the summit climb warns that, "those who have decided to put off the climb for a day in the hopes of better weather, frequently find the weather they do encounter even worse." The string of men and women is there too. It is not a lonely feeling on the Chilkoot Pass summit. The "slender string of men" exists as a dream-like state for the present hiker. With so many relics and

Cutting spring snow steps in the 1890s is a far cry from the boulder-strewn trail we navigate in the summer today. The Chilkoot, however, remains a daunting proposition. *Courtesy of Yukon Archives.*

quality interpretive displays along the trail, the past saga of the once infamous trail is easy to recall, capturing one's imagination with penetrating thoughts of toil and sweat, anguish and joy of accomplishment – emotions easily revisited by tracking this thin line up and over.

Today, the Chilkoot Trail is a well-managed and jointly run (with American Parks Service) National Park that boosts a unique collaboration of natural, cultural and recreational resources.[9]

As a natural setting the park can boast three distinct ecological zones within its small area. Following the trail historically from east to west, American tidewater to the headwaters of Canadian interior waterways, one first experiences the Pacific northwest coastal rain forest with stands of western hemlock, sitka spruce, poplar and cottonwood, then the alpine tundra/meadows set amidst the glacial snow and rushing waters of the Canadian side. Once beyond the 13 kilometres (8 miles) above the treeline, a rain-shadow effect created by the Coastal Range produces a third distinctive zone of fir, pine and spruce, the more open park-like terrain of the sub-alpine boreal forest. Each zone has its own charm that is wonderfully accentuated by the extreme transition in space and time. Average hikers travel through these three zones in three to five days, but tales of one day's hard steady walk/jog duration for the ultra marathon psyche are not uncommon for completing the rugged 53-kilometre (33-mile) hike.

The American side is generally shrouded in cloud and limited for viewpoints. The Chilkoot summit at the Canadian/USA border is distinguished for having one of the lowest incidence of sunshine in Canada. Here the elevation is 1,122 metres (3,680 feet) rising from sea level through to the Canadian terminus at Bennett Lake with a gradual drop to 650 metres. From the summit, the view from the Canadian side is usually free of clouds with an appealing open clean look graced by a gradual slope, a beckoning promised land to the eyes of many a gold seeker and present-day hiker. Amidst the beauty of the sunlit alpine meadows one cannot help wonder if such aesthetic beauty was beyond the singular vision and urgency of the gold rushers.

Culturally the story is a simple one, yet one of wild excesses and extremes. Pierre Berton suggests that calling the gold rush a "Stampede" is a "cruel misnomer." The pass itself, from the coastal thrown-up town of Dyea to the timber-laden and thus boat-building shoreline of Lindeman or Bennett lakes took an average of three months to traverse, if travel was by one's own means entirely.

Once the North West Mounted Police were installed at the disputed summit border in early 1898, an edict went out – one man had to be outfitted in the Yukon with one ton of supplies. This was law and would ideally ensure survival in the Canadian wilds and greatly cut down on any sense of stampeding. Thirty trips were common over the top, with piles of supplies stranded everywhere on the snowy summit. This was only the beginning. From the start of navigation, boats were built by hand to descend the Yukon River from the Chilkoot headwaters to Dawson City, deep within the Yukon interior. While the Yukon is not treacherous, it does have a rapid or two where amateur boat builders would lose their crafts and their ton of supplies they had so laboriously weighted over the pass. Miles Canyon, and the Five Finger Rapids were names to incite a new type of terror and anxiety once the pass was completed, and don't forget John Mattes, mentioned earlier, between Lindeman and Bennett lakes. One rapid, two dumpings over two trips, two lost outfit of supplies, two lost boats and one lost life to suicide. Hard luck stories are not hard to find, though this one documented in the Bennett Lake church records takes all.

My own experiences in this rugged landscape were focused on a slow-paced photographer's dreamland where natural beauty was oddly overshadowed by historical content. The once "poor man's route" to the gold rush is full of riches. At Sheep Camp on the USA side, my journal entry reads:

> A hanging glacier ahead, a 150-metre cascading waterfall behind, a deep valley corridor leading us on, intriguing fog rolling in and out above, and two streams rushing by on each side of us; yet with all this natural beauty, myself and others I've talked with consider the natural secondary to the exciting association with the past. We struggle to picture the saloons, restaurants and hotels of the tent city and the floggings, floodings, rescues, card playing, and other dramas and camaraderies that existed at this exact spot less than 100 years ago...The trees are mostly poplar. At one time it must have been all clear. The timber was used to build tent frames and log structures. One ruined log cabin remains by the water near our tent.

Copied excerpts from historical accounts are kept in a ranger's cabin on site. One 1898 account reads, "a rough spot [Sheep Camp] with scant space for a town site. There was one street, sixteen feet wide and a mile long, winding haphazard along the east bank of the Taiya [River]. There are many saloons, two drug stores, a hospital, fifteen hotels and restaurants, numerous coffee stands and hotels, two laundries, a bathhouse and several stores."[10]

This record paints quite a civilized scene but, to clear up any misconceptions, a Chicago woman, Martha Louise Black, who eventually was elected to the Canadian Parliament, wrote in a letter home of the Grand Pacific Hotel at Sheep Camp, "look at your woodshed, fit it up with Standees and you have the Grand Pacific." Another seeker wrote, "reached Sheep Camp that afternoon; the vilest hole I have ever seen. Not so by nature, but made so by man. The little stream running through the place is full of dead dogs, horses and company."

Over the pass are Lindeman and Bennett, both tent cities (campsites today) and centres of boat building operations in their heyday. Among the relics along the trail are shovels, sleighs, rotting canvas and boots, old stoves, boat frames, two-metre long whipsaws (many found this their most awkward item to carry). A corridor road is all that remains of the summer wagon road between Crater and Long lakes on the Canadian side. A most valuable trail feature is the wealth of historical information available along the route. Apart from interpretive literature at Sheep Camp and Canyon City, Parks Canada has established a photo museum and library at Lindeman and interpretive display at Bennett. Interpretive signs also dot the trail where relevant, often linking old photos with the present scene. It is possible to join a guided tour at Bennett Lake as well.

The human story is a big one, well-suited to this big space, and well-documented in historical travel accounts, even "wearing" on the mind, as Mark Twain might say. In the tent cities there was much stealing which occasionally led to public floggings as men were forced to establish their own law and order. There was both a spring avalanche at the Scales, the base of the Golden Stairs, and a run-off flood at Sheep Camp. These were hazards that awaited those who were not in time for the safer and easier late winter passage. There was boat building to be done on Lindeman shores, a task that many found more demanding than the pass itself. Standing below the scaffolding of the primitive sawmill, working the whipsaw meant sawdust seriously irritating eyes, not to mention its effect on breathing. But mostly there was no gold. When most gold seekers arrived en masse in the boom summer of 1898, they found most claims taken by established operations. Many moved on to the Alaskan gold rush or to Livingstone Creek off the Teslin in 1900. Others stayed and stood their ground, as it were, while more went back home.

Undoubtedly many Klondikers, whether hooked by the land or not, would have a difficult time comprehending the motives of the present-day hikers. No gold, why travel? Either way, likely the stretching of their imagination to comprehend our modern situation would be equal to our attempts to appreciate their circumstance. It is a delight that a new travelling spirit is emerging that values the land not for what we can take out of it, but rather for what we can find in this place – naturally, culturally and recreationally. While today we marvel at the labours and determination of the Klondikers, tomorrow we will rejoice in the insights and determination that secured this area as a National Park corridor window into the past and a gateway to a better relationship with the land.

There are other entry points into the Yukon with stories that help one understand the place as a "place" rather than a space. One such story is "The Lost Patrol" of the North West Mounted Police in the Wind River valley. The dogsledding patrol headed south from Fort McPherson on the Peel River near the Mackenzie River for a 475-mile (764-kilometre) run. Not small change this! But Inspector Francis J. Fitzgerald in December 1910 thought of it certainly as a routine mail run. Experimenting with lighter weight and less food, and not hiring a local guide, Fitzgerald and three others headed out for the Wind River of the Peel River drainage en route to Dawson on the Yukon drainage. The group became lost somewhere up the Wind River headwaters and decided, too late, to return in desperation. In late March, their bodies were found less than 35 miles (56 kilometres) from their starting point. They had eaten the dogs. They had been out 53 days covering an estimated 620 miles (998 kilometres). Temperatures had dropped to -60°F. Exhaustion, hunger, scurvy and frostbite all had a hand in their fate. Certainly disbelief was also a likely factor. Fitzgerald had been an unflappable traveller and leader. Good luck and determined effort had marked his career. He was the epitome of a "we always get our man" and "succeed on the trail" type of guy. On January 12, they missed the correct Forrest Creek Trail to the west. They headed further up the Little Wind River. On February 5, 1911, Fitzgerald's diary ends during their return trip.

I think of Fitzgerald, shocked perhaps that the land had gotten the better of him, sitting on the Upper Wind River pondering his fate. Something about this story echoes loudly for my own winter trip, no matter the setting. Someday I'll travel this Wind River. The echoes then will ring like Quasimodo in his bell tower of Notre Dame.

We also have the Rat-Bell-Porcupine River traverse to the Yukon River. The Rat is an infamous upriver canoe drag from the Peel/Mackenzie rivers, north of Fort McPherson. This was also a Klondike gold-seekers trail. Destruction City, now overgrown with vegetation, once marked a wintering-over site and a collection of boats wrecked in the upriver labours on the Rat. This is also the general area of the Mad Trapper, Albert Johnson, and his strange evasion of a NWMP chase over close to two months duration.[11] The NWMP men knocked on his door on Christmas Day to follow up on a suggestion of illegal trapping. Johnson shot one of the men through the cabin door. So began a long holdout and cabin siege, and an eventual chase up the Rat.

These entry points from the northeast tell lonely stories of loners and single travel parties following challenging waterways up and over mountain passes to the Yukon River lifeline. I'm excited to turn my travellers' attentions to the northeast. Sadly, I knew nothing of these stories in 1980. I passed by the Fort McPherson cemetery without visiting Fitzgerald's grave. Nor did I visit Albert Johnson's grave in downtown Aklavik, just downstream.

All stories from entry points lead into the big Yukon interior. The Yukon is a big space, with suitably big stories. These stories help make this very big space, a " place" one can celebrate with human enterprise, large and small. It all may become "wearing" on the mind, but these Yukon stories at geographical entry points serve as historically echoing entry points as well. I have not, as yet, entered the Yukon from the east. I probably won't. At this stage, my knee couldn't handle the upriver walking/dragging on the Rat River. Still the Wind and Snake rivers afford opportunities to ponder the collective history of these eastern entry points, tripping from the inside out, rather than the outside in as has been my experience in the southwest regions of the Yukon. Slowly I'll make a place out of the Yukon.

4

FILLING CABINS WITH STORIES IN THE LAND OF THE LITTLE STICKS

*In Manitoba there are no straight lines, at least for
the canoeist. Beyond the grain elevators and prairies of the
south there is a paddling paradise of over 100,000 lakes and
rivers, which are wilder than most native Manitobans can imagine.
While researching seventeen of Manitoba's wildest rivers over a
four-year period, I encountered fewer than twenty other paddlers.*
– HAP WILSON[1]

NUELTIN LAKE IS A HUB LAKE of the "Land of Little Sticks." The Seal, Caribou, Thlewiaza, Cochrane, Windy, Tha-anne rivers are all related to the lake that is a maze of islands and bays. In the late 1930s, Nueltin was among the few remaining uncharted lakes in Canada and certainly one of the least known except to its mainly Chipewyan (Dene) inhabitants. Particularly interesting in the 1920s and 30s, Nueltin saw on its shores a mix of white trappers and traders, Cree, Inuit and Dene.

Nueltin Lake is a landscape of transition between a vague treeline and the open so-called Barren Lands, hence the name "Little Sticks." Travelling the lake serves as a gentle transition in terrain, gradually easing one into the tundra.

I passed through Nueltin in 1983, between day 10 and day 20 of a forty-five-day canoe trip from Wollaston Lake, Saskatchewan, to Arviat (then Eskimo Point) just south of the Maguse River, where it empties into Hudson Bay. Nueltin (Sleeping Island) Lake straddles the Manitoba/

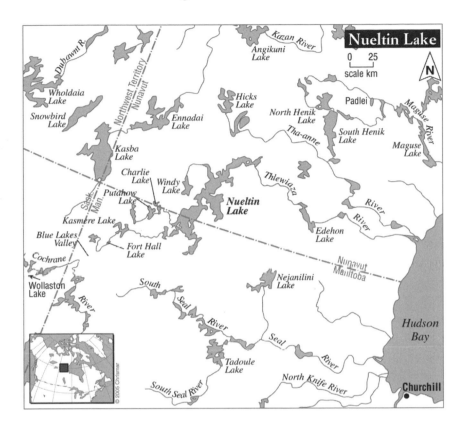

Nunavut border and it, along with the Windy Lake/River complex, forms a landscape etched in my memory and a focus of my imagination of "place" in the Canadian bush, a place that demands return visits.

American nature writer and conservationist Sigurd Olson wrote in *The Singing Wilderness* of his quest for the "perfect lake":

> Always before me was the ideal, a place not only remote, not only of great beauty, but possessed of an intangible quality and spirit that typified to me all of the unbroken north beyond all roads.[2]

Sigurd found it, his perfect ideal lake, with his first glimpse of Saganaga Lake on the Ontario/Minnesota border at the western edge of Quetico Provincial Park. It is easy for me to see why this was Sigurd's choice in the 1950s – a sweeping view, rapids and waterfalls at all of its inflows and outflows, a grand sense of space for canoes and snowshoes. I too had the

Nueltin Lake on a particularly charming evening.

feeling of the perfect lake/river complex with ten days in the Nueltin area – these qualities of the big view, variety of water and terrain and mostly "space." Saganaga Lake is a good choice for Sigurd. I was fifteen years old when I saw it, but remember it well still. However, "the unbroken north beyond all roads" for Sigurd and myself by the 1980s is pushed north. Today Nueltin would have excited Sigurd as it excited me.

I will return to the Nueltin/Windy lakes to travel slowly in an odd wandering circuit. In 1983, I merely passed through on a "move everyday" ambitious linear trail trip. The thought of a slow-moving circuit route to get to know *just* this space is a delightful anticipation and it speaks to a place "getting under your skin," as friend Zabe MacEachren calls it.

Nueltin is a landscape particularly rich in contrasts: from well-treed with surprisingly large white spruce to open tundra; from summer bugs that make sipping a cup of tea next to impossible to bug-free winds that equally make that cup of tea problematic; from high rounded eskers to low-lying meadows; from beaches to rocky shorelines, with summer and winter weather perhaps in the same day; from fast flowing rivers large and small to lakes (so many lakes) large and small of which Nueltin and Windy form a central hub. This description will excite many a canoe tripper. Where I might differ with my amorous gaze is that, while many others prefer the pristine "wilderness" feel to the place, I bring, perhaps undue, attention to those abandoned cabins, grave sites, the well-placed tree blaze, tent rings and a meat cache pile of stones. Mostly it's those now abandoned cabins and trappers' tilts that confound my curiosity.

Filling those cabins with stories is a big part of my particular feel for this particular place. While George Mallory said, when asked why he climbed mountains, "because they are there," I must follow the Gary Larson "Far Side" cartoon twist on this often quoted phrase. If asked, why I seek to fill these long forgotten cabins with their stories, I answer, because they (the stories) are not there. When I started this inquiry following my own 1983 trip, I had in hand, P.G. Downes' 1943 "northern canoe trippers bible," *Sleeping Island*. Some of the people and the stories of these cabins are scantly introduced. But it was enough, thinking again of Mallory's words, to seek out the cabins, graves, etc. because "they are there," and to seek also the stories of these encounters with a human presence because "they are not there" (or rather, certainly not obvious but nevertheless most rewarding when sought out in literature and through local detective work). I will start with Prentice G. Downes.[3]

Prentice G. Downes, a Harvard graduate and schoolteacher with interests in history, cartography and a general fascination for Canada's indigenous peoples, came to Nueltin Lake in 1939 to explore the land. In his own words, "Throughout the trip I had harboured the conceit that I might map not only the route but also the shoreline at least of this vast lake."[4] Quickly Downes and his trapper partner, John Albrecht, turned their thoughts to survival. It seems one must know the general way through before one can map in a carefree manner:

> …we went along for some hours into a headwind, and at last it became apparent that we had run into a long dead-end bay. This was discouraging as we seemed hemmed in everywhere by points and islands.
>
> We began to circle back, coming out on the east side of the islands we had previously passed on the west side; this of course making them practically unrecognizable. It was all very confusing and a little discouraging. This lake has been variously estimated from one hundred and twenty to one hundred and eight miles long, and to be hopelessly trapped in the first three hours was not at all a good prospect.
>
> We at length found ourselves forced back to within sight of our own camp of this morning and last night!
>
> We climbed a hill. What a sight! Islands…bays…channels… islands everywhere, every direction of the compass points, a vast maze as far as the eye could see. What was main shore, lakes, bays, islands,

or points, was all one endless confusion. Both of us wondered about either getting anywhere or back. It is not easy to paddle and map and get bearings all at the same time.

Somehow, somewhere, we had to break through to the north.[5]

P.G. Downes and John Albrecht were on the right track. Soon they found a stone cairn on a ridge, followed by "abundant camping evidence," such as hearthstones, and refuse of camping/dwelling, such as quartz flakes. The Dene would, again, next time in person, continue to show the way, and direct them off the big Nueltin to their preferred Windy Lake route, which rejoins Nueltin at its northern end. Of course, we followed this lead as well, avoiding the maze – well sort of avoiding it – enjoying a richer variety of terrain.

Remember we had maps. And yet due to a mishap in purchasing and photocopying them, we found ourselves missing a significant portion of map for big lake travel. We had to find our own "observation hill" to chart our course north (or at least to the commencement of our next map sheet). For me, this remains a trip highlight, though I have never contrived the situation since.

This Windy Lake route had us passing two significant cabins, those of trappers/traders Windy Smith (perhaps) or Del Simmons and the Schweder family. I'd learned enough from Downes (and Farley Mowat's *The Desperate People* and *People of the Deer* books – Mowat stayed with the Schweder family at the Windy River post in the summer of 1947) to know that more learning about these folks would add layers of meaning to P.G. Downes' words of introduction. P.G. Downes, in his book *Sleeping Island*, gives us stories of the time when white travellers were informed by indigenous peoples living on the land. *Sleeping*

Possibly Del Simmon's cabin at the north end of Windy Lake. The logs are numbered in Roman numerals, allowing it to be assembled above the treeline.

Island speaks of a peopled landscape, when campsites and fur posts were inhabited and both the exploring spirit and dwelling spirit most genuinely played out. Downes is a choice model for ways of being and ways of knowing how to capture the "ways of the north." He wanted to be a part of these ways of the North and once wrote in 1936, "The real people of the North don't love the North; what they cling to is that complex in themselves which is satisfied by their own situation – by the freedom of being their own boss…[by the] wandering irre-sponsibility of it all."[6] His enthusiasm flows freely off the pages of *Sleeping Island*. Indeed it could just as easily been Downes and not fel-low Massachusetts traveller, Henry David Thoreau, who on his deathbed was heard to have repeatedly whispered, "Moose and Indi-ans." Downes, the romantic, would have heard campfire stories about Smith, the pragmatic

Men like Irwin "Windy" Smith did not keep journals. He was of another breed than Downes. We learn from others that Windy Lake is not named for Windy Smith who was a likely occasional occupant of this particular Windy Lake cabin. Rather, the name "Windy" comes from an English translation of a Dene word meaning "windy," while "Windy" Smith is so named for his well-known hot air exaggerations. Windy, an independent trader through the 1920s and 30s, was not well liked. He was known not to have repaid his debt to his local Brochet community trading supplier. He had also shot some Dene dogs that had raided his food cache. Another trader at that time, Syd Keighley, notes, "killing a man's dog was a potential death sentence to his fam-ily." Keighley also reported:

> Late in the war years, Windy started collecting scrap metal out on the land left by the American army, and selling it. He paid the natives to bring it in to him. When, on his instructions, they pulled down an historic monument at Churchill and brought him the copper and brass plaques, he was arrested…[7]

Windy had never gone to school in his hometown of Pittsburgh. Instead he worked in the ironworks. From his various northern homes of Fort Hall, Putahow Lake and the Windy River country, he became self-taught from a set of encyclopaedia. It was believed he knew "everything" that could be found in those books.

Dene graves from the 1920s. Charlie Schweder also witnessed the chilling outcomes of an earlier Dene influenza epidemic.

With stories such as these, one must wonder what else might be said of this character of the North. Imagine finding the lost Windy Smith's journals under a floorboard. As for the Windy Lake cabin, it was well labelled with numbers on each log. Given the fact that it sits above the treeline, all the logs were hauled from the treeline edge of southern Nueltin/Windy country. Location, location, location! I cannot be sure that the cabin we visited on Windy Lake was Smith's, but I'd sure like to think so.

Fred Schweder Sr., a German immigrant along with his Cree wife Rose, eldest son Charlie, and with eight other children in two canoes, arrived in to the Nueltin/Ennadai Lake area to manage a series of fur trading posts for the Inuit to the north and Dene to the south. The year was 1939. That same year P.G. Downes and John Albrecht showed up. P.G. was looking for a pre-arranged plane to take him back to his teaching job. John, the trapper from Brochet, would hook up with others and paddle south. Ahh, the untold stories.

Charlie Schweder was known as "gentle, unassuming, and soft-spoken." Downes had a difficult time getting the 14-year-old Charlie to talk with him. Even the gift of Downes', a copy of *Peterson's Field Guide to Birds* didn't help, but Charlie became quite absorbed in it. Eight years later at age 22, Charlie was in charge of the post and trap line extending between Windy and Ennadai lakes and covering about 80 miles. He developed a keen knowledge of animal behaviour and is known to have influenced a 1947 guest, biologist Francis Harper, to blend scientific and traditional knowledge. Charlie saw much of the ravages of starvation in camps of the Caribou Inuit in the late 1940s and in his diary on July 30, 1947, he commented on a hilltop graveyard with 23

The Schweder family cabin where biologist Francis Harper and young writer Farley Mowat visited in 1947.

picket-fenced graves, near a traditional caribou crossing. Many Dene had been struck down with influenza transmitted from the village of Brochet. Downes informed our tripping group of this sombre spot on the upper Thlewiaza River which we found in 1983. Many picket-fenced graves, borders and wooden crosses were still standing then. For Charlie, at age 22, to experience such events first-hand would surely have influenced his decision to begin a new life in the 1950s, in and out of Churchill. Continuing to trap and travel from his new Hudson Bay coastal town of Churchill, Charlie married and raised eight children. In 1997, I enjoyed an exciting phone conversation with Theresa, Charlie's wife, about the old days and time on his beloved Windy River.

Eskimo Charlie Plenanshek! We know about Eskimo Charlie only thanks to others who mentioned his activities in passing in their records, diaries and letters. The various details found in these "mentions," once compiled, offer quite a life story. Charlie likely arrived in the North in 1907. Although he had spent time previously in Mexico, he was originally of Slavic origin but born in Serbia. He was married in 1915 to a Native woman, Jane Mary Ballintyne from the Churchill River area. His marriage record reports this Central European birthplace, though the name is partially rubbed out and replaced with a town in Mexico. In 1915, the Serbian location would have made him a foreign enemy during the First World War. Syd Keighley met Charlie once in 1927 near his Sturgeon/Weir River outpost and remembered, "He had a small field of wheat and made his own flour. We ate some of his whole wheat bannock and found it very good."[8]

Charlie moved to the Putahow Lake area, just west of the southwest corner of Nueltin, where he is most commonly associated. By the mid-30s "Charlie Lake" became the official name of a lake due north of Putahow. In 1940, when P.G. Downes met him en route to the Little Partridge connection from Kasmere Lake to the Kazan River, Downes noted, "It was an interesting meeting, and I was glad to run into him. He certainly did not impress me as unfavourably as the talk of others had suggested he would."[9] Downes' 1940 journal is rich with information. He reported the following about the Northern loner:

> He has not been outside for 8 years – since he returned from a really remarkable trip by canoe from Windy Lake to the Gulf of Mexico, then around the inside passage to Florida, and up the coast to New York and Montreal. He was married to a Pelican Narrows Cree and took his two half-breed children along with him. The country is full of tales of Charles's escapades. He was arrested and in jail a few years ago for using poison baits. He at one time captured and attempted to train caribou as draft animals. He has always been noted for his fine gardens, and this one was no exception...
>
> In appearance he was a very small, round-shouldered man with a black beard and blue eyes curiously slanted downward at the corners. His clothing consisted of a pair of rubbers, no socks, a very patched and torn pair of pants, and two or three shirts black with mud and sweat. His speech was heavily accented but well expressed and intelligent.
>
> He was very enthusiastic about 'his esker' and the general matter of them. The 'highways of the North,' he calls them, and he is not far wrong. He reminisced about his famous trip. He is a trifle given to exaggeration as to the great crowds which welcomed him, I feel, and extremely vain about everything connected with it, which is justifiable. Talking to him I was struck by his manner and that of Hornby [John Hornby], which had been described to me by people who knew the latter.[10]

Syd Keighley, on a leave from the Hudson's Bay Company in 1926–27, noted matter-of-factly, "We took time off from the autumn chores to explore the Putahow River to the east. We followed the river down to where it entered Nueltin Lake, running all rapids, some of them being very tricky. Later, we were told the rapids on this river were impossible to run."[11]

Keighley records his travel in detail from the outpost cabins on the Caribou River headwaters and the Poor Fish Lake Post, west of Windy Lake and Stanley House on the Churchill River. It is clear that winter is the preferred season for travel. These travels include the mapping of Nueltin Lake and areas west to Ennadai Lake on the Kazan River in 1934. Too bad P.G. Downes didn't know about these rough maps. His overall account of the 1920s and 30s in *Sleeping Island* is peppered with the mention of tripping routes:

> At Brochet we met Jack Lundie, who was taking four freight canoe loads of trade goods north to the post at Thlu-kan-two or Poor Fish Lake in the Northwest Territories. By canoe the distance was a good 350 miles.

Along this very rarely travelled route (the Cochrane River to the Thlewiaza River, to Kasmere and Putahow lakes, and Charlie Lake north to Poor Fish Lake, which is west of the more obvious Windy Lake/ River) he wrote:

> The last portage took us into the headwaters of the Little Fish River, called the Thlu-assee-des [Thlewiaza River, called by the Inuit as Big River] in Chipewyan. The beginning of this river is no more than a creek, and we had to make portage after portage. I counted two hundred and then lost track of the number.

Today, travel north of Kasmere Lake into Putahow and Poor Fish Lake country is very rare, likely for the reasons just mentioned, though it appears to make a good circular route by connecting with Nueltin.

On another trip, between Brochet on Reindeer Lake and Stanley House on the Churchill River, Syd Keighley casually comments:

> At Reindeer River, open water forced me to borrow a canoe, [he had been dogsledding] and we began the tedious process of alternating between water and ice, canoe and sled.[12]

Nothing more is said as to how such a process is actually carried out. For Keighley to point out that this was a tedious affair should suggest to contemporary travellers that it was an intensive undertaking and a bit understated in print.

While Keighley's travels can be followed, those of the independent trappers such as Hugh Mattila are more uncertain and likely more varied. Of the latter, biographer Islae Carol Johnson writes:

> It is next to impossible to chart Hugh Mattila's trapping excursions on a map. Each fall he set out to explore new territories and if his traps line bordered that of a previous year, it was more by accident than design. Nor is it possible to follow his tracks in true chronological order.[13]

It is clear that Mattila's canoe and dog-assisted snowshoe travels from 1929 to 1935 covered a wide area out from Fort Churchill to Wager Bay with a focus on camps up the North Knife and Seal rivers, east of Nueltin. At each new trapping location, a new cabin was built to serve as a base camp. Mattila recalls one hair-raising story of being held prisoner on a floating iceberg while attempting the dangerous shoreline passage around Marsh Point between the Hayes River Channel and the Nelson River. (Today there is a boat taxi service for canoeists that connects the Hayes River to the rail line along the north shore of the Nelson) After five days in mid-July and many scares of being sent further offshore, all ended well, though not before a sled dog, transported by canoe, had to be shot for going mad after drinking sea water.

Thanks to visiting prospectors Harold Way and Sherman Oliver, who were sent into the Nueltin Lake region in 1934 to conduct geological reconnaissance and mapping, we learn about maintaining one's life in this setting. W. Gillies Ross in the fall 1968 edition of *The Beaver* wrote of their time occupying an abandoned Hudson's Bay Company post on Windy Lake. (Perhaps this was the cabin we visited):

> In the fall, preparations for the coming winter absorbed their energy. A wood stove would be burning from September to June to heat the cabin, and they estimated their fuel needs at 50 cords of wood. Hardly a tree existed near the cabin but a stream valley six miles away contained spruce trees of up to five inches in diameter. The

men made dozens of trips to the valley, returning with kamutiks piled high with wood…Preparations for the winter kept the men active but they took well to the life. Way wrote home, "I never felt better in my life. I can run all day behind the dogs without puffing. My strength is becoming enormous – both in physique and odour.

Short days, poor light, snow cover, low temperatures and high winds reduced geological work to a minimum in the winter months. Day-to-day existence, however, required lots of effort and there was no time for boredom. Firewood had to be split and brought in. Water had to be obtained. Stone caches were visited every week for caribou meat. Traps set out to protect their meat caches frequently caught white fox and marten; these were thawed and skinned in the cabin, and the skins dried on frames. Two dozen dogs had to be fed each day. In addition to these chores a limited number of geological trips were made, as well as several trips to lay out caches for the proposed June canoe trip down the Maguse River. [This follows our 1983 trip route.]

Poker games at these northern cabins were common and there was some visiting from other traders such as Alfred Peterson, who travelled with P.G. Downes, and the Inuit trapper Kakut, well-known for his boyhood travels with J.B. Tyrrell in 1894 on the Kazan River.[14] Once, when a visiting NWMP officer arrived by dog team from Athabasca Lake, the prospector Harold Way, in a panic over his illegal furs, stuffed thirty-five marten skins into a wood stove. Ross comically points out, "Six hundred dollars worth of fur blazed away cheerily as he welcomed the policeman."

These men travelled by canoe and dog team extensively around Nueltin and also into the most northerly Padlei Post (established in 1928), and down the Maguse River to Eskimo Point (now Arviat) and, curiously, from Nueltin north to Angikuni Lake on the Kazan River, an awkward canoe crossing at best. Way noted twenty-one portages in thirty-five miles.

The Hudson's Bay Padlei Post was a site for Canadian government relief efforts to curb the starvation camps of the Caribou Inuit in the early 1950s.

They were visitors not dwellers like the two Charlies, but not tourists like myself. They did keep journals and tell us of the ways of the North at this time of staunch independent living. Still my story gathering showed a bias for those "dwellers" of cabins or homesteads of sorts – those "Soldiers of the Border Lands" as Grey Owl called this breed of men:

> "On the outskirts of the Empire this gallant little band of men still carries on the game that is almost played…these are the soldiers of the Border Lands…who, in passing, will turn the pages in the story of true adventure on this continent."[15]

Fort Hall (regrettably burned down by forest fire in 1993) was likely named by Herbert Hall for his father, R.H. Hall. Herbert was a trader for the Hudson's Bay Company. Hall's instructions were to set up a series of posts extending the fur trade north from Brochet into the Land of Little Sticks in 1906-08. His main post at Fort Hall Lake was meant to be at Putahow Lake east of Nueltin. Putahow comes from the Cree meaning, "place where he missed." Hall is one of the many larger than life characters of this land. He was described in the late 1930s, as close to the age of sixty and as "a giant of a man, over six feet tall and weighing nearly 300 pounds…It was said that in his prime he could lift a 45-gallon drum filled with gasoline from boat to wharf."[16] He had dogsledded over the Rocky Mountains, survived a blizzard in 1914–15 on a 500-mile mail route from Chesterfield Inlet to Fort Churchill, traded as an independent in the harsh Ungava region, and set up trading posts for others, such as Windy Smith and Syd Keighley, to follow.

I visited his Fort Hall post knowing nothing of the man and his time. I remember marvelling at the well-built post and wanting to learn more about Herbert Hall, the great trader. Philip Godsell in *Arctic Trader* describes Hall as "preferring the company of Eskimos to white members of his staff, enduring without complaint, hating books and despising discipline."[17] I wonder to what degree such character traits were common to these men? Certainly, Hall stands out among them for his 30 years in the North.

Somehow, such tidbits of information provide an echo that now pervades this region of outposts and outpost men. Were these men "bushed," a state of madness connected to prolonged stays in northern cabins? Likely yes, but in a good way. The Mattila family posted a 'WANTED" sign with the police in efforts to find their trapping relative. Hugh Mattila hadn't been heard from in some time. Hugh was a mite startled to see the sign in the spring after a season's trapping out of a cabin up the North Knife River. One can only guess his response to his family, "Sorry, I've just been having too much fun to make contact." Gerald Malaher, in *The North I Love*, tells a tale of meeting a Scot on the Berens River who had plans to return to Scotland for his six-month home leave "...from the Hudson's Bay Company, but had become thoroughly 'bushed.'" He had said, "the Company would be damn lucky to see him before his time was up," but as Malaher notes, "he was so confused with the hustle and bustle" of Winnipeg that after one week he begged for his return north. Being bushed for some seemed to mean coming to be at home in the remote bush of Canada. It suited these fellows.

There is another side to being "bushed" that is popularized in the Jack London short story, "In a Far Country," in his 1960 anthology *Jack London's Stories*. Two prospectors wintering over in the Yukon eventually killed each other, the only explanation given being that one of them, or both had "gone bushed." From my reading of this "Little Sticks" region, such stories were not common in the lives of the trapper and traders. However, one story I retell each year on a student trip to Northern Ontario involves a trapper called Donald (Curly) Phillips who later became well-known as a mountain guide in the Jasper, Alberta, area.

Curly recorded the murder of fellow trapping partner George Fiester, "his brains blown out with a shotgun." The killer, who may have been "bushed," presumably was never found. Curly trapped in this area throughout the winter but purchased a colt revolver in Biscotasing to accompany him, and eventually left the region spooked. I stop each year with students at a Wolf Lake cabin relic that just might be the site of this tale. We paddle away and leave time and space to consider these earlier times of the lone trapper. I always hope that further questions as we paddle might allow me to share a story or two of the Nueltin "Soldiers of the Border Lands."

I can only begin to touch on the collection of stories that fill the nature of outpost life in cabins that remain standing across the North.

It is sad to think that Fort Hall is gone. The information on any given cabin or person is scant, but, if viewed together, the stories tell a rich tale that echoes throughout the outpost lands of the Canadian North; a North that remains largely unchanged in many ways and accessible to canoe travellers wishing to feel the aura of this bygone era.

What better way to offer a final tribute to this collection of cabin and travel stories in northern Manitoba/Nunavut than by reprinting a tribute written by one of their own. Eddie Engstrom (whose cabin I passed by in 1981 – Eddie wasn't in) dedicates his own book on living out of his cabin on the Clearwater River in northern Alberta as follows:

> To all the lowly, the lame and the humble, who take to the bush in the fall to follow the trails with traps and snares, and with rifle over their shoulders to hunt for the meat they need in order to live – to all the honest-to-God bushmen.[19]

"To all the honest-to-God bushmen." The Nueltin Lake area happily, to my heritage bent, had more than its fair share. Saving my favourite story for last, I actually met the Swede, Ragnar Jonsson, at his Nueltin base camp on day 14 in 1983. He was 84 years old and that summer proved to be his last on the land. Ragnar died in a senior's residence in The Pas in 1988 at the age of 88. He had come to Canada from Sweden due to overcrowding on the family farm in 1923. He had first trapped in the Wollaston Lake area of Saskatchewan and was known then for once selling his seasons' catch of fur for $2,500 after making just five trips around his trap line, this during the Great Depression in 1930. At this time, he travelled on handmade Lapland skiis with one dog pulling a sled. Once in the Nueltin region of the North, he developed a system of living off the land in a series of small teepees, each about two metres in diameter at the base. His main base on Nueltin where I visited had a 10-gallon oil drum converted into a wood stove. He preferred sleeping in cold weather and once commented, "It keeps you healthy. I haven't had a headache in 50 years."[20]

Mail normally reached him once or twice a year. He was a voracious reader of news magazines, well-informed of world events but, as a sidebar to that, once he went two years without speaking to another human being. "No hermit," he maintained. "It's just the way I've chosen to live and I'm quite happy."

In 1972, Ragnar received a scroll in honour of his name being officially selected to serve as a place name for an island on Nueltin where he lived his later years. This island is where we met him and his ashes were scattered there when he died in 1988. Gerald Malaher, in *The North I Love*, wrote, "As the oldest and probably the last of the old-time trappers on the edge of the tundra, Ragnar accumulated much personal information about the North."[21]

I had heard and read of a distinguished trapper of the area, but was amazed to learn from a fish camp owner on Nueltin Lake, that Ragnar was still alive and well in one of his camps five miles up the lake. We approached the site with expectations of a pleasant mug of tea in a rustic cabin with a charming old man from the "Land of the Little Sticks." However, we found

Ragnar Jonsson in 1983. This would be his last season on the land. He was 84 years old, having lived in the Nueltin area for over 40 years. *Courtesy of David Taylor.*

a litter-strewn area and a strange stench coming from inside a scrap metal sheeting and canvas-covered teepee hovel that was his sole shelter. One of our party decided not to join us any further.

Upon my announcing our presence, a head popped out of a canvas door and Ragnar's first words in a jolly tone were, "Ahhh, tourists." The bugs were fierce and his hovel amazingly cramped for one, so we chatted as we were and for only a few minutes. Summer was Ragnar's least preferred season. He is not set up for the short season. A sled dog, which was wandering around on site, looked equally ill-prepared for the hot, buggy summer. Strange, up until that moment, summer was the only time I'd consider visiting this region of Canada.

Chatting briefly outside the mosquito-infested hovel wasn't easy. I remember it all so clearly: the stench of a burning rubber smudge; the uncertain dialogue; the feeling of being a tourist in the presence of the noble outpost man who was too old to properly care for himself. Now, so many years later, I more than value this chance meeting – I treasure it. Meeting Ragnar Jonsson is my only concrete connection with this northern tradition when canoe routes were alive with the travels of trappers and traders, enigmatic and dutiful "Soldiers of the Borderland." He made us feel out of place and yet he helped us understand the place.

It was disconcerting to be labelled as tourists and it was hard to interpret the long awkward pauses between dialogue. We pushed off a bit confused from our meeting with this region's living legend. Now over twenty years later, I realize the meeting was as to be expected.

More about Ragnar. He had up to 11 camps set up north of Brochet to the treeline and had soon become known for his unique and humane trapping style, his success and his general antics. On summer trips down to Brochet he would paddle solo with his dog team running along the shoreline. He always camped outside the town. Once in the winter he sledded from Nueltin Lake out to Churchill (200 miles [322 kilometres] one way) to pick up groceries. He spent about 20 minutes in town, and then headed back to the bush. One lifetime highlight involves meeting the woman he had saved as a baby one winter. Unbeknownst to all others, the bundled infant had fallen from a moving load. Ragnar found and cared for the baby until the anxious parents retraced their steps days later in search of a corpse.

For over 45 years in the Nueltin Lake area he had led a contented life in this land that has captured my imagination, yet in which I had spent so little time. Ragnar had said, after returning from an extended trip "outside" to Winnipeg and elsewhere in 1982 to have a cataract removed from his shooting eye:

> It's a big country up there. You can go and trap and fish wherever you want. Down here there are so many regulations and people keep telling you not to do this or that. This modern civilization is too quick. People go around burning up gas and making a lot of fuss and there's too much noise. I've got to go back to the wilderness where a man can get a good sleep and his solitude.[22]

This return to Winnipeg was after a 59-year absence from the city.

I returned to this region (to the Seal River headwaters) one winter for a two-week sledding trip. Talking with locals, I learned about Ragnar's fate since the summer of 1983 (by summer 1984, he was moved to a senior's residence) and heard more stories, which further fuelled my intrigue and increased my satisfaction of having met this fellow.

While on the winter trail, camped on South Indian Lake on the Churchill River, our party of three, Jim Churchill of The Pas, Zabe MacEachren and I, were about to bed down in our comfortable wood stove heated tent when we heard the familiar distant roar of trappers' snow machines. Night seemed to be a common time to travel, and trappers and caribou hunters were aplenty. Donny and two young partners who were returning from their trapline around North Knife Lake to the community of South Indian Lake, a distance of over 240 kilometres (150 miles), visited us. Again I was greeted with, "Ahh, tourists," and felt unsettled by it. The six of us sat with tea and Dare cookies. Conversation was to the point, spare but not awkward like my earlier meeting with Ragnar Jonsson.

Perhaps from Ragnar or somehow in the passing of years, I'd learned what Hugh Brody in *Maps and Dreams* means, "An awkward pause is a very rare thing among people who accept that there is no need to escape from silence, no need to see words as a way to avoid one another, no need to obscure the real."[23]

A part of this sense of "the real" was my acceptance that I really was a tourist. Charlie and Theresa Schweder, Ragnar and Donny were the kings of this land. I was less than a part-timer and would never describe my travel experiences here with grandiose terms like "expedition" after learning of Donny's regular treks to and from his distant trapline or Ragnar's 640-kilometre (398-mile) round trip for groceries. So I was the visitor from Southern Ontario, the tourist with a knowledge and interest in the region's geography and history, but only an informed tourist all the same.

Donny, Ragnar, the two Charlies, Windy Smith, and Hugh Mattila, (and I haven't even found room to mention Cecil Husky Harris) are the free spirits of our North. They remind me that heritage is not just the cabins but also the people. They remind me that heritage lives, and if I do not call my trips "expeditions," if I don't conquest, don't over "gadgetize" and don't over-romanticize, some of this heritage will be me as well. As awkward as it sounds, some good advice would be, when the going gets tough and you need some inspiration or when you just need some inspiration – think of Ragnar.

When Donny and his mates left our tent for the final 80 kilometres (50 miles) home on their frost-covered snow machines loaded with caribou and furs, I thought of Ragnar Jonsson, then living with friends in Lynn Lake.

Those speechless conversations, the long quiet pauses that are not awkward, staring into the fire, slowly absorbing the heat of the tin fire box, talk of the trail, the weather: this is the "real" Canada. These times seem to solve the problem of knowing this big country. Thanks Ragnar. Thanks Donny.

So Nueltin sits on the Canadian landscape peopled by the spirit of Downes and Ragnar Jonsson, not to mention others such as Samuel Hearne and Matonabbee of the 1770s, the American, Ernest Oberholtzer, and his Fort Frances Native guide Billy Magee (1912), the French Revillon Frères traders of the 1920s, Eskimo Charlie and others. The Dene have now largely settled on the coast or in inland communities such as Brochet, Tadoule and Wollaston Lake. They hunt towards Nueltin in winter by snow machine. The Dene though are not the focus of this particular "filling cabins" story. They appeared to have minimal contact to the lives of the characters, mostly trappers and traders that filled these northern cabins. The Dene are another story but one tied closely to the ones I have touched upon.[24]

And, as for Nueltin/Windy lakes, if you ever contemplate throwing a dart at a large map of Canada with the intent to visit that one spot – (I know someone who has done this) – I don't think you could land up in a much better place than Nueltin Lake in the "Land of the Little Sticks." You'll be just south of the geographical centre of Canada. You'll be in a transition zone on the dominant Canadian geographical feature, the Canadian Shield, on the edge of the treeline between the boreal forest and the Barren Lands. You'll be in the midst of abandoned cabins and trappers' tilts filled with stories of a telling time – itself a transition time between the ancient and modern worlds. And if you're open to these echoes of the past, you may see the truth, beauty and adventure that Ragnar and Charlie Schweder, Eskimo Charlie and others saw.

5

STORIES OUT THE BACKDOOR: A TRAVELLER'S HISTORY OF HOME

The collective process by which a multiplicity of local narratives will eventually get transformed into good practices remains to be negotiated, in myriad ways, at the level of the bioregion.
— SYLVIA BOWERBANK[1]

MY STORIES ARE MOSTLY about travel and history somewhere far or near to home, but apparently rarely home. Rarely home, because, through travel, reading and experiences, I've tried to make all Canada my home or, as my children are inclined to say, "like" home. Hopeless I know, but for me it is a worthy quest. So home, as in a house where I live in a city, is also part of the notion of home as "in" Canada. In short, history is also where you live. In Canada, the grass need not be greener elsewhere. The last thing I'd ever wish to do when telling stories about Labrador or the Yukon is to give the impression that one must chase after the forever elsewhere to explore place, history and excitement. Knowing the local stories about where we live can help us live more meaningful lives there. This might even translate into better "manners" for us at home.

I've lived in Ottawa, Edmonton and mostly Dundas, Ontario, at the "Head of the Lake" (Lake Ontario) between Hamilton and Burlington. Connections to First Nations peoples, to heritage travel (explorers and settlers), to canoes and snowshoes do not jump out at you in Dundas. Geography does! Dundas lies at the end of a significant marsh

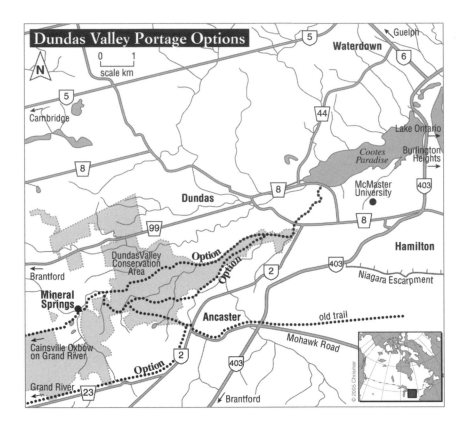

within a glacial valley bordered by ancient escarpment rock. Part of the amalgamated greater City of Hamilton that "should" be boasting of its 15 cascading waterfalls, Dundas is a true valley town. As local Hamilton poet, John Terpstra says, "it's all land meeting water."[2] That's true of one view, out on the glacial sandbar between the lake and the marsh (Cootes Paradise). At the top of the valley it is more a maze of trails and streams and glacial fill. Underneath the glacial fill apparently a river canyon exists, much larger than the Niagara Gorge.

Connected to this wealth of dynamic geography is a relatively forgotten history that will surprise you. I'd suggest that my favourite kind of history, travel heritage stories, are more obvious in Edmonton and Ottawa, two cities both connected to the transcontinental fur trade route. But, I've done my best historical detective work and on-the-land snooping in some very unlikely places at the "Head of the Lake." The history that most excites me in my home town region might not be obvious. The trails and landmarks are faint but still alive.

In *Falling into Place*, John Terpstra describes his book thus, "This book is what happens when one person becomes completely enamoured of the landscape in the city where he lives." If enamoured is the right word for me, it is so because of one thing – the Head of the Lake portage between Lake Ontario and the Grand River. I'll start this story with the big picture and then allow myself to get lost in some on-the-land details.

The 17th century French encounter with the Huron and Iroquois surrounding Lake Ontario involves the "beaver war" in which the southern Five (later Six) Nations Iroquois destroyed Huronia between present-day Lake Simcoe and Georgian Bay, and lay claim over a large area of Georgian Bay and the north shore of Lake Ontario. This encounter involves military, missionary and settlement interests and "marks the first great event in the modern written history of Ontario."[3] It was exciting to learn of my own hometown's role in this saga.

The well-populated Hamilton and Niagara Peninsula was a Neutral Peoples' Confederacy. This Iroquoian group was also taken over by their aggressive southern cousins in the 1600s. At that time, the Five Nations Iroquois set up a string of strategic new hunting and trading villages in the recently vacated terrain. Tinawatawa was the most westerly of these villages, and was strategically located somewhere generally in the vicinity of the canoe portage at the Head of the Lake (*Fond du lac*) between present-day Burlington Bay and the Grand River at Brantford.

Following the intense conflict of the 1640–50s, French explorers and missionaries resumed their travels in the area generally. Specifically, the explorer René Robert Cavalier Sieur de LaSalle and the Sulpician missionary René de Brehant de Galinée and the Canadian-born adventurer Louis Jolliet all converged at Tinawatawa in September 1669.

LaSalle and Galinée, with partner François Dollier de Casson, travelled together from New France, approaching Tinawatawa from Lake Ontario. Jolliet arrived from the west having travelled to Lake Superior and back on orders to ascertain the reports of a surface copper mine "somewhere" in the Lake Superior area. That's a big somewhere. At Tinawatawa, Jolliet informed the two missionaries of the presence of a large group of Natives to the north and west (Upper Michigan State), the Potawatomi, who had not experienced European influences directly. The two decided to alter their initial plans for the opportunity to save souls amongst the Potawatomi. LaSalle went on to the Ohio River and eventually to the descent of the Mississippi.

In Galinée's words:

> We set out then from Tinaouataoua [I have seen four spellings] on the 1st of October, 1669, accompanied by a good number of Indians, who helped us to carry our canoes and baggage, and after making about 9 or 10 leagues [approximately 43 km] in three days we arrived at the bank of the river which I call the Rapid, [Grand River] because of the violence of its current, although it had not much water, for in many places we did not find enough to float our canoes, which did not draw a foot of water.[4]

This must have been some portage, not to mention the chore of navigating on the nearly dry Grand River of early October. Neither the portage or October paddle would be part of any modern-day canoeing agenda. And yet, there is much fun to be had in revisiting this historic portage that was originally a clever alternative to the extremes of the Niagara River as a route between lakes Ontario and Erie. The portage likely inspired John Graves Simcoe as an early road construction project more than one hundred years later: that being of course, the Governor's Road which joined the Grand and Thames rivers to Lake Ontario. It should be pointed out that one of the early translations for the Niagara Gorge portage was,

Bob Henderson standing at the Cainsville Oxbow on the Grand River. This is the closest point on the Grand to Lake Ontario, and possibly the portage terminus from Lake Ontario.

"crawling on all fours." For canoe travel, the more direct Head of the Lake portage to the Grand River was a better route than Niagara. Today, the Grand River is a fine spring paddle with an award-winning Conservation Authority. Parts of the portage are some of Southern Ontario's finest day hiking.

One can speculate that the original Native portage loosely followed the Sulphur Creek route out of the Dundas Valley to Summit Bog at Highway 52. From there, it is but a short seven kilometres of level ground to the current road called the Indian Trail which leads directly to Cainsville (via Johnson Road) at the big oxbow found on the Grand River, marking the closest distance between waters. There is now a walking/cycling/rail trail from Summit directly in line with part of the possible direct routing. An interesting additional option is the possibility of descending the Fairchild Creek (still a fine spring paddle once cleared of deadfall tree limbs) to the Grand. On a spring day, with car, canoe and bicycle, local history enthusiast Wayne Terryberry and I covered this distance hunting for clues of an ancient trail, but mostly enjoying the "idea" of the portage. A highlight was a paddle on a section of the Fairchild Creek and a sideline trip to Westover, west of Dundas, in rolling farm country above the valley. Nearby is one proposed site of Tinawatawa. Here we discovered that a friend of ours actually lives on the site of this possible former village. Friend (with proud United Empire Loyalist bloodlines) Bev Nicol shared with us stories of boyhood exploring with trowel and paintbrush for Native artifacts. He remembers well his father's two rare copper arrowheads, hunted out by early collectors before there was a shared consciousness to report findings and locations to research institutions. Indeed, in the 1960s, an official archaeological dig led by Dr. William Noble worked for a summer in what is now Bev's backyard, 17 kilometres (11 miles) north of Dundas. Years earlier, I had paddled the Spencer Creek downriver to near the spot where it plunges spectacularly over the escarpment at Webster's Falls. I had started this April trip in Bev's front yard, that being the site my friend, Jack Lee, and I believed to be the first point of steady navigable water. The Spencer Creek would once have offered better navigational potential before its two control dams were built at Valens and Christie. Slowly Wayne and I were piecing together the stories of both a changing landscape and its former travellers. Here was a logic to be discerned, a puzzle to solve, with many days of fun on-the-land snooping.

Fathers Dollier and Galinée, after the fateful meeting with Jolliet at Tinawatawa and their gruelling first-reported descent by Europeans down the Grand River, were not to get far without a classic canoeists' embarrassing story to tell – one that would, yet again, radically alter their plans. After wintering over on the north shore of Lake Erie, they departed March 23, 1670, for the Potawatami country. Three days later, they arrived at the now famous landmark of Point Pelee (which in 1670 was at least four kilometres longer and nine kilometres wider at its base than the current measurement). Here I turn the description over to a much defeated, but restrained Galinée:

> Night came on and we slept so soundly that a great northeast wind rising had time to agitate the lake with so much violence that the water rose six feet where we were and carried away the packs of M. Dollier's canoe that were nearest the water and would have carried away all the rest if one of us had not awoke…At his cry we rose and rescued the baggage of my canoe and one of M. Dollier's. Pieces of bark were lighted to search along the water but all that could be saved was a keg of powder that floated, the rest was carried away. Even the lead was carried away or buried so deep in the sand that it could never be found. But the worst of all was that the entire altar service was lost. We waited for the wind to go down and the waters to retire in order to go and search along the water, whether some debris of the wreck could not be found. But all that was found was a musketoon and a small bag of clothes belonging to one of our men; the rest was lost beyond recall….."5

I can only imagine the frustration these task-oriented missionaries must have felt, but I also must chuckle at the commonplace error in judgement that is played out by tired canoe campers in the past and present.

Galinée after this wintering in the Long Point area of Lake Erie (Port Dover) calls the whole region "a terrestrial paradise of Canada." He specifically comments on the grapes, as large and sweet as the finest in France, the profusion of walnuts, chestnuts, apples and plums, the fat bears and the wandering herds of 50 to 100 deer. I surmise he would have been back over the portage a few times to visit Tinawatawa. LaSalle left a man at Tinawatawa who, legend has it, was killed at present-day Webster's Falls by a fellow suitor in a love triangle. Some people say, you can hear the woman's soft crying in the waterfall's roar at the escarpment. The French were in the habit of leaving or sending men to these villages to regain influence after the fall of Huronia. There you have it, a long standing influence over time and a love story, no less. I have students today listening for that subtle cry within the roar of the waterfall after introducing this history to dumbstruck ears.

But where was Tinawatawa and the path of this portage trail? James

Bev Nichol with Wayne Terry-berry, *left*, in Bev's backyard, a possible site for the Native village of Tinawatawa along the Spencer Creek which flows into Dundas.

Coyne, a local historian, in 1903, supported the Westover site as mentioned above. This would make the Spencer Creek a navigation/portage line, or perhaps Tinawatawa was a bit of a detour from the portage out of the valley at Summit Bog. Two maps from the time clearly show the town and portage. The Charlevoix-Bellin map has the village halfway between the Fond du Lac (Lake Ontario) and the river. This map is considered "second-hand geographic intelligence." The second, the Pierre Raffeix map (Raffeix worked in the region from 1671 to 1680), and Galinée's field notes, I later learned after being a "quick to judge" supporter of the Westover theory, suggest that the town is much closer to the lake. Given that Galinée mentions a "fine large sandy bay" as a portage take out (John Terpstra's beloved Iroquois Bar at Burlington Bay perhaps) and a two-day carry, about five leagues (one league equals three statute miles) to the village, with three-days travel for the second half to the river, the village should be in the upper valley of Dundas Valley, not in the flats between the valley and the Grand River. Perhaps the village is as far as the present-day hamlet of Mineral Springs in the upper end of the valley, or perhaps up the Ancaster Creek route and into present-day Ancaster. Both options would allow the Tinawatawa site to intersect with the Mohawk Trail. This Native route follows the top of the escarpment, which Hamiltonians call "the Mountain," from the east (Niagara Peninsula), then dropping into the valley and crossing Cold Spring (Mineral Springs) before heading out of the valley as the portage trail. One thing is for certain, the Native portage trail and town site are showcased on both these maps, making clear the importance of both at the time.

Pierre Raffeix's map clearly shows the head of Lake Ontario and the
Grand River portage. Note that the map is oriented to the south.
The title of the map is *Le Lac Ontario avec Les Lieux Circonvoisins
& Tarticulièrement, Les cinq nation Iroquoises by P. Raffeix.* Taken
from *Ontario's History in Maps. Courtesy of McMaster University
Map Library.*

By the way, both maps also clearly show the Humber and Rouge
River portages with shoreline villages leading to the Toronto Carrying
Place from Lake Ontario to Lake Simcoe. These villages Teiaiagon and
Ganatsekwyagon were, along with Tinawatawa and others to the east
as far as the Bay of Quinte, part of an Iroquian network. These villages
were all taken over by the French-allied Ojibwe and Mississauga peoples by the start of the early 1700s.[6]

I think the Mohawk Trail is significant to this story. Writing of another
Fond du Lac trail at the head of Lake Superior, fur trader George Nelson, in the early 1800s, describes Native "roads":

Finding the people were rather a long time absent, I took their
"road." It is a good road, but as you are not accustomed to these
things yet, you had perhaps better not go. However, I went. The
road was discoverable by the falling leaves being "here and there"
disturbed, from the feet hooking into a root or rotten stick, turning
them up and every two or three yards a branch broken. I made out
however to follow it well for perhaps half or so of a mile; but lest I
might get astray, I thought it most prudent to return. Such are Indian

roads, and many hundred miles have I travelled upon them, with no other indications; but custom, and a little attention to the course or direction of the route, render traveling upon them, comparatively sure. We at last reached Fond du Lac.[7]

The Head of the Lake (I like to say "Dundas,") portage does not stand alone. Early maps and written accounts suggest that Native walking trails were common. Raffeix's map shows extensive trails joining Iroquian villages in the Finger Lakes area of Upper New York State. Geographer Conrad Heidenreich produced a map of the Petun Peoples, southwest of Huronia in the present-day Nottawasaga Bay region south to Noisy River, with over 70 kilometres (44 miles) of trails between tribal villages and Jesuit missions. One trail system followed the Niagara Escarpment, joining the Mohawk and other trails of the Neutral to the immediate south. Clearly there was a hiking trail network that would make a modern day hiker salivate. This is only a part of a much forgotten history.

A western connection to the Thames River from the Dundas portage at its terminus on the Grand River is a relatively easy one via Native roads that follow and/or use either the Whiteman Creek or the Nith River. Both bring you close to the Thames River and thus onto Lake Huron, avoiding Lake Erie altogether. Following their defeat by the Americans at the Battle of Moraviantown near the Thames River, the

Whiteman Creek is a short upstream paddle to the Thames River watershed. A Native trail once followed an interior route between Lake Ontario and Lake Huron, thus avoiding Lake Erie.

British and allied warriors of 1813 under the Shawnee Chief Tecumseh (who died in this battle) travelled east to the Grand River by trail and onto Lake Ontario via the Dundas portage, ultimately camping at the "fine large sandy bay" at Burlington Bay.

The naturalist William Pope, among Canada's first artist-naturalists, having arrived from England to New York City in 1834, travelled by canal boats and stagecoach through the recently completed Erie Canal to Buffalo. From there, he travelled by steamer along the Lake Erie shore past Port Dover and Long Point, arriving at Port Stanley (formerly known as Kettle Creek). It must have been a "bad" trip or put him in a "bad" mood. At Kettle Creek, his journal entry reads:

> The best of Kettle Creek was bad. The meat was bad. The drink was bad. The beds were bad. The wharf was bad. The house bad. The roads bad, and in short, the whole place was bad, damned bad altogether. The only exception may be the people, in any case I hope so.[8]

Time to get back on track – back to roads. Pope also wrote, "The scenery upon this Lake [Erie] is real American backwoods...There appears to be one 'boundless continuity' of dark gloomy forest. The only openings are when roads or concession lines are cut." Soon he would be walking these roads, "like a second Robinson Crusoe to view a little of the country."[9] Walking the Talbot Road from Lake Erie to St. Thomas, he turned east one day, walking twenty-six miles before resorting to a wagon. The route east crossed the Thames River overland to Brantford on the Grand River and on to Dundas and Hamilton. The road certainly followed the same logic if not some of the same specific lines of travel long-known to the Iroquois, the French and Tecumseh's warriors. Today it is used for hiking still, in part. The Talbot Road, Mohawk Trail and Dundas portage are all former Native trails connecting regions the way our roadways do today. Indeed some of our modern roadways follow Native trails directly. But more intriguing are the Native trails and portages within their system that are still walking trails today. Pope describes a section of the forested tract, "the road being not more than six feet in width with trees on either side and a hundred feet in height, quantities of raspberry bushes beneath the large timber."[10] The thought is exciting – to take a modern-day hikers' sensibility back in time to this trail-strewn Southern Ontario – like a second Robinson Crusoe to view a little of the country.

Recently deceased amateur historian Bill Bermingham, to whom this chapter is dedicated, lived on the Mohawk Trail at 919 Mineral Springs Road. I believe, as he reported, his laneway which is still a narrow dirt trail, is a well-preserved section of the Mohawk Trail heading from Ancaster and Dundas and then west to the Grand River via the Dundas portage. Mineral Springs looks like a logical intersection point of these two important trails. Today from this vantage point you'd view a ruin of the first mill of the first white settler to the large valley area, one John Aikman, a United Empire Loyalist. How did John get from the hamlet of Ancaster in 1789 to his 20 acres given by the Crown? He walked to the Mohawk Trail along what is now the Heritage Trail (so named thanks to Bermingham's efforts) of the Hamilton Regional Conservation Author-ity (HRCA). And why 20 acres here? – because the steadily flowing stream found here afforded a means of water power for what became the Cold Spring Grist Mill. Bill once showed me a 1793 map from *Ontario's History in Maps*. The map shows, "a path to the Mohawk Village, Grand River and Detroit," crossing "Cold Spring." These labels are among the very few markings on the surprisingly sparse map.

Bill's laneway and another neighbour's laneway with a small bridge across the creek are part of a meeting of the trails somehow – east to west on the Mohawk Trail and from Burlington Bay south into the val-ley to Mineral Springs. You travel west a bit on the Heritage Trail of the Hamilton Regional Conservation Authority to Powerline Road out of the valley, veering southwest to meet the present Indian Trail Road as noted earlier. Bill remembers discovering corduroy logs bridging a swampy part in the valley in the 1950s, where the Bruce Trail today crosses the headwaters of the stream below a heritage homestead in the valley called Brockton.

These are my favourite jogging routes today. Bill didn't postulate a theory about the location of Tinawatawa that I am aware of, but I will. I think the former village could be at the junction of Wilson Street and Mohawk Road on the edge of Ancaster – or thereabouts. This would make Ancaster Creek off Spencer Creek, running behind McMaster University's Zone 6 parking lot, the end of navigation. Or, Tinawatawa might just be at the current hamlet site of Mineral Springs, and thus at a junction of the two dominant trails of the time 1660 to 1690. Bill believed that the Indian trail at his driveway continued to Sulphur Springs, crossing the road of the same name and following some of the main loop of the HRCA trail system and the current Spring Creek Trail. He argued that both the Natives and the first railway builders took the line of least resistance by crossing a minimum of streams.

All these options I have followed on foot. One exciting find was evidence of an old trail out of the floodplain of Ancaster Creek, a logical beginning for the Ancaster theory. Another highlight of my searching was a tour of Bill's house, part of which was once John Aikman's house – dating back to 1789. Bill's research suggested that this is the second oldest house still occupied in Ontario.

All these details will certainly get a reader lost. For those who know my home in the Dundas Valley, it is still tricky enough. The purpose though in discussing some micro trail searching is to point out the detail and excitement in such speculation. As the British poet, John Keats, once said, "Nothing ever becomes real till it is experienced." The trick is to imagine all this geography without the roads, cleared land, houses, subdivisions, etc. I like to stand on the Picnic Rock Lookout, as it was once called, overlooking the Dundas Valley on the Tew's Falls Trail and imagine all this geography as landforms and contours. Perhaps amongst the Carolinian forest where northern and southern species of trees meet, there will be an odd clearing where the Iroquois fired out a patch of forest to attract deer. In my imagination I can make out a trail and see a wisp of smoke rising through the trees as evidence of a village.

If there is any one person I would like to visit by time machine, it would be David Thompson. But, as for a place and time to visit back-in-time, it would be September 24, 1669, when Jolliet, LaSalle and Galinée were all at Tinawatawa on the Head of the Lake Portage. I could hike familiar terrain along the escarpment rock north to the lake, past the marsh (Cootes Paradise) to the bay and that "fine large sand bar." In doing so, I would pass by my place of work on the flats above the marsh, McMaster University, and the raised beach ridge from an ancient glacial lake overlooking the valley on which my house of eighteen years rests. I could walk by trail to Ancaster, past where the Old Mill Restaurant stands today, where I celebrated a university graduation dinner. I could walk to the Grand River and beyond to the Thames. This would be great. But it is enough to know the old trails are there on this familiar terrain somewhere in the valley, both then and now.

This is a story about the view out my back door, looking east out to the marsh and the bay to the lake and to the west up into the valley. As John Terpstra wrote:

Water, hills, trees and a city – all framed in a rock embrace of the Niagara Escarpment as the escarpment negotiates a hairpin turn around the end of Lake Ontario.[11]

It is home, where history is. Someday I may just find a piece of that corduroy road in a swampy bit of the valley or discover an arrowhead or pottery shard, maybe even some French coins. Anyway – there would be a history here without these travel trails, but it was this Head of the Lake Portage that first truly enamoured me to this landscape and allowed me to explore for details. Now I just have to put a canoe on my shoulders and walk to the Grand River from out my back door. In the meantime, I care more and live with good manners for this home, thanks to the life this seventeenth century story offers the place.

PART TWO

PRACTICES

*Devices, products of our technological culture, fail
to evoke and, in fact, preclude vitally important
experiences that things offer. Things bring the world
home to us and make us at home in it. Experiencing
things enlightens us and enables us to affirm life in a
profound way. Without such experiences, we are apt
to maintain superficial standards and fail to win
through to deeper experiential truths.*
— DAVID STRONG[1]

I remember being dumbfounded by the diamond hitch rope-tying
arrangement used to secure a packed boxes, duffels and everything
else onto the backs of the packhorses.[2] Even after two trips and by day
ten, I was still out of every loop in terms of helping with the "practice" of this travel mode. I couldn't remember which horse could only
be approached from the front or the left side (or was it the right side).
Similarly it was tough, but I was better at determining which dogs had
to be kept apart on the gang line and which dogs required special food
because they were swallowers not chewers. By day two or three I was
comfortable putting harnesses on the dogs, but there were embarrassing
moments where I could swear Blackie was looking up at me thinking,
"Oh no, not another day with this loser."

Yet these practices, horse-pack and dogsled outfitting, were beckoning travel modes that, while one might not master quickly, one can
glimpse into. I had a calling, if you will, to be a part of a vibrant and
distinctive culture of travel. It is exciting to practise a craft of travel
that makes the most sense for a particular terrain. On the eastern slopes
and interior passes of the Rockies, the horse was the historical choice.
On the broad sweeping lakes and open terrain of the Yukon and northern Manitoba, the winter trail called for the dog team. To be a small
part of a great tradition of practice is an exciting prospect. In short,
I'll never be a cowboy, but it sure was fun trying. Horses and dogs;
paddles and canoe poles; winter snowshoes, skis and sleds; canoes and
pointer boats; even hunting for rock art and archaeology sites: these

are *things* and not *devices.* They are part of technologies that enable us to affirm deeper truths about our lives with nature.

The practices I grew up with were canoe tripping and cross-country ski touring. The sea kayak for coastal excursions came naturally. But there are many practices in Canada that demand the attention of a learner, who must learn a way of seeing and/or a way of knowing and being. Learning to see surface archeology and see into the spirit encoded in rock art images is, I dare say, a practice that demands time and attention. Learning the ways of knowing and being involved in river poling, travelling in a 36-foot canot du maître and rowing a pointer boat (or a 40-foot York boat as I hope to do some day) means you have to settle into another way. It isn't canoe tripping in another type of boat. The practice of each involves thinking and acting in a new way with the water, terrain and travel companions. Similarly, snowshoe handhauling toboggan travel and wall tent/wood stove camping establishes a pace and way of being in winter that is really non-comparable with the ski tour camping I started with initially. Those first trips with new travel practices demand much basic learning and attention to detail. Later with all of these practices, be it centred on ways of seeing and/or ways of knowing and being, there is an eventual shift from basic learning to a refinement of technique or, at least, you might have a moment where you "get it" – like an insider.

Mountain ski touring, for a Canadian Shield camper/traveller is, yet again, another practice tough to compare with my familiar winter travel modes. I remember bruising my toes atop the Opal Hills in Jasper National Park by doing jumping jacks with my skis off in efforts to warm my frozen toes. I managed to bruise them which I only learned as they eventually thawed once back to a warm-up lodge. Not all slopes are safe. On Baffin Island, I was set to find the best telemark slope and questioned my friend as to his hesitation only to learn that he had lost three friends to crevasses on an earlier trip. Right, back to basic learning. I started reading our aerial photographs for crevasses with care and learned a new knot or two for tying ourselves to a common lifeline. At Skoki and Mt. Assiniboine lodges I was happy to heed the daily advice of the guide, or travel with one as necessary. We had over 55 centimetres of snowfall in two days while at Skoki. That was different too.

In fact, for new practices, and especially ones that suit the terrain with a strong heritage fit, I have delighted in the company of well-seasoned practitioners. John Dormaar, Dennis Smyk, Peter Carruthers and Chris Blythe have all helped me "see" a language on the land of indigenous cultures. And guides have helped me to first embrace both new technologies and ardent codes of conduct. Books have helped too. They both inform and broaden the imaginative surroundings.

I hope here to share practices that are less common than canoeing and hiking, thinking across all of Canada. One must recognize that the horseback trip is as common in its place as is the river poling trip in its specific place. As well, I hope to show a rich complexity of travel practices when thinking Canada wide. I'll likely never travel in a Beothuk canoe to out islands thirty kilometres off the coast of Newfoundland to hunt seal. The Beothuk have been extinct now for close to two centuries and I've never heard of a replica Beothuk canoe.[3] However, I do hope someday to paddle some of the west coast in a Haida or Salish canoe. I have watched Salish canoes and canoemen paddle into Long Beach on Vancouver Island en route to a western First Nations canoe rendezvous. What jealousy I felt that day! I hope to paddle (oops! row and sail) a York boat on a long wide western river[4] and perhaps even get into a tall ship – an ocean-sailing ship such as Henry Sinclair (1345–1404) sailed on to arrive to North America, to the Nova Scotia coast in 1398.[5] I wonder if any of these, yet to be experienced, practices will reveal their own "diamond hitch" for sure dumbfoundedness to a learner – perhaps, perhaps not. But the fear factor for the Sinclair-type replica ocean-sailing ship for me is a factor I'd be wise to prepare for mentally.

6

SURFACE ARCHAEOLOGY: LIVING THE QUESTIONS NOW

Be patient toward all that is unsolved in your heart and...
try to love the questions themselves like locked rooms and like
books that are written in a very foreign tongue. Do not now seek
the answers, which cannot be given you because you would not
be able to live them. And the point is, to live everything. Live
the questions now. Perhaps you will then gradually, without
noticing it, lie along some distant day into the answer.
— RAINER MARIA RILKE[1]

SOIL SCIENTIST AND AVOCATIONAL ARCHAEOLOGIST John Dormaar and I are walking on the down slope from the Majorville Medicine Wheel to the Bow River, 300 metres away, to search for fossil ammonites called "buffalo stones" or *iniskim* in Blackfoot. The Majorville site is thought to be over 5,000 years old. We are walking towards Falling-off-Without-Excuse, a big bend on the Bow River south of where the river turns significantly south towards the Old Man River. The view is amazing. The river as it comes into clear view is an outstanding curving earth canyon, a massive snake-like trench with a water line that seems strangely alien from this position on the plains. We have walked down from the rolling topped hills surrounding the Majorville surface stone configuration site, some 910 metres above sea level – a good spot for easterners to stand, to learn that the prairies are not, as a rule, flat. The view is breathtaking. In all, I am a bit overwhelmed by the place.

John stops us in our tracks. "What's that," he asks, and points to a small depression in the ground lined with some stones and tall grass.

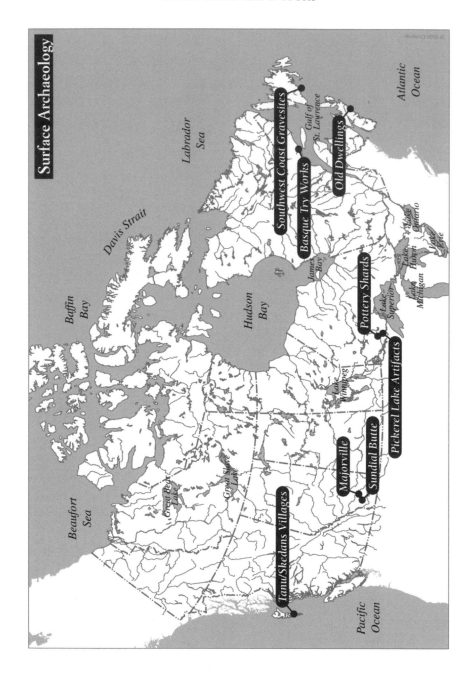

I could tell this is a set up. John was guiding the walk to this spot. "It's an old, very old campfire ring," I say though this seemed too easy. John talks me through why that wasn't likely – no stone tent rings for a teepee, a bit far from Majorville and from water, too exposed. Eventually he shares a theory. "I think this is a boyhood rite of passage site. Here the young brave would sit with a dead rabbit, let's say, for bait in this depression half-covered with some branches. The eagle would fly into the pit to get the rabbit and the boy would snatch an eagle feather without harming the eagle. The feather is a prestige sign of bravery. It's just a hypothesis," John adds.

John Dormaar looking up towards the Majorville Medicine Wheel with the Bow River in the background.

A year later, an archaeologist friend, Peter Carruthers, and I are walking on an offshore island in Georgian Bay, Ontario, snooping about at subterranean dwelling sites when Peter nonchalantly points out the low stone wall on my right. "I've always wondered what this is," he says, "perhaps a duck blind or an ambush site from the 17th century. We will probably never know."

As I recall both these events in my life, I am stunned by the experience. First, the 5,000 year old Majorville stone configuration, and then the strange out-of-the-way rock pit – and those dwelling pits and possible duck blind. I might have walked by all of these features without knowing anything of their significance. On closer inspection I can affirm that these are the work of human hands. The profuse lichen growth on the rocks speaks to their antiquity and sends my usual Euro-Canadian historical time sense reeling. Time seemed to be telescoping away from me faster and farther than my normal perceptions would credit. I was intrigued by the stone structures, the place, the people, but mostly with the practice of my archaeologist friends who immediately recognized things that were hidden from me by my own narrow sense of time and place. The archaeologist is imaginatively living the questions of cultures on the land.

Back to Majorville. Named for Major, a nearby rancher, Majorville is an Aboriginal surface stone structure that is accretional (gradually added to over a long period of time) and composite (made up of at least two or three primary structural elements). These are two common characteristics of such structures generally. Majorville's structures are a central cairn on the hilltop with 26 to 28 spokes radiating outwards for up to 30 metres as if forming a bicycle wheel. The term medicine wheel is believed to originate with another cairn, a spoke-and-circle stone structure on Medicine Mountain near Sheridan, Wyoming. That site became known as the Bighorn Medicine Wheel in 1903. An interesting question raised by Barbara Huck and Doug Whiteway in their book, *In Search of Ancient Alberta*, is which came first. The Bighorn structure was named for the mountain, Medicine Mountain, but was the mountain previously named for the structure? Medicine wheel has become a catch-all term for all stone structures,

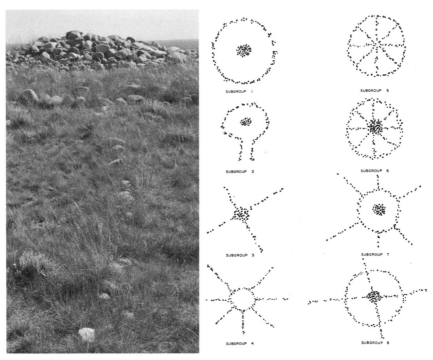

Above left, The Majorville central cairn with evidence of radiating spokes in the foreground. *Above right*, Archaeologist John Brumley has provided a classification of medicine wheel groupings in the southwest prairies.

but in John Brumley's 1988 report of sixty-seven such structures of the northern plains, primarily in Alberta and Saskatchewan and in Montana and Wyoming, he provides eight subgroups of structure types. As stone structures have been increasingly identified in the 1900s, shapes including human and animal (turtle and buffalo effigies) have been added to an intriguing variety of surface stone structure shapes.[2]

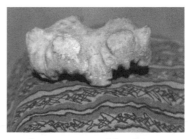

Iniskims, segmented fossil ammonites which are known as buffalo stones because of their appearance.

The Majorville ancient date of origin is based on radiocarbon dating of organic materials from the centre of the cairn and associated projectile point types. Within the central cairn at a particular layer (layer in time) were found *iniskims* or segmented fossil ammonites and baculites that in segments resemble buffalo, hence the name buffalo stones. Archaeologist Brian Reeves has written a conference paper specifically concerning the relationship of *iniskims* (such as those found gathered along the Bow River at Majorville) to the Nitsitapii (Blackfoot) culture. He notes, "iniskims were used by the Nitsitapii in personal, familial and tribal spiritual contexts. It is said that every teepee, had an Iniskim."[3] An *iniskim* gave its possessor great power with buffalo such as knowledge as to which direction to travel to find buffalo. For buffalo gazing, standing atop the hill at Majorville is a good bet too, given the wide prairie visibility from here. *Iniskims* were often kept in personal power sacks or power bundles that provided strong medicine and good luck for its owner. Adolf Hungry Wolf reported that *iniskims* were commonly worn as necklaces and that old *iniskims* are often buried with their owner. They are connected with buffalo-calling ceremonies and often have been found at vision quest sites. There is a Buffalo Stone Lake in Montana, which like the Bow River sloped riverbank near Majorville, can reveal *iniskims*. Along the Little Bow River another stone configuration site, Sundial Butte, serves as tribal gathering and collection sites. Reeves has suggested the place of Falling-Off-Without-Excuse and the sacred medicine circle at Majorville are deserving of World Heritage status as comparable to Piskun, the Head-Smashed-in-Buffalo Jump which has already been awarded this rank.

I visited Majorville twice, once in November with a frosting of snow and biting wind. We approached by car on dirt road exploration tracks. We almost gave up but the repeated "just a little further" paid off. The snow actually aided our visibility of the radiating spoke features. This moment opened my eyes to viewing the prairies in a new way – not as farming lands but as buffalo-grazing lands where glacial stone deposits, rolling terrain and river valleys make agriculture difficult. In such terrain there would be archaeological evidence of the former life of the land. With John Dormaar on a June visit a few years later, the green open shortgrass prairies and expansive view made the buffalo prairie of *iniksim* collectors come alive. This is buffalo country still.

Sundial Butte (Oka-Katzi to the Blood Peoples) is another stone structure I visited that also has avoided the plow and road expansion of the early 1900s.[4] This site north of Lethbridge involves a kame knoll rising 75 metres in a hummocky moraine landscape. Again, like Majorville, the Sundial site near the Little Bow River affords a grand view. Today you may find gifts and prayer ribbons here, which bespeak an ongoing religious significance. Sundial Butte is a different shape from Majorville. One large central cairn forms the core. It has been much disturbed over time, but is approximately (as measured in a 1972 report) six metres in diameter and 1.75 metres in height, being comprised of large stones mostly brought to the site. This cairn is surrounded by two complete rings of smaller stones with a south-facing entranceway lined with stones. It is thought that Sundial Butte is a more recent structure. Again the view is exceptional, (a common quality when structures have an associated large central cairn) and the shape is artistically attractive. That was it. I was hooked. I started researching in earnest.

Why such stone structures and such variety of shapes? The questions are many and have been explored by many archaelogists. Michael Wilson thinks they are site specific in terms of purpose. David Vogt notes that, "they had a plan in mind." There are similarities generally in terms of land features. They tend to be near buffalo jumps, close to water, on hilltops and have evidence of teepee rings and camps nearby. John Brumley and Ian Brace remind us that this is an involved and confusing topic. Brumley reports 150 known stone structures in North America. These are a phenomena, not just a matter of a few sites. But there is a concentration of 125 structures in Alberta and Saskatchewan within a 200-kilometre radius of the confluence of the Red Deer and

Sundial Butte is thought to be a more recent structure than the Majorville site.

South Saskatchewan rivers. Brace notes that 30 tribes representing ten language families likely had some occupancy in the northern plains over the past 700 years. Brumley and Brace both speak to memorials to dominant chiefs. (This is known to be the reason for constructing the "Many Spotted Horses" site).[5] Vogt discusses distinctive places of worship on prominent hilltops. Wilson mentions the homage to animals at Majorville, the 28 spokes might parallel the 28 ribs of a buffalo or the 28 spokes for the lunar cycle. There is a celestial alignment theory as well for certain sites. The *iniskims* at Majorville speak to buffalo-calling ceremonies and associated worship. Yes, from all these archaeologists, hypotheses abound. Whatever the purposes, these surface stone structures are a mystery on the land that can take us back in time with a wink of an eye. When atop Majorville or Sundial, it is a long gaze back made possible through archaeological research, remnants found on the land and a healthy imagination. This long gaze back in time opens the view to a wider perspective on the prairies.

This wider view is important. There is a unifying thread found on the surface of the Canadian landscape that comes from exploring for remnants left behind by peoples who lived there in earlier times. The thread weaves its way throughout the land in space and through time as well. From the thread one extrapolates a story of the place in another time. Archaeology is the closest discipline that examines this surface thread. The thread is pulsating at a place like the Majorville Medicine Wheel and at a Haida former village. The thread is faint when combing a coastline for a 16th century Basque whaling try works site. The common thread found in the remnants left behind opens the way to a richer outlook.

I have experienced this archaeological-based wide view in different parts of Canada. Thinking of friend Michelle Clusiau who, on an archaeological dig at The Pines (a beach site on Pickerel Lake, Quetico, Ontario) found a 500-year-old copper bracelet, I asked Dennis Smyk while on White Otter Lake, just north of Quetico, "How does she do it?" Just how is it done – this finding of projectile points, pottery shards, copper bracelets? In Michelle's case, it is mostly a story of intuition. The group had given up on the day and were back in the boats when Michelle had a feeling, and returned to the beach and made a quick discovery. There is magic in that story. For Dennis, who has found many artifacts and pictograph sites around his local environment of Ignace, Ontario, the answer is simple – "You look." And so I asked Dennis to look with me and my son Quinn one breezy August day. We went to an island with a high bank that was cut back by wind and waves. "Nature is doing the work for us," Dennis said. Within ten minutes I had found small pieces of pottery shards. Gold to my mind. In a twisted turn of events, my four-year-old son left his talking Michael Jordan doll at the site. The site also had unusual pits facing the open south end of the lake, evidence of other probable vision quest locations. Well, perhaps a talking Michael Jordan is a suitable artifact to be found here a century or two from now. The main point I learned here though was the first principle of archaeology to my amateur mind – ask questions and look for answers. Dennis' simple response, I've learned to appreciate as the best one – Look!

On a sea kayaking trip in the Queen Charlotte Islands on the west coast, the looking was easy and a feast for the eye. Our friendship/family group started our trip near the well-known historic Eagle Crest Peoples' town of Tanu. Here, a Haida Watchman, Charlie Wesley, gave us a tour of the haunting site. I had seen George Dawson's[6] photo of Tanu from 1878 with the open flat space filled with totem poles (18 visible) and houses too many to accurately count. We approached Tanu quietly and carefully taking in the fullness of the moment. An intensely green and dark forest has filled the space that I knew as an open village of structures from the 1878 photo. The peoples' work was hauntingly reclaimed by nature. Thom Henley, a sea kayak traveller and effective South Moresby Park advocate, had described this beautifully, "the skeletal remains of long houses settle back into the earth under a funeral garment of moss."[7] From Charlie we learned and observed first-hand, many topics that set the stage for much of our thinking to follow. At one time there were 24 houses here, many sunken

Tanu, a former major Haida village now covered in a blanket of moss, is supervised by the Haida Watchman Program.

terraces descending down into the ground two or even three levels. Terraces were a sign of levels of prestige among members of this proud culture. We also saw fallen mortuary, memorial and house entrance poles that certainly were standing in the Dawson photo. These were poles to serve as elevated tombs (mortuary poles), to commemorate the dead (memorial poles) and to depict genealogical crests of the house owner (house entrance poles). One of the memorial poles had notches cut out of it representing how many potlatch ceremonies that person had had. A potlatch is the ultimate "share the wealth" party that leaves the host poor, but overwhelmed with prestige and honour. In one spot, a 100-year-old tree has lifted up the corner of a former longhouse. The whole site, mostly depressions and massive fallen logs, is covered in a blanket of rich green moss. A new forest towers over all. From Dawson's 1878 survey journal, we learned that he had: "...found it [Tanu] to be the most flourishing of any [village] on the Charlottes." He had witnessed a potlatch there and recorded, "a great gambling game in progress, and a grand dance in prospect for the evening." Only ten years later the population had dwindled from 500 to 80 people. By 1900 the village of Tanu was abandoned for resettlement on Louise Island to the north. We visited another former Haida village, Skedans, by Zodiac when our sea kayak trip was over. I should add here the evocative difference that these two major former villages provide in terms of mood. Tanu is dark and haunting. Skedans is open, bright and as powerfully linked to the sea as Tanu is to the forest. Canadian artist and writer Emily Carr visited Skedans in 1907. In her book *Klee Wyck*, she wrote of the now decaying village site:

...They [the poles] were in a straggling row the entire length of the bay and pointed this way and that, but no mater how drunken their tilt, the Haida poles never lost their dignity. They looked sadder, perhaps, when they bowed forward, and sterner when they tipped back. They were bleached to a pinkish silver colour and cracked by the sun, but nothing could make them mean or poor, because the Indians had put strong thoughts into them...

It was both an exciting and sad moment to witness the few tilted poles still remaining on the village ocean shore at Skedans. Most have been removed to museums.

Near Hot Spring Island, at Ata'na on House Island, and later on our trip at Hagi on Bolkus Island in Skincuttle Inlet, I enjoyed perhaps my personal "deepest" connections with Haida heritage. These two sites are both old settlements, smaller than the larger Tanu and Skedans, and possibly temporary summer habitation. They are both on stunningly beautiful locations for the vista they offer and shelter they provide. In both cases, we simply paddled over for a visit. Camping is not permitted here. The "funeral garment of moss," in our search for terraced depressions and evidence of a ridge serving as a platform for houses, was readily apparent, yet still demanded some investigation. With this knowledge of Haida habitation sites of varied size and purpose "peppering" the islands, I began to realize in a deeper, richer way the former

Hagi, likely a summer Haida village site only, suggests that settlements once peppered the Queen Charlotte Islands.

life of Gwaii Haanas: the ease of fishing and gathering in the lush sea colonies of Burnaby Strait, the wealth in the forest and the easy travel between and among clan members. Here, searching out depressions quietly, I could take the images of Tanu and Skedans from books and from our visit and run with it, as it were. At the quiet, unassuming depressions of long-forgotten Ata'na and Hagi, the Haida culture came alive, and at Tanu, Skedans and Ninstints (which due to harsh weather we didn't see), I felt the power and wonder. At Ata'na and Hagi I pictured a living, thriving forest and sea culture – the Haida for a moment, out of concealment.[8]

On the opposite coast of Canada, the east coast, one archaeological trip highlight involves sea kayaking within the Mingan Islands of the Quebec Lower North Shore. Basque whalers had been visiting the islands for decades before John Cabot's 1497 arrival to the "New World." They were not interested in discovery and politics; commerce and trade appeared to account for their sole purpose. They have left evidence of their presence in the form of circular rock formations, now mostly covered as a mound of grass, soil and crumbling rock walls. Known as the Basque ovens (technically called try works) these mounds exist in the varied highest concentrations along the lower St. Lawrence. I was excited to travel along one of the Mingan Islands looking for a logical harbour for ships to anchor and/or drag whales to land. Sure enough, the small sheltered shallow harbour was obvious and the oven remains were, just as one would envision, on high ground but close to water.

It was a treat to put this story together while standing on the site. A crew of men would fit a huge copper cauldron into the circle of limestone where strips of whale blubber would be rendered into valuable oil to be transported to the awaiting ship. The oil would be used primarily to light the oil lamps of Europe. Fired clay ceramic roofing tiles were also discovered on the site, along with pieces of pottery, pipe fragments, projectile points and a large number of bird bones. Parks Canada conducted archaeological excavations at the site in 1986. Our group carefully explored the area without disturbing any formations. One oven is now largely destroyed by erosion from the high tide ocean waves. It is as if the site were dissected. Here we could examine the construction of large rocks, now obviously somewhat dishevelled, used over 400 years ago. In all, it is estimated that the try works was a 15-person operation. It is believed that the technology, by the 1700s, had

The 16th century Basque Try Works involved the use of rock structures as ovens to render whale blubber to valuable oil. The shallow harbour for beaching a whale can be seen in the background.

advanced such that the rendering of blubber to oil operation could be conducted on the ships. There are similar try works ovens down the St. Lawrence shore as far as Tadoussac.

On other east coast trips, all by sea kayak, my family, well mostly me, have explored for the remaining evidence of settlements/homesteads on the offshore islands of the Eastern Shore – the forgotten shore of Nova Scotia. At Hardwood Island I remember being particularly excited on an evening stroll from camp by the discovery of building foundations of large boulder walls, a sunken root cellar and the remains of a garden. Standing by all of this was one lone conifer tree, likely having taken root in the organic material of the ruin. The island was an open lonely place sloping to the sea. I sat alone, pondering this offshore family life before roads were built on the mainland. The family had likely arrived in the early 1800s escaping the overcrowded settlement at Lunenburg to the south.[9]

Further east, on the southwest coast of Newfoundland, I delighted in the commonplace rustic gravestones on barren knolls of wild-looking coastal camping spots that were once family homesteads or settlements. These graves served as a touchstone for an evolving story of these places. The graves we visited marked the passage of people who gave these much regarded places their names and stories. Local guide George Rossiter of Ramea helped us understand the stories.

Of course, most of the life here centres around fishing. Those graves, be it Deer Island (seven graves found between 1813 to 1957), Fox Island (graves from the 1920s) or Harbour Island within sight of Ramea (with one grave dated 1846 of a man who died in his 80s – born in the 1770s), are all of fisher folk. From the early 1880s to now, one can tell a story of plenty-to-demise in terms of fish stocks and lifestyle. Farley Mowat's 1984 book, *Sea of Slaughter,* chronicles this change from "cod mines" to "the decline of the fishery," with 1992 being the landmark year for Ramea, the year the fish plant closed. Indeed, Newfoundland, as far back as 1497 with Cabot, was known as Baccalaos, Portuguese for "Land of Cod." One 1516 commentator wrote, "the (cod) even stayed [stopped] the passage of his ship." Englishman Charles Leigh, in 1597, reported a catch of 250 cod in one hour off Magdalen Island, near Ramea. By the 1620s there were over 1,000 vessels coming to the Newfoundland banks for a summer and winter catch, using baited hooks and hand lines. This is the same basic jigging technique used today.

The families – Crewe, Dominey, and Peter and Sarah Rossiter – all of whom lived through the second half of the 1800s, all of Deer Island, whose graves we found inside a fallen rotting picket fence within a new forest tucked back on an open peninsula, – all knew the good time of plenty. George Rossiter's father, who lived mostly out of Harbour Island, knew the story of scarcity. Scarcity, following the Second World War, led to a misguided cycle of increased demand, increased prices, increased competition and increased yield (read more destructive scouring of ocean beds), ultimately leading to an all-the-while increasing scarcity.

Fishing, hunting, and trapping stories dominated the recording of these lives of the land. But resettlement was equally omnipresent to our recreation of events of this shore. As mentioned, each kayak pullout involved a cobblestone beach and/or sheltered cover with a substantial clearing – good camping. Being close to the sea for quick access along with the above physical features were the criteria for settlement for single to multiple families. The population seemed to be determined by the space available at the time of Newfoundland's Confederation in 1949; there were 1,200 settlements peppered along nearly 10,000 kilometres (6,214 miles) of shoreline. Joey Smallwood's 1950s vision for Newfoundland was to move people from outpost communities to "growth centres." Deer Island, Harbour Island and Fox Island were all outposts. Ramea and Burgeo were area growth centres. Now over 300 former communities exist only as choice (and rare) camping sites. They were relocated. To a keen eye, or with George's active memory, flattened grave-

The stunning physical features of Fox Harbour Island make it an
ideal camping site today. There are several gravesites to be found on
the island.

stones, rutted cart tracks and the odd cabin foundation are all visible.
Many homes were moved on ice pans to Ramea. While learning about
the ten-family community of Harbour Island, George pointed over to
Ramea across the channel, and said, "that was the last house to be here;
it's over there now, moved twenty years ago on the ice." The mind reels
in considering the community labour involved in such a task.

Fox Harbour Island, though, truly captured my imagination. We paddled in for a shore lunch of stewed cod. The kids had caught the cod.
My partner Kathleen and I had paddled into this amphitheatre of cliff
walls containing a small Fox Island as if we had landed on a nest. Appropriately there is a local story of a rock slide destroying a small vessel in
the night in this cove. As the story goes, at times you can still see the
lights of the ship against the cliff wall. On the hilltops were graves –
exposed, beautiful and haunting. I later learned we missed the main Fox
Harbour Island cemetery site atop and over the dominant island hill.
What lives were lived here? I was happy to get a glimpse – the graves
serving as a window for stories brought to life by our local person.

I have never volunteered at an archaeological dig, though I would like
to do so. My archaeological practice has been easier stuff, surface stuff.
I have travelled by kayak, canoe, car and on foot, often with a friend

trained in this field, learning to be open to possibilities of living imaginatively with the questions of the past in the here and now. Your investigations will take you to dynamic places. Majorville Medicine Wheel on the open prairie immediately springs back to mind. You must look. A friend found a hundred-year-old glass medicine bottle of a gold seeker, behind a shack on the Teslin River, Yukon. That one was by chance. I have found an old cart with a well-preserved wagon wheel in the Algonquin Park bush in Ontario, neglected for over 100 years from former logging glory days. A well-researched inquiry led to the definite location of Jasper House, using a Paul Kane painting of the fur trade depot with its distinctive mountainous backdrop. Aligning the painting with the actual mountain backdrop today was the predominant finishing touch to the find. (Thanks to Ian MacLaren for that one) I found teepee rings by a fresh water source on the Labrador coast and gravesites in the barrens on the Maguse River flowing into Hudson Bay, evident from the river only because of a precious pole of wood purposely left at the burial site. I've started looking.

I hope to visit the large stone dwelling structures in the high Arctic that Farley Mowat believes are connected to the Albans, a Celtic peoples who arrived to North America fleeing Norseman raids, but which British researcher Gavin Menzies believes are connected to the Chinese fleets of 1421.[10] I have read too much about this now not to go there. As historian journalist Stephen Hume put it, "Don't rely on any book, you have to go there."[11]

I remind myself, as I pointed out at the beginning of this archaeology-focused chapter, I am not to my mind particularly good at such investigations, the surface investigations on the land. I marvel at the insight of the practice of archaeologists and am thrilled to have shared the trail with a few, and aspire to pursue my own amateur practice. The rewards are as the Rainer Maria Rilke opening prose expresses, to "Live along some distant day into the answers." Answers or not, living the questions is magical. For me, American poet Wallace Stevens put it best, "Imagination, we have it because we do not have enough without it."[12]

7

CANADIAN ROCKY
MOUNTAIN HIGH: BACK
COUNTRY SKI HERITAGE

*These places are pretty good the way they are. Maybe people
need to adapt to the place; not the place to adapt to people.*
— SEPP RENNER[1]

IT WAS A VERY SATISFYING FEELING. I had arrived by helicopter
with my family on March 5, 2003, at Mt. Assiniboine Lodge set
just on the British Columbia side of the Continental Divide south
of Canmore, Alberta. It was -30°C with a heavy snowfall. We were suddenly in a land of mountain passes and meadows, close to the edge of
the treeline with mountains of blanketing snow and rock all around.
The jewel, Mt. Assiniboine, was as yet obscure from our view. It was
white and grey everywhere but for the copse of trees and the almost
submerged scattering of small buildings.

We were in a land of warmth and hospitality. Inside the lodge was
the good cheer of other like-minded guests – great food, hot drink,
plus the stories of Sepp and Barb Renner and their son Andre. Barb
was out to greet us before we could wonder – what happens next?
Well, of course, hot drinks, and then we were skiing.

Inspired and well-prepared, having studied the history of the lodge
and its key players over time, I rose during our first dinner to toast the
very first ski tour in this region. I toasted the then soon-to-be lodge
operator, Erling Strom, his adventurous friend Marquis Albizzi, and
their first backcountry ski tourists. This early group, consisting of guides

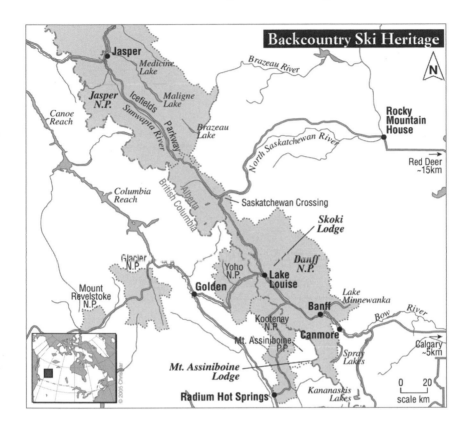

and tourists, departed from Banff on March 5, 1928, seventy-five years ago *to the day* for this same cabin which then had recently been built by the Canadian Pacific Railway (CPR). It would take them three days to arrive. Banff, the nearest neighbourhood then, was 64 kilometres (40 miles) away. (Now folks can ski in or out from the end of the Spray Lakes Road or from the Sunshine downhill ski area. Most people take the helicopter ride and more ski out than ski in uphill.)

Veteran horseback outfitter and guide, Tom Wilson, had met Erling on the main street of Banff and scolded him for his foolishness in planning to take tourists up there in the winter. As a trip – a tourist trip – it was truly a first of its kind in the Canadian Rockies and marked the initiation of a long-standing and much charmed back-country ski lodge tradition. Skiing was not unknown in the Rockies. Ski jumping was popular. Ski racing was common in the 1920s, ski touring was new.

Mt. Assiniboine Lodge sleeping cabins with the mountain in
view at –30° C.

The Banff Ski Club was formed in 1917 using Tunnel Mountain and
later Mt. Norquay as its base. Camrose, Alberta, given its large Norwegian farming settler population, also had a ski jump platform like
those back home. Ski touring into the mountains along the summer
horse-packing trails and passes was an extension of a more local hill
event-based idea. Mt. Assiniboine Lodge and cabins had been built by
the CPR as part of a set of backcountry summer facilities for horse-
packing outfitters and guests, in support of the high-end luxury hotels
such as the Banff Springs and Chateau Lake Louise, positioned along
the rail line. It took a Norwegian and an Italian/Russian adventurer to
conceive of Mt. Assiniboine as a winter destination.[2] It has been receiving ski touring guests for seventy-five consecutive years.

A few days later on our trip it was still snowing, but we were much
warmer and more tired having just skied over two mountain passes, (Boulder and Deception passes at 8,000 feet from Temple Lodge at the Lake
Louise Ski Resort – a distance of about 11 kilometres or seven miles. We
were now in the cozy confines of Skoki Lodge built in 1930. The lodge,
now designated a National Heritage site, was built by the Ski Runners
Club of Banff to promote backcountry ski touring where mountain touring conditions were at their best. Members of the CPR imported Swiss
guides fraternity recommended the area across from the train stop (Laggan) and from Lake Louise, the Chateau. There was no downhill ski area

then. A bunch of Canadian keeners from Banff took up the challenge. And the rest is...well...history. And what a history![3]

At Skoki, I rose from the candlelight dinner table surrounded by happy ski touring guests. Having the ear of the lodge operators, Blake O'Brien and Jennifer Lee, I read aloud a quote of significance. All of the early enthusiasts – Erling Strom, Peter and Catharine Whyte (the first Skoki Lodge hosts) all those keen Banffites and likely most of those 1930s guests and backcountry ski packers (such as Ken Jones) who brought in supplies – all read *High Speed Skiing* by Peter Lunn in 1935. Peter and his British father, Arnold, wrote articles and books on ski travel and techniques in the 1920s and '30s, and they became known as the first "fathers" of snow science. Peter, then a member of the British ski-running team, wrote the following to close his book:

> But the artist and the sportsman know that their work is a justification in itself, and they will continue in it, not because of its effect on civilization or international politics, but because it enables them to break through the barriers of this material world and to taste, if only for a moment, the happiness which lies beyond.

I only wish I'd had a round of "cougar milk" for those in the room when making those toasts. Let cougar milk be my first of the small number of stories I can share here. As the story goes, Erling and ski touring

Skoki Lodge

buddies couldn't find the butter for their hot rum toddies after a full day ski en route into Mt. Assiniboine Lodge. The answer, as substitute, was Eagle Brand sweetened condensed milk. Eureka! It was deemed preferred and a tradition was started. The recipe is easy to remember – a finger of rum, a finger of Eagle Brand and a cup full of hot water. I drink cougar milk on winter trips everywhere, now using it as a springboard to sharing stories of those pioneers on skis.

Beyond the lodge operators (not owners given that these lodges are leased from a provincial park in the Assiniboine case, and a license of occupation for Skoki under the ownership of Parks Canada with shared responsibility for the Lake Louise Ski Resort), there were the ski and horse packers who faithfully brought in supplies winter and summer. All told, these groups, operators and packers, form the foundation of rich history of ski touring pioneering.

Erling Strom in the early Mt. Assiniboine years. *Courtesy of The Whyte Museum, NA660-1366 (V612/LC).*

Erling Strom had arrived in North America following an honourable discharge from the Norwegian Army because of some misconstrued command given during marching drills. Apparently the ever-confident Strom had a stammer. For a man who had ski toured from Estes Winter Park in Colorado to Steamboat Colorado long before such an activity was heard of, and had a winter ascent of Mt. McKinley, as well as becoming North American's first professional ski instructor working at Lake Placid, New York (where he later owned a cross-country lodge, while also teaching at Mont Tremblant, Quebec), this was problematic.

The army discharge story is simply referred to as the "stammer incident." I'd love to know more about this one. Strom, in the 1930s and for "fifty" years after, returned in March to Mt. Assiniboine for the spring ski touring season (once the eastern winter season was waning) and for the summer hiking and horseback outfitting. His daughter Siri had the lodge for a few years in the 1970s, but for the last twenty years the Renner family has run the show wisely, preserving the history through story and careful maintenance of simple living traditions and buildings. Imagine that, only two families running the lodge over a 75-year period.

Skoki has seen a larger number of operators and an intriguing crossover of characters with Mt. Assiniboine Lodge involved in the day-to-day operations. Together these lodges may not have been the first ski lodges in Canada (Swiss guide Emile Cochand opened a lodge in St. Marguerite, Quebec, in 1917) but they were the most westerly and most remote. Peter and Catharine Whyte first operated the lodge from 1931 to 1933 and were heavily involved throughout those formative years of the thirties. One is easily taken with the smooth fit of the artist/skier/hosts that began the Skoki legacy. Peter and Catharine went on to become leading members and supporters of the Banff community and Rocky Mountain traditions through their art, skiing and service. The Whyte Museum and Archives and Banff Library are all connected to their influences. Photographs of the young Catharine in the 1930s at Skoki show a lively spirit with a big smile and an inspiring *joie de vivre*. She had written in her diary at age 15, "My ambition in life is to be loved by all and to be able to be good and help others to be good and to do good to others. I don't wish to be a burden on this world, for there are enough of them."

I can't help think in some strange way Catharine set the ambition for the spirit of lodge operators and packers to follow. How I would have loved to ski with her and others that followed. Their wide skis, bamboo poles and distinctive low stance for "straight running" are well-captured in 1930s photographs and art. They had straight-running speed, control and a healthy amount of jumping. Telemark, named for a region in ski-crazed Norway, and the Christie, named for Kristianna the former name of Oslo, Norway, were not widely used in Canada as yet. Indeed, Erling Strom certainly had much to do with the emerging development of downhill, heel-free techniques. Looking back, for Skoki the 1930s were magical.

Lizzie Rummel, always Lizzie in the mountains, though she was the Baroness Elisabet Von Rummel if she so choose, hosted Skoki Lodge from 1942 to 1949. She then went on to run a back-packer hiking retreat and ski-in camp at Sunburst Lake, two easy kilometres from Mt. Assiniboine Lodge, with an equally elegant view of this "Matahorn of the Rockies" (not that I ever saw this mountain despite my three days of straining my eyes through the ice fog of -30 degrees C or the heavy snowfall). Lizzie came to Canada with her family from Germany for a summer of "pleasure ranching" in the Alberta foothills.

Lizzie Rummel and Ken Jones packing supplies into Skoki from
Lake Louise in the 1940s. *Courtesy of The Whyte Museum,
NA660-1108 (V554/893/PA).*

When she was a teenager, ranching, by the necessity of the First World
War, became not pleasure but work. Their assets were frozen and soon
Lizzie's dream of running a guest mountain ranch provided her direction through life. Lizzie worked for Erling Strom at Mt. Assiniboine
Lodge and, at age 46, took over the Skoki license. At 54, she acquired
the Sunburst Lake Camp, leased from the famous Brewster family,
the major tourist operator family in Banff during the 19th century.
Lizzie was a fine skier and had a Canadian National Park ski guide's
license. Throughout the 1940s, she guided and hosted ski groups
around Skoki Mountain, through the Red Deer Lakes meadows to
the Douglas Glacier and also onto Merlin Ridge, all routes that inspired
the early Swiss guides and keen youthful Banff Ski Club members.
These same routes inspire us still.

    Ken Jones, fellow packer and host, would later say of Lizzie, "She
ran a good show, good food and good entertainment." Others would
talk of her legendary good cheer and company for all who arrived to
her backcountry settings. Such a simple set of words of praise by Ken
and others, yet there is so much spirit and character behind these simple qualities. Indeed, Lizzie received the Order of Canada in 1980 for
her "good show" in the Rockies' backcountry.

Another host, Ray Legace, took over Skoki in the 1950s at a time when downhill skiing with lifts was taking over. These were lean years for backcountry lodges, but repeat guests, mostly easterners still returning from the 1930s, and local drop-ins kept the tradition going. Ray was an infamous non-skier. Given the ups and downs of Deception Pass, this is an odd and fun image. Ray's "show" didn't involve good food either. As the story goes, Ray would watch for skiers arriving from the window and shout out to the kitchen, "Open another can of pork and beans." Jim Deegan and John Porter were ski packers in the 1940s. Both worked for Lizzie. Jim remembers his toughest load to pack in – a new 50-pound battery in his standard Trapper Nelson wood-framed pack. From Temple Lodge (where the downhill Lake Louise resort Temple Lodge stands today) for eleven kilometres he struggled with that dead weight. On 1940s paraffin-waxed skis, he ran the final down hill into Skoki flats from Deception Pass, only to have a spill in the meadow and have to race into the lodge and engine shed to change the battery quickly. He then examined the six-inch-wide acid burnt hole through his three layers of clothing. Skoki would have lights again. But for some reason, sometime after this, Skoki returned to the 1930s candles and kerosene.

Jim, or Timberline Jim as he was also called, estimated the total winter inventory into Skoki in 1946 was five tons, all to be packed in on skis. Perhaps we modern skiers with internal framed packs and well-cambered skis might wish to consider returning to the Trapper Nelson pack and wood skis. It seemed to have done the job with little grumbling. And remember that in Jim's time at 100 pounds (45 kilograms) per run, it was a $10 day wage.

You've heard of cowboy poetry, well, Jim and John wrote ski-packers poetry. An example adds colour to ski tracks everywhere; though particularly to the roots of these words – the Skoki Lodge trails.

From "Code of the Mountains" comes:

> ...*Come, ye maids of the vanity box,*
> *come, ye men of the stifling air;*
> *the white wind waits at our door and knocks,*
> *the white snows call you everywhere.*[4]

And from *Timberline Tales,* "A Night in the Cascade Bar":

> *Have ever you stood*
> *Above the wood*
> *On the top of a mountain divide;*
> *And you're full of gut-rot*
> *With nerves half-shot;*
> *And an avalanche after your hide?*

Ken Jones and Sam Evans must be saved for last. For longevity reasons alone, at both Mt. Assiniboine and Skoki lodges, Ken and Sam warrant the lion's share of wood stove evening storytelling and toasts of cougar milk from us, the fly-in and car-assisted guests. Now Skoki guests receive a car trip around to Temple Lodge from the downhill ski resort, an 11-kilometre trip rather than 20 kilometres to the train station.

Ken was a kid from Golden, B.C., raised on a ranching homestead. As I write this story in April, 2003, Ken is at Skoki Lodge for his traditional St. Patrick's Day visit with many friends. He is 93. Ken learned to ski from the local Swedish kids in town. The Canadian kids used snowshoes to get to school; the Swedish kids had skis made by their fathers. Ken and others had a pair made so the hills around Golden became playing fields for all. Ken remembers that the Swedes used a piece of salt herring for waxing. In Ken's words, "apparently the salt kept the skis from back slipping and the oil from the herring kept the snow from sticking."[5] Ken also remembers they used one firm stoat pole for skiing. It would serve as a rudder for downhill runs. Ken didn't see two poles in use till the mid-1920s.

In October 1936, Ken had just finished a hunting trip in the Banff area. Skoki was getting a facelift with an addition and second storey being added to the main lodge. Ken could use the work. He arrived at night and was immediately dispatched the next morning to hunt for a ridgepole to be 60 feet long and at least nine inches wide. He had to walk seven miles into the Red Deer River headwaters to find such a tree. Legend might have it that he and Sam Evans carried the pole back, but no horses were used. Ken and fellow packer Sam Evans, also still alive at 94, do hold a legendary record, a long part of Skoki lore now. In 1936–37, together they packed supplies over the 20-kilometre (12-mile) distance between Lake Louise Station and Skoki for 63 consecutive days. On a good day the Skoki to Louise run took them two-and-a-half hours and four hours to return loaded, their route rising from 5,100 feet (1700 metres) at the Louise Station to 8,000 feet (2666 metres) at Deception Pass. Over the exact same trail though a lesser distance, my family enjoyed a double-the-time ski out – can't complain about the ski conditions either. Upon arriving at our car, none of us could then imagine returning with a load of, say, boxes of eggs (45 lbs./box, 30 dozen to a box). This was Ken's least preferred load. Ken was famous for his flapjack pancakes and was known now, both at Skoki and Mt. Assiniboine Lodge, to enjoy cutting snow steps and shovelling off roofs despite his great age. It was with regret I learned of his death, a stroke, in January 2004. It was in 1997, on my first ski trip to Skoki, I met Ken at Boulder Pass. He was heading out on a snow machine. We talked

Ken Jones departing Skoki in 1997, having worked on cutting new ski trails. We had a brief chat atop of Boulder Pass – a special moment for me.

briefly at one of the two worst locations, given weather, to meet on the trail. It was both exciting and regretful that I didn't have more time. In 2003, I missed him again at Skoki by a day.

Ken had run Skoki in the winter of 1960 and was the first park warden at the Mt. Assiniboine Park cabin near the lodge. In 1939, he and Sam Evans met Herman Smith "Jackrabbit" Johannsen, a guest of Erling Strom. Ken was the first Canadian-born registered mountain guide and took part in many of the early Banff and western ski races. He has guided that healthy mix of locals and mostly wealthy easterners through the 1930s to '60s, working for Strom, Lizzie Rummel and Jimmy Simpson. Until his recent death, he lived in Nanton, Alberta, and loved to return to these backcountry lodges, sometimes with Sam, whom Seppy lovingly calls, "the first ever Canadian Rockies ski-bum."

A remittance man, of sorts as I understand it, Sam Evans came to Skoki for a New Year's party in 1933. He soon moved to Banff and since has never been long gone. Together these men fall into the living legend category for anyone who has skied into Skoki and Mt. Assiniboine lodges. Seppy remembers their last ski into Mt. Assiniboine together in the late 1980s. They travelled light with oatmeal, tea and a billy (cooking pot). A young warden was refusing their continuation up the pass for fear that these two old-timers were not adequately prepared. As the story goes, the warden phoned news of this up to Seppy who suggested the young warden join them overnight and for the rest of the ski in, to see how its done.

There is so much more to tell of these pioneers on skis. Have I mentioned that Erling's old room upstairs in Mt. Assiniboine Lodge is haunted by Erling's presence? And Halfway Hut, en route to Skoki, is also haunted with the presence of the odd avalanche victim in the area. It is said they play cards at night by candlelight. Have I mentioned, too, Erling's crazy ski races, across the lake and back before breakfast or the Skoki slalom ski races in Lizzie's day on the slopes of Pika Peak? In those days guests measured their stay in weeks, not days. Have I mentioned arriving for the winter season to discover part of the roof had blown off? – a story true of both Mt. Assiniboine and Skoki lodges.

These ski pioneers of backcountry mountain skiing set a high standard of joy for skiing and simple winter living traditions. If you're lucky, Sam might tell you the odd story first-hand, but you can now take delight in the hospitality and continued story-telling tradition of Blake

Descending Wonder Pass to Mt. Assiniboine Lodge. It had warmed up to -20°C.

Inside Skoki Lodge. "These places are pretty good the way they are."

and Jennifer and the Renner family at Skoki and Mt. Assiniboine lodges respectively. You can also learn from the places themselves. Absorb the feel of the "way" of the place. Know it has changed little since Lawren Harris (of the Group of Seven artists) and Jackrabbit Johannsen were guests in the 1930s. I think you will learn that this minimal change is good and that, as Seppy said to me, "These places are pretty good the way they are. Maybe people need to adapt to the place; not the place adapt to people." As you adapt, you can feel the blanketing weight of all this ski heritage that beckons you to the ski trails as a "code of the mountains." As John Porter wrote in one of his skier poems, "Grant to this vagrant heart of mind, a path of wood where my feet may go...."

This weight is not a burden. Like the snow blanket we experienced at both lodges in March 2003, the snow was magical and omnipresent, factoring into all our actions, including our getting to the outhouse. At Skoki and Assiniboine, ski heritage can be the same – a presence that is magical and omnipresent. Thank goodness that Erling Strom, in March of 1928, did not listen to the non-skier outfitter Tom Wilson on Banff Avenue.

8

ON THE HORSEBACK
OUTFITTER TRAIL
WITH MARY SCHÄFFER

There are some secrets you will never learn, there are some
joys you will never feel, there are heart thrills you can never
experience, till with your horse you leave…your
recognized world, and plunge into the vast unknown.
– MARY T.S. SCHÄFFER[1]

ISTORIAN MICHAEL BLISS once stated, "We have to find a
way to make history smell again." Well, Michael, I agree. Let's
take those office-library-laden butts of ours and put them on
a canoe seat, behind a dogsled, or mounted on a saddle. The "fragrance
of the past" awaits those who eventually (once adequate study is complete) leave the enclosed space and move beyond a reader's yearning
for a sensual experiential rendering of the past as a "living history"
recreation. You can still do this in much of Canada. And yes, history
really can smell. No travel mediums are more renowned as pungent
for this than travels by dog team or horseback.

Living in the west, as I did for a short while, with a keen eye for heritage travel practices means that sooner or later you will turn to a
horse-packing outfitted trip. It can be pricey, but it was once *the way* to
go. Today, it is still, as you would expect, a fine way to go, a way that smells
of the past and has a culture all to itself.[2] To be a small part of this culture
with its particular travelling practices was a personal goal. There was also
the richly told travel accounts of pack horse explorer Mary Schäffer.

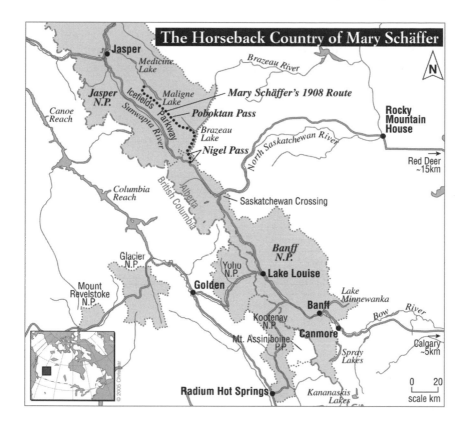

The Horseback Country of Mary Schäffer

Mary Schäffer Warren (1861–1939) was born Mary Sharples to a wealthy Quaker family in Philadelphia. She had been exposed to science and "higher" learning in her youth and had developed interests in natural history and art. She had also travelled with her family to California and Alaska, and to the Canadian Rockies by rail and ferry. Here she developed, what she called her "fever" for Native Peoples. Undoubtedly this interest advanced her longing for ways of life that sought a rediscovery of a more primal authentic being with nature and a deeply felt disgust for the ever-advancing industrial progress into this western frontier. Both these sentiments emerge strongly in her later writings.

In 1889, Mary married the much older Charles Schäffer and, from 1891 to 1902, the Schäffers were to visit the various rail stops of Banff, Laggan (Lake Louise) and Field to conduct field botanical studies, as Mary noted later, "within the sound of the shrieking engines."[3] Her camping experiences were predictably taxing. A fear of horses and

Tom Wilson, Mary Schäffer's guide for her early trips. *Courtesy of The Whyte Museum, NA660-848 (V86/PA 178–99).*

bears, and the ever-prevalent chilling temperatures, pervaded all thoughts. Mary noted that horseback outfitter Tom Wilson "simply dragged a poor little delicate tourist to points she would not have reached." This sounds a bit like "delicate-bum-Bob" and friends with their version of Tom Wilson in modern-day guides Ron and Lenore Moore. We were called "prune pickers" by our outfitters. I never did learn the origins of this fun-loving mockery. But how times would change for Mary and friends – but not so much for us. Rudyard Kipling during a grand tour of the Rockies on one late August day in 1907 would notice Mary (Yahe-Weha-Mountain woman to the Stoney Peoples) and comment in ignorance from this passing carriage, "Indians on the move, how characteristic."[4] It was clear that of our party, he might have commented, "greenhorn dudes with cowboys."

With the sudden death of her husband in 1903, and her apparent study motive for western trips gone, she quietly continued her husband's work from her Philadelphia home. She completed her botanical sketches to accompany Charles' classifications and saw to it that a finished product was published, albeit with less credit going to her husband than she anticipated. More significantly, she returned to the west the following summer and each subsequent summer to continue her acquired lifestyle. Seeking the appropriate guide, she soon found Billy Warren and a partnership quickly developed that eventually led to her so-called "little journeys" that were also major explorations of new routes in what is now Jasper National Park. This partnership also led to marriage with Billy in 1915.[5] She had already established permanent residency in Banff in 1913.

Mary's first trips with friend Mary (Mollie) Adams and Billy Warren's outfit consisted of tours of the hinterland. She later wrote of these days, "Moraine, O'Hara Lakes, Yoho, McArthur Pass – each one of them a stronghold at civilizations limits, each one of them a kindergarten of the at-first-despised camping life." After three summers of such rambling, she and Mollie must have taken stock. "Early precursors [men, of course]," she noted, "all men – then we looked into each others eyes and said, 'Why not?'…So we planned a *BIG* trip." And what a trip they planned. Her "little pat answer" was "the Saskatchewan and Athabasca source," but she had a more general exploration in mind. She did indeed explore much of Jasper National Park, travelling to Fortress Lake at the headwaters of the Athabasca and travelling through Wilcox, Cataract, Athabasca and Yellowhead passes, "Though Chaba Imne, Maligne Lake was to become her key imaginative exploration spark." And mine too, eighty-four years later.

My trips by horseback were two. One via Moosehorn Lake from Brule to the Devonian Flats near Jasper. This trip, despite being in late June, was based on avoiding river crossings and high country, given the heavy late snow load and rushing rivers. The next summer in 1991, a more normal summer season allowed us to travel with Mary's words, thoughts and trials, to Maligne Lake on a classic route now known as the southern boundary route of Jasper National Park. In Mary's day it was exploration. For us, it was exploration still, but it was the practice of pack horse outfitting that was our first study.

Other trails and travellers can inspire one's horseback travels as well. Cliff and Ruth Kopas' 1933 honeymoon trip from Calgary to Bella Coola at the Pacific Coast over a period of four months comes quickly to mind. The Kopas' drew their inspiration from, as Ralph Edwards called them in his book, *The Trails to the Charmed Land*, "the wonderful co-operation of a small body of men…the corps of guides and packers working out of Banff, Lake Louise and Field."[6] All seem to defer to

By 1907 Mary Schäffer was exploring the Rockies. In 1991, we greenhorns were exploring the pack horse outfitting tradition.

the likes of "a tribe" of horsepacking outfitter guides, Tom Wilson, Bill Peyton and Jimmy Simpson.

One particularly interesting trip involves the flamboyant Marquis Albizzi's early 1920s guided horseback trip planned south from Banff along the Continental Divide to Estes Park, Colorado, with sixteen guests, plus packers and about forty horses. All went well until he learned at the Canada/U.S. border that the horses had to be quarantined for thirty days as a rule. Without missing a beat and without telling his "clients," he headed into British Columbia. One morning, a guest noted the sun rising in the "wrong" direction. An infamous story from the 1920s, it no doubt became part of the cowboy banter/performance for years.

Mary Schäffer's true colours shone with her ability to put her explorations into perspective. She never seemed to aspire for that which she was not. She would never have claimed to be an explorer, an anthropologist or an artist, though her writings and her artworks confirm she was talented in all of these areas. Mary remains Mary, a curious wandering traveller thriving on the campers' lifestyle. Once describing her party as "four picnickers," she wrote of her travels and destinations, "to be quite truthful, it was but an aim, an excuse, for our real object was to delve into the heart of an untouched land." This reads fine today, but in Mary's day, trips in such country had a clear purpose, either scientific or exploration based. We, as a 1990s group, were comfortable picnickers learning the insights and technologies of pack horse travel and camping.

To Mary, the Native Peoples of the area, were "a part of the whole," exciting and authentic to the land. It was the white men and women who came to the land as outsiders, as explorers, and, in so doing, saw the land as an obstacle. Mary did what she could to change that. Her travels suggest a strong desire towards an indigenous flavour to travel within the place. She wanted to be a part of this whole and travelled accordingly. She wrote in a letter once, "they like to say 'explorer' of me, no, only a hunter of peace. I found it."[7]

Today's traveller can learn from Mary's engaging spirit. Her reasons for travel fit more with recreational travellers today than other explorers of her day. Mary was not there for science. She was not a big game hunter. She was not after a first ascent, a motive that opened many new routes in her time. In fact, she had a disdain for climbing and only rarely joined her "billy goat" guides Sid Unwin and Billy Warren on their big-view reconnaissance climbs. For her time, Mary did not have an "acceptable" reason to be in these wilds. But like so many today, she sought, in her words, "an *emancipation* from frills, furbelows and small follies." I sense she came to know a significance and meaning to her being in these mountains. She learned to discriminate between simple fulfilling needs and excessive wants and she learned to laugh at herself as an avenue to understanding. She captures, in her writing, this significance and understanding as a humbling participatory consciousness of animals, land and companions. Her travels of two summers completed, she finished her book thus, "...the last day's play was done."

Unlike so many, both then and now, she had not fallen victim to objectifying nature, to proclaiming her omnipotence against the adversary. Mary's call to the wild had a minimal agenda, such that the wilds could be heard and experienced whole. As T.S. Eliot once wrote, "we had the experience, but missed the meaning." But not Mary Schäffer and perhaps not me, through Mary's guiding influence. Emancipation from too much civilization is a factor, but there is a flip side. Finding something is also possible – time with oneself perhaps, time with these fine animals, time with this particular breed of human being – the horse-packing outfitter. Mary's favourite word for this time with self, setting and companions, was equanimity. Today, such a traveller is likely to say, "I had a great relaxing hard-working trip." We leave it at that and perhaps miss the deeper meanings.

I discovered Mary Schäffer by catching the title, *Old Indian Trails of the Canadian Rockies: Incidents of Camp and Trail Life, Covering Two Years' Exploration Through the Rocky Mountains of Canada*, on a library shelf at the University of Alberta in Edmonton. Having recently arrived in Western Canada, I felt like a lake canoeist out of water. There was so much to learn. Here were mountain passes in mountain parks, travelled by familiar names like David Thompson and new characters like Bill Peyton, Curley Phillips, the Earl of Southeast, and – well, Mary Schäffer. There were mighty western rivers for epic continental-type canoe planning in keeping with the fur trading days of old. East or west, north and south, the map told of a geographical history for re-creation. Such are the joys of Canada! Study quickly began to fill the map with names, stories and a plethora of specific routes. There was many an epic tale – Alexander Mackenzie to the Pacific, David Thompson's dealing with mutiny on the Athabasca Pass, and climbers' first ascents. But, it was "incidence of camp and trail life on old Indian

Bob Henderson reading Mary Schäffer's journal on the trail, doing his best to look the part.

trails" that came to spark my greatest fancy. Mary Schäffer's writing and travels captured the fragrance I was seeking and quickly became the western travellings with which I most wanted to connect. But it wasn't just Mary. I wanted to experience the ways of the pack horse outfitter, the cowboy-wrangler-packer-camp cook, old smelly saddles, cowboy coffee, the diamond hitch knot, canvas kitchen tents with pack box seating, and, above all, a new language and new practices.[8]

Mary Schäffer travelled by horseback with an outfitter. Her extended summer trips of 1907–08 to search for the coveted lake of the Stoney Indians, north of the Brazeau, blended in with a more generally rambling style of travel – quite an unusual orientation as mentioned. In 1907, the party came to a dead end of glaciers and mountains at the north end of Brazeau Lake. She had missed the route through Poboktan Pass on the west side of Brazeau Lake as August storms signalled the need for the return journey for Banff to commence. On this return, Mary enjoyed a trip highlight. She spent four days, idyllic days, camping and visiting with Sampson Beaver, a Stoney, and family on the Kootenay Plains. Her 1907 photograph of the Beaver family, known as one of Canada's most recognized western images, is housed at the Whyte Museum archives. At the Kootenay Plains she acquired a rudimentary map for the northern lake from Sampson, which only strengthened her respect for Native Peoples as a part of the whole of the landscape. She would return with this map in 1908 to explore what remains today a classic travel route in Jasper Park, over Nigel Pass to Brazeau Lake, to Poboktan Pass and finally over Maligne Pass into the stunning beauty of Maligne Lake. This was the route our outfit of wranglers and dudes (clients) travelled in 1991.

Sampson's map of 1907 was crude. It did little more than confirm Chaba Imne's (now Maligne Lake) existence and offers that critical change of direction at Poboktan Pass. Our maps were detailed and our outfitter guides knew the route inside out. Mary would be on the trail for four months and return via the Sunwapta and Bow valleys, which is now the corridor for the Banff-Jasper highway. Our travels took ten days. We arrived at our trailhead by car and, where Mary's guides had retired their exploration advance due to the difficulty of the bushwhack, we drove by truck over these footsteps back to "our" outpost, the Jasper town site. But why focus on the differences when the similarities are there for exploring. With one all-at-once imaginative gaze out into Nigel Pass at the trailhead, a journey begins out of time, off the beaten track of linear thinking. The adventure is not to be solely measured in distance or days, but with the relationship of the travellers and the travelled. But this relationship defies measurement and recording. It requires interpretation.

Outfitters' technologies and their language were two mediums through which we shared Mary's experience. Mary and Mollie were, in today's lingo, dudes. Granted they were very accomplished dudes by 1908. We clients were also dudes, albeit good dudes, regular dudes. Our knowledge of packing up a horse for the trail, or setting up an outfitter's camp and tending to the horses was, at best, at novice level. The diamond hitch knot, really a sequence of knots, could only be marvelled at given our limited time on the trail. The language of the wranglers' day placed us firmly in our proper visitor's sub-culture. Latigo – a leather strapping on the saddle; a sawbuck – a type of pack saddle; a wreck – a violent reaction of a horse reminiscent of a two-year-old child's fit; "get a tarp" – "no not that tarp, that's a…"; jingling – rounding up the grazing horses at dawn; distance measured by number of smokes – all these spoke to our adjustment. You don't make morning coffee – you "build up the

Nigel Pass, then and now. I quickly grabbed for my camera and took a quick picture, having recognized the mountain's profile. *Courtesy of The Whyte Museum, NA66-1402 (V415/LC).*

coffee." And by the way, you drink it black – very black. I preferred the dude's peach juice, which came with a healthy teasing by cowboy banter. It was a delight to be part of the out-of-place sub-culture in a traveller's life that makes so much sense. The challenge was to become involved without getting too much in the way. We learned early on we would not join what historic outfitter Ralph Edwards called, "the mystic circle of the diamond hitch." By our tenth day one could be quite involved, as involved as Mary was. But one doesn't become a horse-packing outfitter or wrangler overnight. In fact, Deb Muldoon, a horse-camp cook and wrangler, put it to us straight, "you're not made into an outfitter's life, you're born into it." Living on the trail with Deb Muldoon, Rick Picray, Sandra Temple, Wendy Reade, Dave Flato and Skyline Trail Outfitters, owners Ron and Lenore Moore, proved solid testimony to that score, whether they were born into it or not. Meanwhile, us dudes from eastern Canada, the United States, Belgium and Germany stumbled our way along, enjoying our displacement and the kindness with which we were welcomed. Even the horses seemed at times to understand our predicament, or at least David Barwise from Whitby, Ontario, still talks favourably about his trusted horse, Sally, which he simply couldn't part with after day one. My horse, on the other hand, on day one walked away from me at a short stop, just fast enough that I had to walk, then jog, then run to retrieve her. I failed. Wranglers rounded her up and I was from then on, a goofy canoe tripper.

Dudes, wranglers, outfitters – we travelled together for ten days reading Mary Schäffer's words of the trail at mealtimes, and, like all travellers, we were not without our own "incidence of camp life." On day one, a horse wreck did in my trip guitar. Five years of canoe tripping with only a scratch. Later, dudes challenged wranglers to a Brazeau Valley baseball game. Dudes brought ball and glove (just one) while cowboys brought mugs of coffee. Still later, we saw two grizzlies, Mary's greatest fear, while on a day hike. Mary never did encounter a grizzly, though she did find a favourite tree in each camp for the ever-possible quick escape. She also noted that, while grizzlies cannot climb trees, neither could she. It seems she never resolved this issue. We enjoyed exciting polar bear style dips in lakes Brazeau and Maligne. Wranglers never swim. They just change shirts. A birthday was celebrated with boundless spontaneous energy and gaiety. Wrangles don't roast marsh-

Camp life today, looking very much as it would have in Mary
Schäffer's time.

mallows either, or rather, "only when we're alone" whispered Ron. At
one point, a deer joined our camp and spent the evening wandering
in and out of our midst. One dude learned the backflip quick-exit dis-
mount, thanks to a spruce limb backlash. The stories go on.

However, in the main, there were notably few incidents for dudes
and wranglers alike. There were full days of riding (by dude standard),
time for reading, hiking, endless coffee, campfire chats and, as a connection with 1907-08, there was time to wander and wonder. In fact,
my first night's journal entry begins with the following field note:

July 22 Brazeau Valley, Four Point Camp
I'm looking down the Brazeau Valley to the east. Somewhere down
here there is a big beautiful lake but it looks quite a way. Mary would
have looked too with this same view and likely the same feeling.
"Where is that lake?" Not that I'm in a rush to get there, but I can
appreciate the difficulties of exploration in these mountain passes
more, once I'm in them. The view from here isn't promising.

To appreciate the difficulties and the delights of the explorer's experience demands time to wonder. Robert Pirsig in his thoughtful book,
Zen and the Art of Motorcycle Maintenance, suggests, "reality is always
the moment of vision before the intellectualization takes place. There
is no other reality." The moment of experience when the past is felt
and can be brought to the present is this pre-articulation moment. In

such moments, the fragrant smell for the rigour and joys of the dusty trail through time are made real. But there must be the time and a knowledge base to wonder, to make that moment of reality concrete. Mary's writings as a regular presence (a pre-dinner grace of sorts) served as a common knowledge base to our travels. Together we came to learn much through Mary's lead.

Mary grew to love horses. Their efforts and follies are a constant part of her narrative. Individual personalities emerged, enriching the travels with humour and character. Of course, one has to be receptive for these gains to occur. For Mary, Pinky was an intriguing and problematic horse worthy of regular journal entries. He was, "a little white rat of a horse," who was, "to shine as days went on." For us, it was Applejack. He was a massive draft horse, a latecomer to the outfit without many friends by this point. He was also a "smudge horse," who looked to join our campfires with his big head directly over the flames at every change. We took great delight in his fire-singed eyebrows. He was a great pack horse. Others in the group required different respects. "Don't tie up Buckwheat," was a forceful and regular reminder. Then, in a softer tone, we'd again be reminded, "he doesn't like it." Mary helped us learn that, like people we must respect the individual personalities of our horse outfit, although our horses were also teaching us this all the while. And I must remember too, that, Sid and Billy were teaching Mary and Mollie. Deb Muldoon is long remembered for her kind suggestions to us canoe-tripping easterners. Margot Peck and I still guide university trips together off and on, and easily find a way to relive and share with others "incidences" from our pack horse days. These days seem quite exotic when paddling a familiar northern lake.

Mary's influences also tended to be felt in a more general way. She wrote, while still approaching the Brazeau in 1907, "the ease and comfort of such an existence has taught me that there is a lot of unnecessary fret and worry in civilized life." Another sample: "and they ask, if one grows lonely. Lonely? How can one, when all Nature sings the evening hymn." It was clear to us all, dude and wrangler alike, that Mary Schäffer had much to share and that we had much to learn. To let the rich ambience of Mary's simple travels and pack horse outfitting practices take hold was my personal adventure at the outset. However, Mary's narrative cast its perfume over all the cast on our romantic retracing, and at trip's end, when "the last play days were done," we all felt a deeper conversation with the land, this place, and another time. And for us dudes, we had also learned another way of travel, so suited to these mountain passes.

There has been an attempt made here to capture and describe an ambience, or, for Michael Bliss, a perfume. What an example of serendipity it was then, that, when thinking of writing about this experience, I read Bliss' comments that encourage us to find a way to make history smell. With over thirty horses, well-worn gear and wranglers who merely dust themselves off, our history-inspired trail life certainly smelled. And it was filled with the right ambience. Also in my field notes there was a quote that read, "there is a perfume in the air when someone is in sync with a place." The quote is not my own. I had been reading *Krishnamurti's Notebook* while on the trip. (To my defense, for Krishnamurti as the eastern philosopher is not exactly cowboy poetry, I also had in the saddlebags a variety of western horseback tales besides Schaffer's *Old Indian Trails*). Here was a quote that succinctly touches the spirit of travel that Mary Schäffer and I both sought. Here was the adventure quest, to discover a perfume in sync with the place of travel, with the mode of travel and with another time with that place.

This Krishnamurti thought now serves as a signpost for coming travels in the same way that much of Mary Schäffer's thoughts will be carried along in the reflections of her 1990s compatriots. As for the following passage from Albert Einstein, I had to look it up, but it serves as a fitting conclusion, "He who finds a thought that enables him to obtain a slightly deeper glimpse into the eternal secrets of nature has been given a great grace."

Thanks, Mary, "a hunter of peace" indeed.

9

DOGSLEDDING: OLD CANADA AMBIENCE

In order to really enjoy a dog, one doesn't merely try to train
him to be semi-human. The point of it is to open oneself
to the possibility of becoming partly a dog.
— EDWARD HOAGLAND[1]

DOGSLEDDING, FINALLY. There I was, on the first moments of a twelve-day dogsledding trip in northern Manitoba's Land of the Little Sticks, heading towards the headwaters of the Seal River. The "ways of the north" as experienced through this particular special mode of travel was my goal: just absorb all this old Canada ambience, the sounds, the work, and the movement over snow and ice – the smells, the *smells*.

There I was, but my slip-knot wasn't. My slip-knot didn't slip, as the third and last team to depart in our train to commence our dogsled trip. The slip-knot tied to a tree close beside the sledders' standing platform is a final safety anchor. I was left to contemplate trying to rip a tree from its roots, lose my fingers while fidgeting with my knot under intense tension from the pull of out-of-control dogs, or simply watch hopelessly as a team of seven days careen into a mania of pent-up excitement. By now, the dogs already knew I was a goof, not a musher to be trusted. My team, newly out of the truck dog boxes, looked back annoyed at their confounded novice between outbursts of frenzied protest. My friends would soon be out of sight and the local kids of the community of South Indian Lake were laughing themselves to exhaustion. Poor souls.

Clearly I had to act quickly. I "sucked it up," as the saying goes, and a careful fidget worked. I was off, dogs free to run, and I looked like

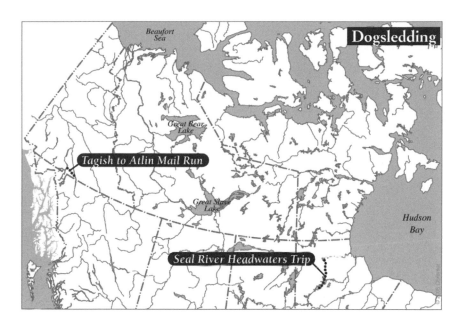

a cartoon character vanishing stage right in a whirlwind. Surprisingly, and so gratefully, I stayed on the sled. This would not be a dog walk in a city park.

I also enjoyed watching the other greenhorn in our group of three, Zabe MacEachren, dive for safety in a snowbank as her team sped on around a curve on a "training run," leaving her stranded. The dogs eventually stopped. Zabe also relieved my sense of incompetence, when during one of many toboggan-wrestling runs following a tight trapper's trail in search of caribou, I would turn to see her hat blocking her vision totally. She never told us if this was accidental or a purposeful move – "Better not to see the trees fly by." By the way, her slip-knot always slipped too soon – another type of problem. We had lots to learn to join the ranks of our outfitter Jim Churchill.

The clearest proof of "rookieism" was on day 4 when I jumped off my toboggan to "reprimand" two fighting dogs (was that Digger or Alvin or Buster?). Anyway, booting them in the butt with my heavy Sorrel boot was the suggested technique for breaking up a dogfight. The only problem was it triggered my trick knee. The anonymous dogs quit fighting, but I was left rolling in the snow in pain.

Now Jim is not an incompetent leader. He knew if we were going to drive our own teams for close to 500 kilometres into caribou country, north from South Indian Lake, that we had to learn for ourselves and learn quickly. Jim believes in "experiential education" and while I can hardly claim to be a pro, I was, at trip's end, now experienced enough to appreciate Arctic explorer Knud Rasmussen's endearing sentiment for all "us" dog mushers, "Give me winter, give me dogs and you can have the rest."[2]

From December 5 to the 20, 1987, I joined a friend, and fellow outdoor educator, Zabe MacEachren, and commercial dogsled operator Jim Churchill of Churchill Sledding Expeditions, for a two-week pilot trip into caribou country from the South Indian Lake town site north into the upper reaches of the Seal River. It was an "up and back" route following the yet-to-be maintained South Indian/Tadoule winter road and a variety of trappers' snow machine side trails. It was Jim's first time guiding a trip in this area. Travel statistics don't usually impress me much, but this time I was impressed – over 500 kilometres (311 miles) in 12 days of travelling; averaging 25 to 30 miles (40–48 kilometres) per day, 45 on a good day; 10 to 16 kilometres per hour; carrying 600 pounds (272 kilograms) of dog feed (total at start); pulling 500 pounds (227 kilograms) per toboggan load. Now, I'm not talking human propulsion here. The sleds were sturdy toboggans made of half-inch oak planks with steel foot brakes and an upright backboard. They weigh 100 pounds (about 45 kilograms) each and with our personal gear consisting of heavy felt-lined boots, parka and more underclothing than I'd ever thought conceivable, each of us weighed close to 200 pounds (91 kilograms). So the general emphasis of these statistics is, travel "heavy but cover great distance." These thoughts, of course, are not often linked with winter travel as I had come to know it as a hand-hauling snowshoer.

When I asked Jim why the early season focuses north of South Indian Lake, he responded in a word, "Caribou." The Kaminuriak herds migrate into these forests from their breeding grounds in the barrens south of Baker Lake. The most southern extension of their winter range is the northern edge of South Indian Lake, about an eighty-mile trip from the Southern Indian Lake community. The western winter limit of the herd is usually around the Phelps and Snowbird Lake area, well out of range of Jim's Pelican Narrows home base in those days. Jim has since moved to The Pas. This caribou migration information is also very tentative. The caribou may follow another course altogether, or, as we

Our sleds fully loaded weighed in at approximately 227 kilograms (500 pounds), including driver.

luckily learned to be the case this year from area trappers, the caribou can on rare occasions travel on South Indian itself. Spirits were high at the outset for dogs and people. It seemed a certainty I would finally observe lots of caribou. The animals do not gather into extensive roaming herds until the summer months and tend to travel in groupings of ten to thirty animals, preferring the open lakes to the forest and deeper snow inland. I envisioned lakes peppered with caribou groupings, as did Jim who even surpassed me with his excitement for caribou.[3]

Caribou were important, but I was also there for some imagined visceral understanding of a dogsledder's way of the North. This state of mind started to become real for me when I felt I could begin to see the travel from the dogs' perspective – even if just a hint of this alien view opened up for me. For some dogs more than others, there seemed a great joy in running and pulling and an equally great joy in resting – a kind of "animal lazy" we humans so rarely attain. When the dogs settle into the day's pace on a big lake there is a meditative quality to this travel. That is, until a biting wind reminds you that you should have a quick trot beside the moving sled in effort to warm up. Still, "be like those dogs," I remember thinking. Become at home here. To gain such comfort, however, there was an involved set of techniques that had to be learned experientially. The practice of dogsledding was new. So much for me to learn on the job, as it were.

Beyond the excitement of seeing caribou in winter (it finally did happen), I was living out two strong desires. Firstly, to do a dogsledding trip of equal distances and length to a summer canoe trip has been one of those hard-to-fulfill dreams, given I live in Southern Ontario without much by way of dog teams and snow. Secondly, I had hoped to return to the Land of Little Sticks, the place that for me is an island of voicelessness in the historically rich and beautiful Canadian North. I am attracted by its remoteness, not from the road-head so much, but remoteness from lack of attention. This region rarely makes the national news. There is a genuine "old world" North here. It is a good place to travel by dog team. It is a quiet meditative place with long horizons and distant bands of whitened eskers. "The dogs must love it here," I thought. Of course, for the people who live in the area, this would all seem senseless. But I first felt this authentic old world North paddling the Thlewiaza River in 1983, and my attraction to the North Knife, Caribou, Wolverine and Seal rivers has only amplified.

Our plan was simply to get into this region by following the trails of the early trappers and hunters, to explore caribou country. Jim's racing dogs, turned bush-travel dogs, need a trail to follow. "Gee" and "haw" (right and left commands) work only on occasions, with little rhyme or reason. So "explore" is the proper word for any dogsled travel in new country unless you are prepared to break trail for the dogs all day, drastically reducing travel distances. In our setting there were

A peaceful-looking image of winter camping. What you do not see here are dogs yapping for their evening meal along their gangline to the left of the tent.

options with often no certain route destination. We would follow area trappers and hunters off the main line winter road. As it was, ridiculously unseasonably warm weather (+5° C) early on forced us to both grunt it out and wait it out. We did some trail-breaking, "raising the road,"[4] which in Jim's words "screws up the dogs' heads" and also waited patiently for area trappers to zoom by in their snow machines, providing a narrow ribbon of hard-packed trail.

To be in this vanished trail predicament was abnormal. It was brought on by the warm weather and very large lake. Dogs can usually still feel out the trail following moderate snowfalls (also unusual here). We cursed our strange circumstance. But with the upcoming fur auction in Thompson, Manitoba, area trappers were in transit. So new trails were soon to be had. There is a clear historical lesson here. It was easy to understand why, despite the "heavy load but good distance" rule, dog teams were not totally relied on for winter travel, particularly in more southern latitudes where thaws and heavy snowfalls are more frequent. I'd often wondered why the winter packet (our early mail delivery service between trading posts) was often moved labouriously by hand-hauling toboggans with snowshoes. Now I was learning why and I gave thanks to the increased population in the region these days. When reliant on established trail systems you explore new country with a, "well let's follow this one" attitude at times. On side trips, guessing exactly where we were going via what routing from our 1:250,000 topographic maps in, relatively speaking, featureless terrain, was always exciting. At one point we had to decide whether to head east on Waddie Lake, part of the North Knife River headwaters, or due north along the winter trail to the Chipewyan community of Tadoule on the Seal River. Such major decisions I am used to making long before I'm on the trail, though I think I prefer this luxury of the spontaneous way, or in Native terms simply "going out on the land." The lack of definite destination, yet with great distances covered, seemed a strange and wonderful novelty. In the end, the Tadoule route was chosen, which meant less wrestling with sleds on narrow winding portage trails. "Something to do with more experience," I thought.

Now in retrospect, it was dogs, plain and simple, that made this trip so special. Jim's version of communicating with his crew stands out as a special highlight. Jim would always be quick to reinforce, "these aren't pets." The overall comedy of being with 21 dog companions was the pleasant surprise of this particular excursion.

Bob Henderson with Alvin, the gregarious dog. *Courtesy of Zabe MacEachern.*

By trip's end I could hear a bark from inside our wall tent and likely know which dog's name to shout to seek quiet. I could identify all dogs from the front and back. Floppy and/or pointed ears are a common indicator beyond colouring. The backend view recognition is particularly important for when their tails lift and their legs spread a bit while running – more of this later. I knew which dogs I could play fight with, which was a slacker and which loved to pull. Fred was the movie star, seeking attention and complacent with humans, but sporting many a battle scar from fights with other dogs. Alvin was the most gregarious sort, always keen for playful wrestling matches. Sinner was a growler and subsequently got yelled at a lot. Lyle was older, distinguished, and deserved respect. Healer avoided all human contact. I was told to make special note of this. He had to be dragged onto the ganglines everyday but he was a good puller. Tellie was wildly enthusiastic, a real screamer with a deafening high pitch, yet with a second gear that was all whimpers. He was always getting in ridiculously frustrating tangles on the line – the most loveable dog on the team. Molly, his sister, was equally loud and high-pitched. No, she was worst. Dougie was a no-nonsense reliable lead dog. Best of all, for humour, was Buster. Every trip has a Buster, I was told. Buster, on two occasions, reached over just off the trail, and gripped in his teeth a snack of caribou meat or bone: once with Cree hunters watching in shock. Buster was no dummy. He nipped a tenderloin cut. Buster seemed all play, all little boy. In a group size of 21 (humans that is) you're bound to enjoy the company of many, not care for a few and not really get to know others. I found it just the same with 21 dogs.

Jim's dogs consist of former racing breed dogs that "don't have the top end." This means they are less speedsters and more slow-paced endurance animals. In Jim's words, "they are great working dogs but as race dogs they lose the spirit quickly." Jim had been in and out of dog racing for ten years so he knew what he wanted in a dog. The inspiration for starting a commercial business followed his support of Will Stegar's Minnesota to Alaska dogsledding trip in 1985. Jim helped by guiding the The Pas to Pelican Narrows stretch of the trail. From Jim, I learned something played out time and time again with other dog mushers I have known, such as Dave Freymond of L'Amable, Ontario, – canoeists or hikers may go on a trip now and then, but dogsledding is a way of life.

I learned first-hand through Jim's guiding philosophy to understand his 50 to 60-pound (23 to 27-kilogram) canine partners – "A good dog has two goals; one is to eat, the other is to work." Zabe and I saw plenty of both. Arctic huskies average 80 pounds (36 kilograms) in weight and have heavier coats than Jim's troop of racing mutts. Those heavy, woolly dogs would fry in the balmy winter temperatures of this particular north. As it was, our temperature range was from an unseasonable five degrees C to an appropriate -25° C.

The dogs pull our load, but once we arrive at camp our work begins and most of it evolves around dogs. Once the wall tent, stove, fire, dinner etc. are in order, there is dog feed (chicken skin and fat) to heat up on an outside fire in a 20-gallon drum. Each dog ate two to three pounds of feed per day. Dogs were served a broth with solid chunks that are chopped into pieces for individual serving bowls. One must be careful serving the daily feed, particularly with Big Al.

Getting 21 dogs to and from the camps, stake-out lines and running ganglines, and in and out of harness represents considerable work, not to mention the loading and unloading of sleds. It seemed like a lot for three people each day, but I came to look forward to it.

Most impressive was Jim's knowledge of his crew of twenty-one. We were quick to learn all we could to follow Jim's example for a smoothly running team. Jim knew all the dogs by sound, by sight from any angle, by behaviour and literally by "shit." He could tell who's being a "lard-ball," who deserves a "good dog" pat on the back and other more lavish endearments, who will fight with whom if beside each other on the line, who pulls sideways when on the right of the gangline and who tends to relieve himself when and how into the day's run. Knowing all this is important to efficient travel. Knowing these so-called toilet patterns seemed a marvel to me, but it sure can prevent frustrating tangles.

When your lead dog tries to stop "to go," you are best to be ready to encourage his need while on the run and not at his "suggested" stop. For the dogs this is possible, but difficult, particularly for the wheel dogs (last on the train) who get dragged a bit in the process. You have to be watchful for this and other "moments" along the way.

Overall, the ease with which we travelled, even with experiencing a few major tangles and a few travel redirections, helped us tap into the ways of dogsledding. The general keenness of our individual teams of seven dogs bespeaks Jim Churchill's abilities as both a teacher and a trainer – for all – people and dogs alike.

From the novice point of view, there was a lot to learn in this unpredictable world of dog mushing. At first, the lead dog was a bow dog and wheel dogs were stern dogs. Buck was Buster or was Buck Diamond. I was hopeless. Harnessing took twice the time it should to loop the gear around the fidgety legs of 50 pounds of hyper animals, because I put the harness on inside out. It is much easier to put on a diaper, and I thought I'd met my match with diapers. As well, each dog has a particular harness so there's lots of "where's Tramp?" "where's Tellie?" Then there was my slip-knot, as if that wasn't enough drama to start the whole affair.

The question remains, did we see caribou? The answer is "yes." But a more intriguing question for us as we travelled north became how would the dogs respond. Would they charge the always frightful animal? Would they bark, howl or whimper? (I was sure Tellie would whimper.) Well, they simply ran on, cool to the excitement we were experiencing. Caribou peppering the lakes was not a reality. We saw fewer than ten animals and this only from a distance. Signs on the lakes and in the bush did tease us in the extreme and we learned that caribou are elusive. And so they should be, and we'll just have to return. The bottom line of course is that the search is more important than the result. I was thankful I was not a hunter or wildlife biologist. Though if I were, undoubtedly I would eventually have more success.

The following journal entry from the closing moments of the 1987 trip captures my trip end sentiments:

Day 13 Near Long Point – Southern Indian Lake
I sit up in my sleeping bag enjoying the first blasts of heat from the stocked-up wood stove watching the fire reflecting on the walls of

this make-do log shack used as a shelter by area trappers. A pleasing change of pace from the wall tent. Today will be my last day dogsledding for I don't know how long. After twelve consecutive days of running dogs through the Land of Little Sticks, when I unhitch my team that will be it. It is a hard pill to swallow. My feelings are similar to that last stroke of the paddle for another season or the last ski glide on wet exhausted snow. But it's still December. The first snowfalls in my hometown in Southern Ontario perhaps are still expected. I have all winter to think of the quiet steady push of the dogs and my wandering gaze into white, green and gray of the seemingly endless lake and spruce country.

Other than many day trips, mostly with university students (which allows me each year to relive that greenhorn excitement), I have only been on one other dogsled trip. It is worthy of mention though for its traditional links to the past and continued tradition now in modern times.

In 1990, I joined the 120 kilometre (74 miles) Commemorative Mail Run by dog team from Carcross, Yukon, to Atlin, British Columbia, via Tagish and Atlin lakes. Unlike the quiet Manitoba trip, this historical retrace with specially stamped envelopes for mailing was a grand party with an official count of participants at 37 dog teams, 46 people and over 300 dogs in total. Let me tell you, that's quite a party.

The Commemorative Mail Run idea is credited to Yukoner Bill Thompson to whom, in fun, I personally hand delivered my mailbag

Bob Henderson, *left*, ceremoniously presenting Bill Thompson with the Tagish to Atlin mail delivered by dog team.

in Atlin. Bill retired as event organizer in 1999. The annual event began
in 1975 and over the years has grown into a season end social function
for local and some distant dog runners. The Commemorative Mail Run
is also a charity event. In 25 years, Bill and his wife Millie have raised
more than $100,000 for local charities. *Up Here* magazine in May/June
1999, reported the silver anniversary run sold close to 3,500 special
edition commemorative envelopes to be carried to Atlin by dog team
before being placed in the normal mail system. I still have the enve-
lope I mailed to myself in 1990.

The 1990 run I participated in was the fifteenth. As a true outsider,
I joined in with an outfitter keen to make the run, a little bewildered
by the mayhem of it all. This busyness was particularly evident in the
mornings, as the many teams would head out on the trail in turn. Now
rather than one dog of a team getting tangled on its lines, it was possible for teams to get tangled with other teams. Fortunately my slip-knot
anchor technique was perfected by then. For this trip, timing was an
all important ingredient for success. One must hold the dogs in check
until an open lane with good lead time became apparent. Timing is
everything. It sounds easy, but it wasn't.

In 1901, following the Klondike Gold Rush, Norman Fisher took
the commission to service a mail run to remote Yukon centres. Dogsled
guide Wendy Bush, of Jasper, Alberta, in her celebratory book, *Ascent
of Dog: Working Dogs in the West,* records the ways of travel here
through the seasons:

> In early November each year, when the paddlewheelers tied up for
> the winter, canoes were put to use. When the ice started to form,
> canoes carried the mail, freight, two or three dogs and a sled. The
> sled carried the canoe over the icy sections and the canoe hauled
> the dogs and gear over the wet segments. Until the middle of Janu-
> ary, a team of dogs hauled the entire trip, when the ice was thick
> enough to hold a team of heavy horses. In spring, when the ice began
> to candle and rot, the dogs were put to use again.[5]

By the mid-1930s air freight bush plane service replaced the dog team
and canoe, but I had to wonder. While on my 1990 commemorative
run, I remember passing a major southwest bend in the expansive Tagish Lake. Later a fellow I'd chanced to meet on a plane sent me a

photograph of a small mailbox nailed to a tree at the point of this bend. It seemed that mail by boat and dog team continued to travel over the 30-kilometre run to this halfway box. Good traditions die slowly.

Dogs do have a rich tradition connected to travel throughout much of Canada. Various Native Peoples used domesticated dogs to transport gear and firewood. Dog packs, like saddlebags, and dog travois (two wood extension poles with a platform for gear strapped to the dog's shoulder) were employed. Wendy Bush reports on fur trader John McDonnell, in 1793, noting a large Husky-type dog hitched on an Assiniboine dog travois and hauling loads of 100 pounds.

Explorers, fur traders and the North West Mounted Police all took up the practice of dog teams. David Thompson, in June of 1807 and later in 1810, noted being forced to eat one or more of their hauling dogs during hard times for hunting in the eastern Rockies. Thompson used dog teams in exploring both the Howse and Athabasca Pass. Winter packeteers were mail-runners for the fur trade. Basically, the dog team took over from the canoe in the winter months. And while there was much less travel activity between remote posts and headquarters in Fort William and Montreal, the mail, just as with the more acknowledged Pony Express in the American West, would arrive. Indeed it would arrive often read by others all along the way, by people craving any news and information. I can imagine the odd juicy love letter causing quite the stir while secretly being read by candlelight in a remote trading post. The usual means of travel involved two or three men, their supplies and 70 pounds (32 kilograms) or so of mail. Four dogs per team of two teams were most common. The men often broke trail or ran beside the dogs. Sixty-four kilometres (forty miles) per day were apparently not uncommon. Fort Carleton in central Saskatchewan served as a transfer point to all places west and north for the winter mail service in this country. Certainly there were times when the sledding was good but as the literature suggests, when the going was tough with dogs, it was particularly tough, mostly I would suggest, because of the heavy loads being hauled.

A traveller in 1800, the Reverend J.A. Mackay, made a candid statement useful for all over-romantic types like myself to remember:

Wednesday, 15th – I reached home [Stanley Mission on the Churchill River, Saskatchewan] this evening after a tedious journey of seven

days from the Ile-a-la-Crosse. Two years ago I accomplished the journey in four days with much more comfort. I have sometimes seen
illustrations of winter travelling in this country. The traveller generally represented comfortably wrapped up in his sledge with his
dogs going at full speed over the snow. A more truthful picture would
represent the dogs floundering through the snow and the unfortunate driver with one pole behind the sledge pushing to assist the
dogs. At all events such has generally been my experience and particularly throughout this journey. I was thankful on arriving home
to find all safe and well.[6]

A favourite story for my winter campfire with students now is the North-
West Mounted Police "Lost Patrol" story of December 1911. Inspector
Francis Fitzgerald with three other men, and with dog teams, set out
on a 765-kilometre (475-mile) patrol from Fort McPherson to Dawson City via the Hart and Little Wind rivers. Their purpose was to
deliver mail. First opened in 1904–05, this was the established route.
The dogs were malamutes, the Mackenzie River breeds weighing 80
to 150 pounds (36 to 68 kilograms). The men got lost (they had no
local guide), were poorly supplied (their choice to go extra light as an
experiment) and, some surmise, they had felt themselves "indestruc-
tible" under Fitzgerald's command. Some three months later, on March
21, the leader of the search party, Corporal Jack Dempster, found two
of the four bodies. Fitzgerald's and guide Sam Carter's bodies were
found on March 22, downriver on the Peel River a day later. The mail
had been carried up to 80 kilometres (50 miles) from its destination,
a sign of the NWMP legendary devotion to duty, I'd say. They were
less than 40 kilometres (25 miles) from a safe return to Fort McPherson, having likely been lost for weeks in the Wind River country.
Fifty-three days on (and off) the Mountie dogsled trail, and over 1,000
kilometres travelled. As historian Dick North notes, "Lesser men would
have quit sooner."[7] Most of the dogs were eaten; they shot one dog at
a time as necessary. Fitzgerald's February 3rd journal entry makes this
clear, and highlights the trip leader's optimism:

> Killed another dog tonight, and had to feed some of it to the dogs
> as we have no dried fish. Men and dogs very thin and weak, and
> cannot travel far. We have travelled about 200 miles on dog meat,

and have still about 100 miles to go, but I think we will make it all right, but will have only three or four dogs left."[8]

The four men started with twenty dogs, five per team. Why this story? Well, it's a "brave men against the odds" story. Nature wins. In Canada, nature usually wins. Along our winter trails today, I'm happy to help keep such stories alive.[9]

Our hosts for two nights on that 1987 Manitoba trip were Bill and Shirley Hicks of Leaf Rapids. They lived then on the outskirts of town, boasting a dog yard of over 100 animals – packing dogs, race dogs, you name it. They seemed to acquire and trade dogs as though they were hockey cards – favourite hockey cards, mind you. Jim and Bill talked long into the night. Dogs, dogs, dogs! As Zabe and I finally parted company with our hosts, Bill smiled and said, "Dog mushers are a breed apart." I'd heard a lot about breeds over two weeks, but, "a breed apart"? I have heard that expression used a hundred times regarding everything from chess to football. But this time, I paused, and thought, "It really is true, dog mushers are a breed apart." I had gained a glimpse into this "breed apart" and the "ways of the North," their practices still being celebrated today. It is a trip back in time but also an eminently practical way to travel on well-trailed systems.

Sometimes when out for a winter walk in the city in the crisp winter night air, I can bring back to my senses this old Canada ambience: the sounds of yapping and growling dogs, the good work of running alongside the sled up a steep hill and forever moving dogs from haul lines to gang lines, the romantic floating-like movement over snow and ice, the northern stories, and those smells, those smells.

10

ROCK ART: A LIFELONG
QUEST AND MYSTERY

*There was a time when I wondered – do I really believe all of this
[leaving offerings for the spirits at pictograph sites]. After a while
such questions stopped mattering. Believing or not believing, it was
all the same. I found myself compelled to behave toward the world
as if it contained sentient spiritual beings. The question whether
or not they actually existed became irrelevant. After I'd stopped
thinking about it for a while, the ritual of offering tobacco became
comforting and then necessary. Whenever I offered tobacco I was for
that moment fully there, fully thinking, willing to address the mystery.*
— LOUISE ERDRICH[1]

LOOKING AT PICTOGRAPHS on lake cliff faces was my start. It was
the start to all that this book involves – the seeking of the human
stories and presence on the land. You might say it hit me like a
rock. It was like staring through a porthole into the grand mystery of
the Canadian Shield wilds and her indigenous peoples. I was a hopeless foreigner – still am – but that's okay. I was fourteen then.

Today, thirty plus years since my first gaze at the Lake Superior Agawa
site and my canoeing through Quetico Provincial Park, visiting many
well-known sites throughout the region, I've learned that when it comes
to Native rock art, pictographs (printing) and petroglyphs (carvings),
we are all gazing into a spiritual world. Experts and amateurs alike
(and there are plenty of both) will acknowledge that there are more
questions associated with Native rock art than answers. Still, there are
many "best guesses" out there which adds to the excitement of the
mystery. But note, best guesses do not solve the mystery. The mystery

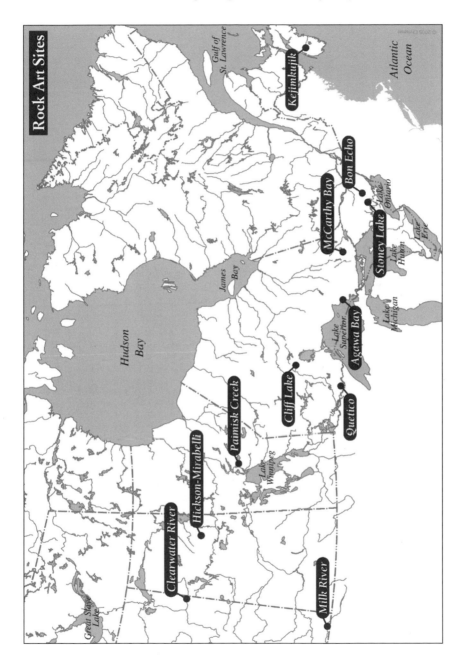

is paramount to viewing rock art. Novelist John Fowles, quoted in Wayland Drew's *The Haunted Shore*, concerning Lake Superior, captures the important qualities of mystery well:

> Mystery, or unknowing, is energy. As soon as a mystery is explained, it ceases to be a source of energy. If we question deep enough there comes a point where answers, if answers could be given, would kill.[2]

Selwyn Dewdney, Thor and Julie Conway, Grace Rajnovich, James Keyser and Michael Klassen, Tim Jones, Dennis Smyk, Michael Furtman – I've learned from all of them in reading or in conversation. They have been the bridges to gazing through time and into culture. Mostly, though, you learn about rock art from going to the sites with the goal of simply staring wide-eyed into the porthole of this now mostly lost

world and taking in the aura of the overall environment. Within is the aspiration to ponder the meaning and ways of the human relationship with the cosmos. And it is good to wonder about such things. Cataloguers can record and report. Artist can seek the aesthetic. Dreamers can ponder the meaning. The canoe tripper might embody some or all of these, though certainly rock art sites add spice or even definition to one's travels, whatever your particular persuasion. Like the canoe itself, exploring rock art in the wilds acknowledges the centrality of Native Peoples to the Canadian canoe trip experience. There is always this presence of an indigenous way "to be" on the land. There is teaching here. Perhaps rock art allows us to glimpse into other ways to be well-suited to travel and camping. Rock art opens us up to sound possibilities for expanding our personal relationship to land, water, animals and story. From American writer Louise Erdrich, referring to Lake of the Woods pictographs, comes, "The rock paintings are alive. This is more important than anything else I can say about them."[3]

Ceilidh Henderson, proud of her Churchill River rock art sketches.

Beyond those early first explorations of the ever impressive Quetico and Agawa sites, I have followed Selwyn Dewdney's lead to other highly concentrated sites on Cliff Lake, north of Lake Nipigon, the Bon Echo

Park site on Lake Mazinaw and the Hickson-Maribelli Lake site near the Pink River/Paull River headwaters north of the Churchill River in northern Saskatchewan. Dewdney claimed these were the three dominant sites on the Canadian Shield. There are many other sites scattered throughout the Shield for pictographs and I'll always go out of my way to visit, be it to see some of Dennis Smyk's finds on White Otter Lake while I'm there, or those sites reported on maps and in books or mentioned by fellow canoe-tripping friends. That interest became a central motive for route selections. Ric Driediger from Missinipe, Saskatchewan, told me about the Larocque Lake site, north of the Churchill River which I'm hoping to visit soon. Indeed the University of Saskatchewan's Department of Anthropology and Archaeology had, by the 1970s, recorded over 480 symbols on over 170 separate rock faces mostly in Saskatchewan. Dennis Smyk tells me about new finds in northwestern Ontario. He says, quite simply, he is discovering unreported pictographs because, "he is looking." Simple as that!

Snowshoeing to the rapids' rock art site on the Clearwater River in Alberta was a highlight. Here winter proves the best time amidst the otherwise convoluted channels of fast water to view those images. An icy spring walk south of Canmore, Alberta, revealed an excellent collection. Another highlight was a driving excursion to a rock pile outside Tucson, Arizona. The images were strangely both different and familiar. Likewise with petroglyphs on the Milk River, on the shoreline rock in Alberta at Writing-on-Stone and in Kejimkujik Park, Nova Scotia, one can explore images from a wide variety of First Nations peoples. Seeking rock art sites is a practice for me now. Like snowshoeing or canoeing, this is an activity for lifelong learning. There is a technique. I question when I travel, "Is there rock art here?" My aspiration is to see that ancient skiing rock art image from northern Norway – but alas, I daydream.

One special site for me is located on McCarthy Bay of Matagamasi Lake, northeast of Sudbury. Every August, for over twenty years, I have visited this site with university students. Each year I'm grateful for the opportunity to introduce pictographs to others and follow the age-old ritual practice of leaving an offering on the site with our departure. Don Godwin, from the Cree Nation and former mayor of Norway House, Manitoba, has said of the Paimisk Creek site specifically (but I assume with general application), "Anyone who goes there and uses it [a rock art site] for whatever reason, a payment of tobacco and food

The McCarthy Bay, Ontario, large rock art image is likely a *Maymaygwayshi*.

is simply the way of returning the peace and tranquility."[4] I think returning the peace and tranquility today should also involve first a hearty
discussion of the key questions. Who painted these and why? How old
are they? How have they lasted so long? And, of course, the "biggie"
– what do they mean? Each year I revisit these questions, seeing each
question's mystery renewed for me in the eyes of the newcomers. I like
to tell P.G. Downes' account, in his 1943 book *Sleeping Island*, involving northern Manitoba, of the *Maymaygwayshi's* revenge on three
irreverent canoe trippers who did not show due respect to the "ways"
of the North. *Maymaygwayshi* are tiny, hairy rock men who live in the
fissures and cracks of rocks. They can wreak havoc with a canoe tripper's progress if they so choose – an Ojibwe and Cree equivalent in
some ways to the Irish leprechaun. If you have a dump in a big wind
or feel mischievous mishaps befalling your travels – perhaps there are
Maymaygwayshi at play. Happily, there is a fine example at this McCarthy
Bay site of an image commonly believed to be a human-like figure with
bent outstretched arms and fingers, possibly depicting a *Maymaygwayshi*. This is a man with horns. Horns denote a spiritual being. If the
human figure, generally speaking, is meant to denote a shaman (spiritual leader or advisor), the rock art image is more likely to have a
thunderbolt or other objects protruding from the head area. This small
Canadian Shield site also has figures in a canoe and a depiction of various animals. Both are common motifs in Canadian Shield rock art.[5]

I like to refer to cultural historian Paul Shepard's assertion that rock art sites are "Earth Temples." In his book, *Thinking Animals*, he states, "We are what we are because we think animals." This is no doubt true of the hunting/gathering cultures responsible for rock art sites through Canada. But it is no less profound to consider a modern western urban culture and the prevailing presence of the non-human. Think of a child's bedroom for the use of animals as metaphors in our language, and in our art and sport motifs. Animals are everywhere still, despite their apparent waning in our immediate thought-world. Viewing rock art is a special time for thinking about animals and our mythical, once overt but now more subliminal, attachment to animals. When I see figures in a canoe, I sense this is detail told to initiate a story. It could be a teaching or a dream depiction. Louise Erdrich writes that rock art refers to a "spiritual geography." This reminds me of that mysterious quote by Paul Eluard, "There is another world, but it is in this one."

Although mostly outside the Canadian Shield, carved or etched rock art images were recorded through time, in the style we call petroglyphs. There are a few key Canadian sites; the Blackfoot and other Plains Indians carved their outstanding writing-on-stone images in the Milk River Valley of southern Alberta. James Keyser and Michael Klassen

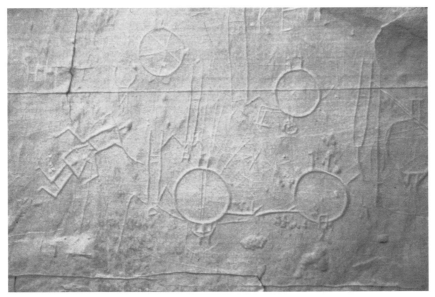

Writing-on-Stone Shield Warrior figures and images.

state there are nearly 100 separate sites, representing at least five different rock art traditions, in this one area of concentration connecting the Sweetgrass Hills with the soft sandstone cliffs and rock pillars in the Milk River Valley just to the north. Here, it is believed, fasting and the seeking of a guiding vision in the Sweetgrass Hills or table-top plateaus of various rock pillars were followed by a descent into the valley to record the images and stories gained.

In the Maritimes, the Mi'kmaw petroglyphs from Fairy Bay in Kejimkujik National Park, Nova Scotia, present a comparable site as a cultural mecca. Here early evidence of European/Native encounters is recorded in the soft rocky shoreline. Sailing ships are a dominant motif. In Ontario, the teaching rocks, *Kinomagewapkong* at Petroglyphs Provincial Park north of Peterborough, near Stoney Lake, are another archeological treasure. As a sacred site for Algonkian-speaking peoples for some 600 to 1,100 years, this site on the southern edge of the Canadian Shield was "rediscovered" in 1954 by Dr. Walter A. Kenyon of the Royal Ontario Museum. Park literature confirms there are more than 300 distinct images and perhaps as many as 600 now eroded images. The site is a flat marble rise in the land and now is encased with a protective chamber and a visitor centre. Like the Lake Mazinaw rock art site in southeastern Ontario's Shield fringes, the 'teaching rocks" are an intriguing highly accessible location as is Writing-On-Stone and Kejimkujik in Nova Scotia. To use Selwyn Dewdney's words, these "age-hallowed places" can and should be visited as tourist attractions to develop reverence and a greater depth of understanding of Native Peoples' inspiration (and depth of feeling) for the land. But true to a canoe tripper's sensibility, I prefer the remote sites that pepper the lakes on the Canadian Shield. I have a few remote favourites, and so many still to explore.

CLIFF LAKE, NORTHWESTERN ONTARIO

The route along the Big River system had been a difficult one, full of taxing blazed trails and shallow rapids. The final approach to Cliff Lake involved leaving the low boggy spruce lands north of Lake Nipigon for a rugged 75-foot (23 metres) elevation gain. This is a strange phenomenon in this low-lying terrain and a big part of the attraction to Cliff Lake, both for us as recreational paddlers and earlier, I assume, for Native

Fairy Bay, Kejimkujik Park, where a bow and arrow hunter petroglyph can be found.

groups, as a spiritual and sacred spot in some way. In a land of few Shield rock outcrops, Cliff Lake rises up from a 100-foot (30-metre) canyon portage to a narrow six-kilometre (four-mile) lake virtually lined with wall-to-wall cliffs. But this was only the minor attraction. This odd off-the-beaten-track lake with dynamic topography and extreme concentration of Native rock art had captured me. It is the Native pictographs that distinguish this northern lake from others of its ilk. To explore Cliff Lake was a fulfillment of a personal spiritual quest.

The trip had been in my mind for over ten years since my childhood Superior and Quetico introduction and Selwyn Dewdney's seminal large-scale introduction through his just-released 1973 book, *Indian Rock Paintings of the Great Lakes*. Canoeing friend, Gordon Hommes, and I thought we would visit Cliff Lake en route to "a bay trip" continuing north via the Attwood and Witchwood river systems to the Albany River. Once on the Albany, we were excited at the prospect of visiting the Mamatowassi-Wonderful Stone, but that's another story for elsewhere. We'd finish at Fort Albany by James Bay in early June.

The pictograph concentration at Cliff Lake is exceptional, obviously linking the lake to some special significance in former times. I reported in my journal that there are 17 groupings of Native art work on six different cliff faces. In total there are well over 50 individual drawings. The most common drawing type is that of a large canoe with over six paddlers. One has 12 passengers. The next most frequent subject drawings are various moose forms, though no representations are as vivid and life-like as the Lac La Croix and Darky Lake moose drawings in Quetico. The Cliff Lake sites also contain many thunderbirds, a variety of stick figures and tally marks. Somewhat unusual here are the many smeared blotches of pigment.

The most unusual site had three distinct colour differences: a purplish man-like figure which due to fading appears the oldest; many brick-red drawings most common to this lake and other Shield locations; and an orangey vivid quality drawing suggesting a more recent time.

That this was a much-returned-to rock art site is likely evident in the variety of styles and the use of three colours which at times over-lap. Dewdney refers to the orange pictograph image as the "dreamlike legs that walk by themselves." The single most striking painting to my mind is a human-like figure with five fingers clearly delineated and a curled projection extending from its head. Such projections have been interpreted as shaman (medicine men) representations. Andreas Lommel in his classic work, *Shamanism: The Beginnings of Art*, credits the tribal shaman as the magician priest, the interpreter of the spirits for his people, and the central main rock art artist. To understand the Native Ojibwe quest and motives for the drawings, one must begin by imag-ining a spirit world that permeates all actions and matter in the natural world. It is a worldview where one has to tap the force of the universe to receive individual power. One interprets the spirit-natural world and portrays or understands his inner images and mythology in an artistic, often decorative fashion.

Was Cliff Lake chosen as a site for such personalized art because of its quality natural canvas – the cliffs – or is the lake as a whole a man-ifestation of the power and grace in the universe? Perhaps the two ideas are complementary? While I could not claim to have a state of mind capable of tapping the universal force, I could lay claim, in a vague, incomplete manner, to being closer to the spirit world the Ojibwe shaman knew. Cliff Lake had been a worthy quest.

A full day was spent slowly inspecting and recording each cliff face on both sides of the sliver-like lake. Our conversation focused on the exciting study of the intangible. Combining our study of Native Peo-ples' cultures with a healthy amount of imagination, plus the benefit of Dewdney's and Kidd's previous interpretations, we had enough pic-tographs here to keep us pondering for days. Could these odd stick-like human figures be *Maymaygwayshi* those tiny, hairy folk who can put a curse on you and your canoe? Why twelve in a canoe – surely not in this part of the country? Perhaps the hairy folk ancient beings are travelling. Why the three colours and the overlapping of the paintings at one site? Is Dewdney's description of the "dreamlike legs that walk by themselves" correct, and what about the animal figure with a long tail and distorted hump? Could this be a bison as Dewdney suggested? Perhaps it is a serpent – in Cree, a *Misikinipik.*

Attempting to solve these mysteries is great fun, but we both knew the excitement remains in the indefinite nature of the study. When studying pictographs one is reminded of the Zen sayings, "A life with no questions is no life."

HICKSON/MARIBELLI LAKES, NORTHERN SASKATCHEWAN

About ten years after this James Bay trip via Cliff Lake, Grace Rajnovich released a most valuable book, *Reading Rock Art: Interpreting the Indian Rock Paintings of the Canadian Shield.* This 1994 book, along with Thor and Julie Conway's *Spirits on Stone: The Agawa Pictographs,* began to answer those thorny questions of who, why, when and how. Mostly these authors attempted, with Native counsel, that all-important "best guess" informed by years of study. With such reading behind me and many sites visited by now, I decided it was time to visit the last of Dewdney's big three destination – the Hickson/Maribelli Lakes site. Dewdney had stated that the northern Saskatchewan site at the narrows between Hickson and Maribelli lakes was one of the best. Our topographic map suggested the same. Canoe-tripping partner James Cottrell and I would fly into the Pink River watershed to visit this now-remote non-mainline canoe route. Though likely, as with Cliff Lake in Northwestern Ontario, mainline canoe routes can change with commercial and lifestyle patterns. The Wathaman/Pink/Paull rivers are a main route between the important Churchill River and Reindeer Lake. Once it would have been a main trading route. There was a feeling here of travelling a historical connection that is no longer needed now that the days of air travel and winter roads have taken over from the canoe. Today there are a few fly-in fishing lodges along the route from Deception Lake down to our take-out at Missinipi, but one can still enjoy challenging rarely used height of land portages to add a special quality of this "age-hallowed place."

The Hickson/Maribelli pictographs are mostly a vivid red orche (iron oxide). This colouring is standard in Shield rock art, but I was first struck by the intense, almost radiating images standing out brilliantly from the rock background. It is more common for rock art images to blend into the rock subtly with evidence of fading. Not here. Thunderbirds and animal images figure prominently, but a most striking image

The Hickson/Maribelli pictograph site. The images here likely represent *Maymaygwayshi* rock men figures. *Courtesy of James Cottrell.*

is a *Maymaygwayshi* with wild hair. This has been an image that specifically has most captured my imagination. Another human or human transformed to animal figure appears to be in a dance with other shapes in its surrounding. The well-preserved quality of these images reminded me of those first gazes into the rock at Agawa on Lake Superior and in Quetico Park. It is fulfilling to arrive and relish in the moment after close to thirty years of imagining. Thanks, Selwyn. You didn't let me down. And thanks to the few or many artists, dreamers, storytellers – those who were part of a living culture and a sacred custom that fills one with wonder and admiration. Yes, these paintings did seem alive.

Is it wrong to be a voyeur into a culture that is not your own? Is it wrong to reproduce such images, say on your paddle or pack? Perhaps. I, for one, however, believe that with study and genuine respect and admiration, we can wisely, together, both Native and non-Native, continue to learn of this sacred heritage and see through these pictograph/petroglyph portholes into a grand mystery and enthusiasm for the human enterprise of relating to the earth. We can, and should, respect and celebrate the presence of rock art on the Canadian landscape.

Now it is time to plan canoe trips that involve visits to my secondary list of rock art sites. There are many in Saskatchewan such that a long trip in the Churchill/La Ronge area with pictograph visiting as a focus would be fruitful. I'm certainly grateful for that first Quetico trip of 1972 that organized this focused way. The Bloodvein River, east of Lake Winnipeg, is also known for striking images. As well, a most unusual image at Paimish Creek near Norway House, Manitoba, has captured my fancy. Archaeologist Jack Steinbring has commented on a boat image in which there are both human and animal passengers – though I believe the image more likely depicts a townsite. This site has over one hundred drawings and is also noted for near-perfect acoustics. The rock outcrop itself is shaped like a human being. Such attributes might account for the rock art concentration, suggesting that "any-old" rock cliff would not necessarily do.

I wonder what attributes might account for the Hickson Lake and Cliff Lake sites. What did I miss as a wide-eyed "outsider"? The unknowns here seem to have no bounds. But that's the intrigue and fun. I may have to find my way to Norway House, soon.

11

TRADITIONAL WARM WINTER CAMPING: FOLLOWING EXAMPLES

Night comes, and at last the tent is up, the fire going, enough wood cut for the night, bare sleds stuck up, snowshoes hung on a limb, guns and axes upright in the snow, a waterhole cut and brimming kettle on the stove. A moment more of cold is immaterial. Numb hands and dead feet count for nothing now there is warmth for them. One last look at the bleak river, growing terrible in the darkness of the deep hills, a valley taut with cold, under icy starts. Now, Old Devil, be as cold and blowy as you like.

— ELLIOTT MERRICK[1]

WARM WINTER CAMPING is not about winter survival, it is about winter comfort. Certainly there is a physical comfort of employing an external heat source (that is, other than what your own body can muster), at the end of a day of travel. But, there is also a psychological comfort of establishing a cozy warm home each night that meets all your immediate needs. Once the tent is up and wood stove fired up for dinner, one can rest in a warm glow of satisfaction for the day's work and snowshoe travel well-spent. Once settled, you can stay a night or stay a month. I know of few feelings as satisfying in the bush.

Warm winter camping involves hand-hauling supplies and your camping outfit with toboggans and sleds, and using the resources of the bush to provide both warmth and poles for the portable wood stove and cotton wall tent. But mostly, for me, warm winter camping

involves the satisfaction of establishing a warm home each night that seems
a shame, each new day, to leave, that
is, until you have started on the trail
again for a new "winter home" down
the trail. It is a practice with a long tradition, very widespread and part of the
psyche of various Native and white
hunters and trappers, explorers, sur-
veyors and now recreationalists and
educators. Quebec bushman Paul
Provencher, thinking of hauling loads
rather than carrying them (but certainly he would add warm wall tent
camping to these sentiments) wrote in

James Cottrell relaxing on a winter's
night.

the 1940s, "Remember that the Indians, who live in the forest and master bush lore better than we do, [he was writing about the Montagnais
of the north shore of Quebec's St. Lawrence River], haul everything
that weights over ten pounds on toboggans. Why not be wise and follow their example?" Indeed, following the example of wise indigenous
travellers of the winter trail should not be overlooked. When trips were
measured in weeks or months or perhaps the season, there is a certain
embedded wisdom to the techniques employed. Today there are certain camping impact issues that need to be addressed though. While
I doubt it is true that there are more people in the bush today, when
"the bush" is used as a generic term for "the country way back in," it
is true, I think, that there are more people in specific bush areas. Traditional warm winter camping must be well-conceived and attentive
to the problems of frequent and return visits.

This long-established bush technology of warm winter camping is a
practice steeped in a mystique of dwelling and travelling well in winter. Survival is always there in the back of one's mind (in the front of
most first-timers to any winter camping). But a cozy warming contentment of making "home" and following a sound tradition overshadows
the fear of Elliott Merrick's "Old Devil" – the cold winter's night.

An equipment list for such a venture would include: snowshoes, narrow toboggans and flat sleds, a 10 x 12 foot sail-silk wall tent with 3
to 4 foot walls, a tent fly, a portable wood stove, an axe and saw, shovel

and other more obvious camping gear. The list need not include the warmest possible sleeping bag, nor the over-stuffed down jacket. If all this seems wildly foreign and impractical, consider that it was once the norm at a time when self-sufficient winter life in the north was far more common than today.

How would it work today? The ideal group size is six for a 10 × 12 foot tent. Members would snowshoe, hand-hauling either by flat toboggan, *Nabagodawban* in Ojibwe, or sleds with runner for rigid items such as the stove. One member free of a load would break trail. When camp is needed to be set, a flattish area out of the wind, with a good wood supply and some tall, sleek dead timber for tent poles, is selected. The selection of camping spots is where experience is key. Seven poles need to be cut for a standard wall tent, firewood gathered, the tent and fly put up, stove and stove pipe set in position and a water hole cut. Then the regular routine of personal needs can be attended to. An efficient, practiced group can do the job in a little over an hour. There is no question that this is a lot of work, but the rewards far surpass the effort for those who prefer this traditional method.[2]

There are techniques for hauling uphill and downhill, dealing with slush on the lakes and reading ice strength. Time on the trail teaches what load to put where and on what sled. There is the "dancing stick," a one-metre pole hand-held while travelling, to help with forward momentum and to knock caked snow off one's shoes in certain conditions. Throughout the woodlands there was *aki-a-gun*, a lost technique of leaving snow messages for others along the trail. *Aki-a-gun* is a language, of sorts. The use of spruce branches, for example, one cut pole leaning on another vertical stick means, "we are one day's travel in the direction the leaning pole is pointing."[3] There are snowshoe designs of all descriptions to suit the terrain and condition; this includes variety in the babische (webbing) thickness and pattern. Both functional and aesthetic considerations are involved in the design. All told, the snowshoe and hand-hauling technology is a sophisticated affair that has little need to see much by way of changes over time. For Canadian Shield travel, Native Peoples created the snowshoe for the predominately waterway travel and also forested deep snow trails. It is no surprise that the ski is a product of the genius of northern Europe with more open forests on mountainous to hilly terrain less dominated with waterway travel. On the Shield the snowshoe is the product of genius. Today, a much modified clamp on a metal-framed small snowshoe is well-suited to the windblown mountain regions of the Rockies and terrain like the Chic Chocs in Quebec. But in such areas, the ski is king, as early settlers learned from their Scandinavian neighbours. In the Shield, generally the traditional Ojibwe (rounded frame) and Cree (pointed frame) shoes are best. The rules of foot is easy; find out what Native travellers used and now still use to support snow machine travel – why not be wise and follow their example.

The travel camp is taken down in the morning, and snowshoe travel commences again, or the camp may serve as a base camp for local exploring or cross-country ski travel. Daily distances that can be covered by such snowshoe travelling are 10 to 20 kilometres on open terrain in early winter with short daylight hours.

That all sounds so matter of fact though. But this traditional winter camping approach can stir the cockles of the heart. While touring a wall tent campers' village at the "Snow Walkers Rendezvous" conference in Vermont, well-known traditionalist camper Garrett Conover was so moved (and with tongue in cheek) to lovingly reference wall tents as "chapels of independence and nomadicness."

It all sounds so easy too, when put to print in a how-to-do-it writing style. It is necessary to add to this, a more descriptive prose – Elliott Merrick again:

> It's devilish hard work, but its never futile or unworthy or petty, and it makes one very strong.... But even better is the roaring stove within and the roaring wind without on howling winter nights. Every birch chunk was cut with your own hands, and if it hadn't been cut, you would be frozen to death.[4]

The trade-off between the traditional warm winter camping and the modern survival camping, with portable gas stoves, snow shelters, open tarps or nylon winter tents with snowshoes or skis and backpacks, makes for great debate. To go light and fast gets you home faster with less work. While wonderfully enjoyed by so many, it is always survival camping, to my mind.

The heavy loads of traditional travel and longer camp set-up and break-up can be called into question. The work is hard and long, but there is no sense of grin and bear it while you are out. Winter can offer

Hauling supplies over a summer portage route and lake in
Algonquin Park, Ontario.

a home, and extended trips are easily possible with such a traditional
approach. It has been, and still is, the way of the North in the colder,
less accessible regions of northern Quebec and other Shield locations.
The warm winter camping technology also is so much more dependent on natural materials. The connection to the land – to winter – is
much greater, and the feeling of a fit with the land and its tradition
creates a warm endearing reflection. Such an evocative connection of
means and ends is rare in our culture of high convenience demands.
Find the wood, cut the wood, make the fire, stay warm – means to
ends. This is a far cry from your home's "flick of the switch" central
heating. The wall tent's warmth is certainly burdensome, but it is also
engaging. The central air of the modern house or office is certainly dis-
burdensome. It is easy, instantaneous and ubiquitous (it fills the whole
space). The thing is, we need the richness of connecting means and
ends in engaging ways. We need more than just convenient and instantaneous. We need, occasionally anyway, the burden of work for our
needs. We need the actuality of working for our warmth and huddling
around it together as if at the hearth of old. There is a deep satisfaction here largely missing in most people's day-to-day lives. I see this

deep satisfaction often working as an Outdoor Educator on winter trips.[5] The experience is good for the psyche.

This raises another commonly asked question. Traditional winter camping is not no-trace camping, but it can be low impact camping. Much wood is used each night in quantities that would soon strip an area clean over time. But the forgotten element is that the ideal winter campsite is the equally less ideal summer site. Swamp country with dry, dead, standing timber is a winter haven, sheltered and with all the needed natural resources. People who frequent a site cherish their tent poles that lean on a tall tree in waiting, ideal for repeated use. With knowledge of winter wall-tenting sites and wise use at such sites, when compared to the overall global impact of high-tech camping equipment, the high impact criticism can break down. Or, at least, a healthy debate ensues concerning impact and differing ecological and philosophical frames of reference. It is a good debate.

The warm winter camping style is adapted from Native Peoples who are still using this basic equipment as they did in the 1800s. It is the way to *live* in our winter, not merely survive in it. Craig Macdonald, a leader in disseminating the virtue of warm winter camping, has a golden rule: "Life without an external heat source for a sustained period in snow belt areas is not possible."[6] For sustained living to be anything other than survival, you have to have periods of warmth to preserve optimal physiological and psychological states. External heat sources must be enough to bring the temperature up to above freezing.

Concerning life in the far North, igloos and snow shelters can offer an external heat source with the addition of candles and seal oil lamps. Inuit Peoples would drive up the heat to roughly 20° Celsius for short periods to rejuvenate lacking bodily functions, those which slow down with continuous time in extreme cold. With dinner brewing on the airtight wood stove, temperatures easily exceed this in a properly set up wall tent, providing heat for drying wet clothing and a balmy living space.

The comfort of this winter outfit creates a spirit or ambience of cultural fit with winter. Put simply, there is no survival anxiety and constant struggle against the winter elements that is a more common sentiment with cold camping practices of lightweight tents or snow shelters with gas fuel stoves. Not that it isn't fun too. I certainly do enjoy cold winter camping from time to time. But warm and cold camping practices have very different effects on the psyche.

It is so easy to turn to Elliott Merrick's writings of his time in the "country way back in," inland from coastal homes in Labrador. He was travelling with winter trappers, learning the ways of winter living. He closes one travel account, "Snowshoe Trail," so elegantly:

> I am thankful to have been a little part of this, to know the ever new-ness of such a way of life. And more than all is the land, the backdrop against which these lives are tempered, taught, crushed, made strong or beautiful. The long white lakes, the mountains and rivers, the space and the northern lights, the spruce forest and birch hills, the cold and the terrible beauty of it when darkness is tightening like a grip of iron; nothing in my lifetime will be more satisfying to have glimpsed than the heart of all that.[7]

To be just a "little part" of this travel/camping practice (minus the trapping in my case) brings an added element to the romantic reading of Merrick's travels on a Labrador trail. I am grateful to Hugh Stewart who ran Headwaters, a winter travel educational program out of Temagami, Ontario, in the 1970s. Hugh shared *True North* by Merrick as if it were a northern winter bible. It is for many! I was happy then to count myself among those caught by the romance. Here is Merrick in *True North* capturing details of the snowshoe trail:

Cathy Weber in a familiar scene.

We had a cold bright spell that lasted nearly two weeks during which the snowshoeing was perfect – a good crust with an inch-deep carpet of soft snow on top. The familiar webs that had grown so much a part of me seemed to have a spring of their own as though the day could never be long enough. I often used to stop on a hillside to look back at the trail streaming from my heels, flowing back astern, scarring the lonely, limitless snow as a ship's wake might scar the Pacific. Over glistening white hills and marshes and lakes it winds, a darker serpentine ribbon, scallop-edged, filled with tumbled blue shadow markings. And every individual print is a beautiful thing, a bit of sculpture, endless impressions of an Indian craftsman's masterpiece. Here is the broader webbed babische of the close-knit middles, here the finer knit tibische of the heads and tails molded into the snow, perfect in the very finest line; there the round-curved frame of strong white birch and the lip of the tail, the head bar and the tail bar, the toe hole and a small cup scooped from the snow where my toe pushed through the hole at the end of the step; the blurred mark of the dragging tail, then another perfect, graceful-lined pattern printed in blue-white marble.

This is Merrick extoling a philosophy of the trail upon his arrival to Unknown Lake, Ossokmanuan, "the Indians call it," way upriver from the Grand River (now the Churchill River) – the great moments on the trail:

On the fourth morning…standing tiptoe on our snowshoes we could not make out any limits to the lake. I've never been happier than that morning on the hill. I thought to myself, "This is the place in the world where I would like most to be, and I am here." People say it is no use poking off to far corners, that you are still you and you see but yourself through your own eyes. Well, they lie, poor things. I am a thousand different persons, and today I am the freest, strongest, happiest of them all. I can feel the charm of a city park, that oasis of green amid the stone, but it is not like this and why pretend it is. Why be satisfied with half a loaf, with half-beauty, with half-honesty, with half-life. This moment is worth months of pain and fatigue and hunger mixed with the tight cramp of cold. This moment is worth twice what it cost.

I always like to temper such glowing writing with reminders. Here is one as recorded by Osborne of the voyageur reminiscence of Michael Labatte in a 1901 issue of *Ontario History Papers*:

> I often had Mal-de-Racquette [a snowshoe related ankle ailment]. I would sharpen my flint, then split the flesh of the ankle above the instep in several places, and sometimes down the calf of the leg for a remedy.

It is good to remember such examples to help guide conduct today. The lesson – if acute ankle pain from snowshoeing is persisting, stop and rest. Presumably Labatte couldn't.

While I was romanced by Merrick's writing, I have also been equally influenced by the eminently practical and detailed mind and the friendship with Craig Macdonald of Dwight, Ontario. Craig has spent decades learning the Ojibwe language, trail routes with place names and techniques of travel from those who remember the bygone era of snowshoe, hand-hauling travel before snow machines. For years, Craig ran workshops on this means of travel for educators like my students and myself. In 1985, Craig produced an historical travel-route map of northeastern Ontario. His map shows both winter and summer routes. Winter routes were certainly a novelty to see plotted so clearly. The map lists 661 traditional place names for the region acquired largely from over 200 Anishinawbe elders.[8] The Conovers, Garrett and Alexandra, follow neatly in the traditional pattern of Merrick and Macdonald and others. From their northern Maine wall tent home, they run winter snowshoe, wall tent camping trips. It is no surprise that they are keen on extended trips in Quebec and Labrador's "country way back in," following the ways and routes of the traditional families living on the coast. Their book, *A Snow Walker's Companion: Winter Trail Skills From the Far North,* is a sound companion indeed.

I have my students read Merrick, Macdonald and the Conovers. They watch the 1960s film "Attiuk" (The Caribou) produced by Crawley Films for the National Film Board of Canada. The film shows the connections across the caribou, the hunt, the drum and the snowshoe march inland for the Montagnais Peoples at LaRomaine on Quebec's Lower North Shore of the St. Lawrence River. All these influences in their own way, show the practice of travel and dovetail together to convey the mystique of a way to dwell well in our Canadian woodlands in winter.

This mystique is also conveyed through stories, usually of the extreme in travelling exploits. Think of Samuel Hearne, the explorer, setting out in December 1770 from Fort Prince of Wales (Churchill, Manitoba) with Chipewyan guides. He gave up using snowshoes with the June thaw. He didn't really know where he was going (to the mouth of the Coppermine River to look for copper, but how he wasn't sure) and he didn't know the language or customs. He travelled 5,000 miles (8,000 kilometres) over three trips (there were two aborted attempts). The travel ways of the Chipewyan peoples on the land is compelling, but the human drama in considering Hearne's experience is beyond reason.

Think too of the snowshoe journeys of Jean-Baptiste Lagimodière and John Pritchard. Both travelled with the same basic message – the threat of armed conflict between the rival fur trade companies (HBC and NWC) at the new Red River Settlement, near present-day Winnipeg. In 1815–16, Lagimodière carried this message of warning over 1,800 miles from Red River to Montreal. He followed a route south of Lake Superior in order to avoid North West Company fur trading posts along Superior's north shore. Lagimodière travelled light. At night he would dig out a pit, line it with conifer boughs to insulate him from the snow and maintain a fire at the pit's centre. Pritchard meanwhile was taking this message from Montreal to Red River via a route north down to Abitibi River in Quebec, along James Bay and up the Nelson River to Lake Winnipeg and south. Lagimodière was eventually taken prisoner. We must pause and consider our own personal routes when thinking about such exploits – a sure tonic from self-aggrandizements for distance travelled and hardships endured.

Finally there is a favourite story for a rest stop along the trail. Arctic traveller Peter Frenchen, in 1923, once rolled his sled over a small hole in which he lay to evade a blizzard. Later he awoke to realize he had dug his own grave. The snow had mounted over the sled and compacted. Frenchen cursed his stupidity in not keeping his snow knife close at hand. First he sacrificed one of his frozen hands as a digging tool, then took a piece of frozen excrement to use as a chisel. Finally he got out of the hole by sucking on a piece of bearskin he had, using it as a scraping tool. The story goes on and on. He eventually chops off his toes with a nail puller and hammer and lived to tell the tale. He later said of this event:

Pain is a peculiar thing, a luxury in which one indulges when he can afford it. When something of vital importance must be accomplished, the pain fades away.[9]

Then there is the snowshoe walker John Rae. He is noted as saying, "A long day's march on snowshoes is about the finest exercise a man can take." Well, John Rae was fit. His first job out of medical school in Edinburgh was as a surgeon on a Hudson's Bay Company supply ship. The ship became winter-bound and Rae stayed. As a clerk and surgeon for the company, he became noted for his "house calls." One trip of 105 miles (170 kilometres) from Moose Factory to Fort Albany in two days seems to have initiated the travelling speed and endurance image he well-deserved. The notion of travelling light by employing indigenous techniques was one championed by Rae and also much scoffed at by the British Arctic explorers of the day. Vilhjalmur Stefansson would later call Rae's initiative "wise" and he, too, followed the local peoples' example. Attention to detail was also a trademark of the frugal Rae. Biographer Ken McGoogan in *Fatal Passage: The Untold Story of John Rae, the Arctic Adventurer Who Discovered the Fate of Franklin*, often writes of Rae's meticulous nature. What follows is one example that I cannot fathom undertaking for the efficiency of any trip:

> To locate weaknesses and determine the speed at which he might travel, Rae timed his men hauling loaded sledges over a measured mile. He too practiced over that distance, hauling his sledge with 120 pounds on it. He set aside the fixed ration he proposed to use and, along with the men, tested it for four days.

In 1981, on a two-week trip for six people travelling by snowshoe and wall tent from La Loche, Saskatchewan, to Fort McMurray, Alberta, via the Clearwater River, I'd thought we were meticulous in noting certain details of menu and travel distance. But compared to Rae, it was merely a feeble gesture at efficiency.

Using the "Rae Method," Rae travelled, it is estimated, over 10,000 kilometres (6,214 miles) during four Arctic expeditions, both surveying and searching for the third Franklin expedition lost years earlier "somewhere" in the Arctic. In retrospect, it should be little surprise, that the fleet, snowshoe-footed, meticulous, indigenous-minded Rae would find evidence of the ill-fated, aged British naval tradition-minded Franklin party.[10]

While travelling along the Clearwater River in1981, or on regular snowshoe trips in Temagami and later Algonquin, I think of characters, stories and the Native ways of this travel practice. When the hauling is slow and hard, you can draw strength, perhaps even in the form of a pilgrimage of sorts, from the accumulated knowledge of the teachings of Merrick, Macdonald and the Conovers, and the stories of snowshoe-hauling travel. This knowledge can add that needed resolve to not only keep going on the trail, but to keep going *well*, "as part of a continuing tradition."

With traditional warm winter snowshoe camping, the more you follow examples and become part of that continuing tradition, the more you will hear and be within the echoes of this particular mystique of the trail.

12

OLD WAYS:
NEW PERCEPTIONS

With the loss of cultural history, we have no choice but to learn
from technological history. Will its deep ironies prompt us
to realize that the first lesson it has to teach is repentance?
— I.S. MACLAREN[1]

THE CANOE AND PADDLE are king in Canada. For many it is part
of the Canadian psyche. Indeed in Scandinavia, the canoe is called
simply the Canadian. This is well-justified, given our canoe routes'
history. However, there is a rich sub-text where conventional canoe
and paddle travel is replaced by other forms of travel with distinguished
heritage lines. Three such related heritage travel modes will be explored
briefly here: river canoe poling, travel by canot du maître and logging
pointer boats.

RIVER CANOE POLING

A phone call came out of the blue. I missed it. The message was to call
Gerry LeBlanc, whom I hadn't heard from in five years. Gerry had
recently finished paddling and poling the length of the Tobique River
(160 kilometres or 100 miles). "Not one portage," he later told me.
But wait, that's upriver!

I first met Gerry in the spring of 1998 at the Bathurst, New
Brunswick, train station. Gerry was going to drive me across the
province to the Upper Tobique or Little Tobique at Nictau from where
I had planned to learn to pole my canoe solo up the river, over the
height of land and down the Nepisguit River back towards Bathurst.

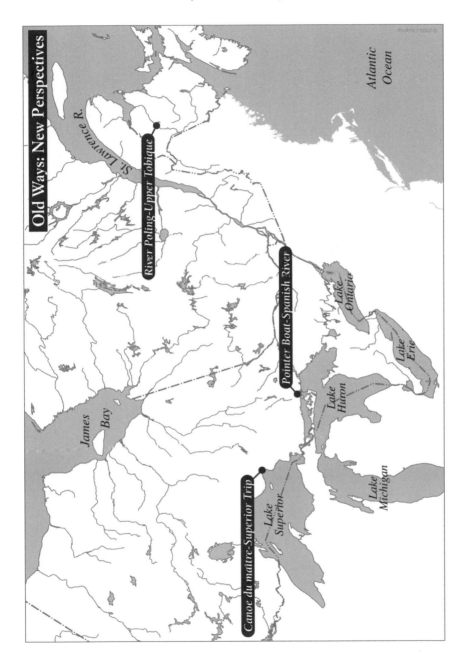

It was a bit too ambitious. Gerry would spend one day with me show-ing me how to pole. Now five years later and, perhaps with a bit of a spark from the memory of a silly Ontario non-poler, Gerry had accom-plished something I thought eminently noble.

In New Brunswick there are still people poling the shallow rivers upstream to fishing holes and to other river connections, but the days of the full-length up-river "run" is past. Whether done as a single trip or over many free weekends, the Tobique accomplishment is a physi-cal one. Poling is hard work, but surprisingly relaxing. I learned from Gerry, though I didn't really understand until years later with quiet time on a local river back home, that poling up river must be a calm watchful activity. You move slowly on the river. You must see details of the bottom and shoreline – where to place the pole to thrust, where to nudge just enough into the main current to miss a river sweeper. There is a meditation to canoe river poling. You cannot be in a rush. I didn't have it in 1998 on the Little Tobique. Gerry did. At least I saw what it should look like.

Gerry's 2003 accomplishment goes beyond the hard work. Medita-tive work is also spiritual for its connections to the heyday of river poling. They were called Tobiquers, those men who poled wealthy Americans up the Tobique River to the mountain-clad Nictau and Nepisguit lakes in north/central New Brunswick. Both the canoemen and tourists came to fish and hunt. Their heydays were the 1890s through into the 1930s. And while you won't recognize the names of the canoemen (among them Vic Miller, Tom Bear, Ned McAskill, Fred Paget, Percy Sinnott), you will recognize the names of their charges – among them Teddy Roosevelt's son Archie, a Rockefeller, Hollywood's John Barrymore (who credited his Macbeth Scottish accent to the Tobique River guide Jock Ogilvie), and, perhaps the most famous of them all, the baseball legend Babe Ruth. It was a good living. Gerry now knows the river guide's life in a way few others do today.

I had hoped to tap into this mystique for the physical and spiritual. The closest I came to it was watching Gerry as I fumbled on behind him, trying at least to match the technique moves and his line up the river. The amazing history of river connections in New Brunswick wasn't my only interest.[2] I also had in my thoughts the upriver poling of canoemen throughout the country on rivers like the Albany and Athabasca. I have paddled "downriver," of course, on parts of both. On the Albany, I

Gerald Le Blanc joined me for my first full day of river poling. We ascended a section of the Upper Tobique River, New Brunswick.

was intensely aware that I was only doing the easy part of the river run. I would finish at Fort Albany twenty days out (ten on the Albany), but the hired canoeman would return to pole and perhaps winter over back upriver. I remember Gordon Hommes and I travelled over two hundred kilometres in four days on the lower Albany in the spring current. I couldn't imagine, then, the upriver trip. I can imagine it now and certainly Gerry's story on the Tobique helps.

When you've floated down rivers like the Albany and Tobique, your respect for "old ways" canoemen and your humility for your own outings run high. My respect for Gerry was great in 1998, but leaped forwards after our enthusiastic "polers united" phone call in 2003 that allowed me to share in his adventure on the Tobique. For me, this was an opportunity to suggest to him that I had learned, with time, something of the mystique for the old ways, the skills and temperament of the bygone era canoemen. In the interim years, I have done most of my poling on the Eramosa River near Guelph, Ontario.

Gerry had poled the 160 kilometres over a stretch of eight-and-a-half days, mostly on weekends as time allowed, starting in the snow on May 10. Some sections he poled with his wife Debbie, but Debbie told me she knew poling is easier solo, so she backed off a bit for later trips. Gerry figured he averaged two kilometres per hour, but one day near the town of Plaster Rock he travelled 27 kilometres (17 miles). He marvelled at the strength and skill of the old-timers to whom he is connected by kin. He told me he was "in tune with the past," a past that, as he was well aware, was "fading away with time." It was only in 1976 that Ted Weymand, the New Brunswick Canoe Club provincial associate president, said, "Canoeing in New Brunswick is a means of transportation rather than a sport in its own right. One sees more poling than paddling on our rivers."[3] Now there are lots, *lots* of bush roads in New Brunswick. Gerry says that people assumed he was just going around the bend. When they heard otherwise, they, like Gerry, were proud of their particular river heritage. The old ways had inspired a new, more vibrant perceptive for their local waterways. Thanks to Gerry, Captain Campbell-Hardy's 1850s words would echo for years to come with folks watching along the bank:

> It is very interesting to watch from a distance the motions of the canoemen, when using their poles in shallow or rapid waters. They perform every action in concert, and the white poles, removed dripping from the water, glisten in the sun as they are raised aloft for a fresh purchase. Leaning with their whole weight against the poles, which are planted in the river bed, they make the canoe shoot forward under them, till you fancy they must lose their balance and fall backwards.[4]

Bye the bye, my poling trip on the Little Tobique lasted two plus days. Bill Miller at Nictau suggested to me, politely, as I started out, that "the Tobique was running high at present and [I] should come again in a few weeks." I didn't. I came back in three days and arranged to enjoy downriver paddling on the Nepisquit. Still I had been inspired. I knew that the 1904 *Scribners Magazine* quote I'd read before departing was only true for beginners: "To a person unfamiliar with the setting pole it is a demon of perversity, and the canoe acts worse than a frightened pig." You can see me now on my local rivers such as the Eramosa and the Grand, practising old ways and gaining new perspectives of the elegant canoe moving on the water as only the canoe can.

River poling is not the only old way fading away into obscurity. In 1997, I tried with family and friends the new perspective of canoeing big water (Lake Superior) in a big canoe (36-foot voyageur canot du maître), also called a Montreal canoe.

CANOT DU MAÎTRE

There would be much to be made of comparing our trip with similarities to the days of the fur trade, exploration (geographical and scientific) and early tourism. After all, that was, in part, a leading reason why we were here. To be on Lake Superior in a voyageur canoe with our own *gouvernail* (sternsman guide) was to bring us closer to the great Canadian tradition of voyageur canoe travel. It was the canoe itself that was the chief catalyst for connecting with canoe heritage – a heritage documented in the paintings of the British Victorian painter Frances Anne Hopkins, herself a part of this heritage in the 1860s. We would be the voyageurs on this trip – well, sort of. *En avant.* (Let's go!) I could hear the call to paddle in unison. This was it, the big one – on Superior, in the big one – the canot du maître.[5] I will explain some similarities to the days of regular transcontinental canoe travel (1790s to 1830s), then offer some humbling differences.

Peter Labor, then of Wawa, our gouvernail (the sternsman and thus captain of the ship, so to speak), who had served in this role on the Mackenzie Sea to Sea Expedition of Lakehead University, pointed out the blackish line on the water horizon and noted, "sloppy seas today." Head winds and rough water were no strangers to us – still, this was Lake Superior and "sloppy seas" was not our standard way to forecast the canoe-tripping day. When asked, with tongue in cheek, by one of us early on, "Do you ever do canoe over-canoe rescues with these thirty-six-foot canoes?" Peter answered simply, "You don't dump in these canoes." I remember thinking, "presumably you can swamp though."

Later that day, our *avant* of the day (our bow paddler who is critical to the day's cadence and progress) and I wondered how much water was needed to flow over the bow before we'd head for shore or swamp, as the case may be. After about six such soakings (trivial we were later to understand), we headed for the nearest beach and called it a day. For the modern voyageur wannabes in the stern "area," our bow shrieks were a source of hilarity. We were learning the ways of the voyageur canoe. Five-foot swells could bring in gallons of water. White caps and swells are okay, but when you add "chop," now that's difficult canoeing. For those times, the voyageurs had a full-time bailer appointed with sponge in hand. After paddling for many hours in such waters (for us, it was mere minutes), it is possible to see how a voyageur's ration of one gallon of rum per man for the whole trip might be consumed in a single go – if given the chance.

While discussing the details of voyageur canoe travel on Lake Superior, it became clear that we had no canoe standard reference points other than our gouvernail's uniquely qualified position of experience and whatever could be gleaned from the writing of the non-paddling *bourgeois* (those elite passengers in the middle being escorted to fur trade posts throughout the country). Indeed, Peter Labor has largely developed the canot du maître guidebook while on the job. I , for one, would certainly have floundered at organizing the group's pulling the mighty and dangerous weight of his canoe up onto a cobblestone beach on a windy day. Get between this beefy canoe and a hard place and it is serious. I didn't have to ask Peter what those solid four-metre poles leaning out of the stern of the canoe were for. I'd find out on that particularly windy day. They hold the boat safely out from shore so loads can be ferried to land. One puzzle solved.

J.D. Elliot Cabot, in 1856, wrote about "manners" needed or not needed for travelling. He wrote of paddling in cramped quarters, or rather, he wrote of the voyageurs' manners in these ever-present circumstances. (It should always be highlighted that the written word of the fur trade is virtually never that of the voyageurs themselves.)[6]

> For this is remarkable about these men, that obliging and respectful as they are in general, there are certain things for which they stand out, and will have their way. John, for instance, though the

Heading out for a new day on Lake Superior—the right way—in a canot du maître.

best fellow in the world, would never allow the due sweep of his oar
to be obstructed even by an inch, and anyone whose back or head
came in this way was reminded of the impropriety by a dig from the
end of it at every stroke until he withdrew within his proper limits.
About these matters (which however were confined entirely to the
management of the board and respected exclusively the public interest) they never argued nor attended to argument, but quietly persisted
in doing as they thought proper.

Such polite writing. Hmm, I wonder? Certainly we could sympathize
with the odd polite "dig."

Sir George Simpson, the governor of the Hudson's Bay Company in
the 1820s through to the 1840s, himself a veteran bourgeois noted for
demanding a most gruelling travel schedule, commented on the number one difference between ourselves and the voyageurs who were always
at the forefront of our heritage travel muse. He wrote of the standard
sixteen to eighteen hours per day on the water, "This almost incredible toil the Voyageurs bore without a murmur, and generally with such
a hilarity of spirit as few other men could sustain for a single forenoon."

This leads one to remember the differences that, in the end, are more
exciting to consider than the similarities we felt. Our trip was a friendship leisure trip. We covered about one hundred kilometres out and
back from Michipicoten. The voyageurs were the workhorses of the
fur trade. Their out and back trip on Lake Superior involved closer to
1,500 kilometres (900 miles). Our stroke rate was in the range of 48–52
strokes per minute. This fast, very fast, stroke rate is required to maintain the heavy craft's momentum in the water. Their stroke rate was
faster still. The biggest, even comical, difference is our three to five
hours per day on the water compared to their fifteen to eighteen (wind
dependent for both groups, now and then). After our filling breakfast,
our gouvernail would gently encourage our hasty departure to beat the
afternoon winds. The Lake Superior travelling voyageur would be off
without morning sustenance, not stopping for his breakfast of corn
meal mush till sunrise after several hours of paddling. Big distance
became possible with such routines. The explorer David Thompson
is reported to have travelled 4,000 miles (6,437 kilometres) in one ten-
month period by canoe and on horse – preparing his great map of the
Canadian North West.

Quinn Henderson and Kate Harrison were quite taken with the
"kids' den," a play area in the middle of this very stable canoe.

Our group had fifteen members in total, including three children of
ten and under, who sat in a makeshift "kids' den" reserved historically
for the lofty status rank of the bourgeois. This alone highlights the sta-
bility of this very wide canoe – kids free to frolic. The original voyageur
paddling crew was typically eight to ten men. They had more gear, but
were far from "gear-freaks." Their gear on the way out from Montreal
to Fort William (or Grand Portage depending on the time period in
history) consisted of trade goods meant for the more distant posts in
the northwest interior of the Athabasca/Mackenzie and Columbia River
districts. They would return east from the Great Rendezvous on the
western Superior shore with furs, wrapped in ninety-pound bundles,
from this same western interior. Their total baggage would measure
up to four thousand pounds. Our baggage (even with the odd gear
freak among us), including personal bits, amounted to a little over two
thousand pounds. Still, when all was loaded, we were an unusual sight
of packs, barrels, wannagans, cameras and happy "elbow rubbing" faces
ready for the mysteries of the lake and the canoe, and it all did seem
particularly weighty. This unconventional way of travel would take some
getting used to. Our gouvernail on our first morning would clear his
throat and shout, "Prepare...ah.... Let's go, Bob. *En avant!*" With this,
a new day would begin with our engrained images of the Frances Ann
Hopkins' voyageur canoe life paintings and our new understandings
of all this filling our present.

Frances Anne Hopkins (1838–1919) captured the twilight years of the canot du maître in the 1860s. We know little about her, but most of us on the trip have her paintings as cards or reprints framed in our homes. Her work served as one of our entry points into a broader vision of time for our own voyageurs' canoe trip. Peter Labor, then of Naturally Superior Adventures, was another entry point. (This company is still running Voyageur Canoe guided trips out of Wawa, Ontario.) His stories, crafts, songs and guiding – all to period (circa 1790s to 1830s) kept us ever marvelling both at the delightful similarities and differences of our crew and those of days gone by. Both Frances Anne and Peter framed our trip for our own personal imaginations. Lake Superior provided the awesome setting. Frances Anne's paintings of voyageur canoe life didn't sell well in 1870s Canada. As noted in the catalogue accompanying a major exibit of her artworks, she herself had written, "I have not found Canadians at all anxious hitherto for pictures of their own country. I sent some very nice ones out to W. Scott and Sons, Fine Art Dealers in N. Dame St. (Montreal), but they did not sell." At that time, the canoe represented a past that Canadians wished to forget – as the steamboat, urban growth and the dream of a transcontinental railway were all progressing. Frances Anne would be pleased to know that the canoe, however, has endured and that her canoe images are commonplace and are exhibited, studied and enjoyed.

Canadians are now "anxious" for pictures and experiences of this part of our heritage. We now realize the unique qualities, beauty and possibilities in the epigram of historian Arthur Low who once said, "Canada is a canoe route." And there are many canoes, each suited to the terrain of travel or the circumstances involved, such as moving large volume of supplies at great speeds. The canot du maître did both for us as recreation or play. But for about one hundred years it was work for voyageurs in the fur trade. This is an old way that sheds new perspectives on our experience of "playing" with fur trade history.

THE YORK BOAT AND THE POINTER BOAT

I have always wanted to do a trip on a western river, ideally the North Saskatchewan or the Hayes, down to York Factory on Hudson Bay in a replica of the latter-day fur trade York boat. These were the Hudson's Bay Company's answer to the canot du maître and North Canoe, (used in the northwest interior) as the competition for fur escalated, and the HBC was forced to go to the people and fur rather than have the people and fur come to them. The wide (beam of 2.7 metres with an inside depth of 0.9 metres), stable, dory-like boats were durable and required less skill from the Orkney Islands men hired for a stint in Rupert's Land. With a crew of six to eight trip men, a York boat could carry over 2,700 kilograms – that's about twice the load the North West Company North Canoe might carry. The boats were built at stations between James Bay and Fort Chipewyan. Fort Edmonton, a recreated fort, which now has a number of replica York boats of various sizes, saw its first York boat built in 1795.[7] While living in Edmonton, I tried to organize some sort of excursion. But it was not to be, or, rather, became a dream still to be pursued. However, a different, yet similar and equally rewarding, opportunity did avail itself with some friendly inquiry.

In the summer of 2001, I joined a few history buff friends and "Captain" Bill Blight for a short run down the lower Spanish River in Ontario's Near North. We wanted to row a replica 32-foot pointer boat built and owned by the Friends of the Spanish River. Like the York boats, we would row, not paddle. Likewise, we would be together in the one big boat. For the canoeist and sea kayaker this was an exciting difference – for a while. For Bill, then well into his 70s, this was a homecoming. His first pointer boat camping trip was three decades earlier when employed by the area logging company.

Bill Blight knows the Spanish River because he worked in the logging industry from 1945 to his retirement in 1992. Bill knew many of the great lumberjacks and river men, and their stories. But mostly, Bill knows the boat – the pointer boat.

We knew what a pointer looked like, but that's about all. It somewhat resembles a York boat. This trip would greatly enhance our knowledge and give us a fresh perspective on river travel and lifestyles that endured for more than a century. The last spring logging drive on the Spanish River was in 1967.

On the Spanish and Sable rivers, the first drives were in the 1860s. Lumber drives in the Ottawa River watershed, including Algonquin Park, began earlier. The flat-bottomed V-shaped pointers, also called bateaux or dories, were the riverboat of choice from the 1850s. And by the 1870s, pointers were also being used in the Lake Huron region.

Bill Blight led our group on our first and only pointer boat trip,
teaching us logging history along the way.

Today, signs of these spring log drives are everywhere, not only on the
Spanish River, but also on the water and shorelines of the Dumoine, the
St. Maurice, the Petawawa and the Sturgeon. There are still old jams at
many rapids, iron rings in the shoreline rock for holding logging booms,
and field and tote roads that are now overgrown. In some places, you
can even spot alligators – those amphibious tugboats (developed in Simcoe, Ontario) and used on the lakes, like the two on the Dumoine River
and the one on Chiniguichi Lake on the Sturgeon River watershed.

Ruins of logging chutes still abound. It's said, for example, that there
were as many as one thousand different logging chutes on Algonquin
Park waterways. On our Spanish River trip we found an old crosscut
saw, the type that replaced the axe in the 1870s as the primary felling
tool. It was embedded in the shoreline mud.

We had a few surprises. Bill had made the boat's two replica paddles,
one each for the bow and the stern, from solid red oak. Each was about
seven feet (two metres) and weighed in at 25 to 30 pounds (11 to 14 kilograms) with a three-inch shaft width. You don't paddle these paddles.
You don't draw. You pry. That's it. Bill controlled the steerage from the
bow. The sternsman helps, but, given that he faces the crew, he felt like
the group storyteller of the day. We changed over this role often.

The oars we used were originals, used in the last river drive on the
Sable River in 1938, and then stored in a barn in Massey. Only recently,
they had narrowly escaped being turned into fence posts – and good
fence posts they would have made – 10 feet of solid spruce.

How else to put it? This was serious, sturdy equipment. The equally sturdy pointer boat was made from 8″ spruce, 3/8″ thick, overlapped by 2″ with epoxy. Our oarlocks were two-to-four-inch spaced wooden pegs.

We carried gear for eight, a table for campsites and precut firewood, all of which Bill ensured was traditional. But these more modern traditions, common "these days," were not as interesting as Bill's stories about the use in "those days" – the days of the spring river drives.

Throughout the Great Lakes watershed the great pines were cut in winter. The lumberjacks, also called shantymen, were housed in the practical caboose camp – one-room shelters for fifty men with a central, open fireplace. Donald MacKay's quintessential historical treatment of the logging era, *The Lumberjacks*, claims that by 1880 at least 234 eastern Canadian rivers were being driven, and that these drives employed over half of the male workforce in Canada.[8] These men developed their own lingo. Some say there were upwards of 4,000 expressions in use in the logging trade. "In a jam" is one of the most enduring.

Logs would be stacked by the water's edge to await the spring thaw. With the ice gone and the river swollen, the men who had signed on for the spring drive began the process of "watering the wood." With peaveys and pike poles, they worked logs into the current and cleared them from shorelines. Most often, dams and chutes were created to adjust water levels to suit the downstream flow of logs.

Generally, the early square timbers were rafted down the Ottawa River to Ottawa and Quebec City, then shipped on to Europe. In the 1870s, Lake Huron timber had a ready market in Michigan, and the Chicago fire of 1870 created an intense demand for timber from the Spanish River region. During the drives, pointer boats of various sizes worked as support boats. Half pointers, 20 feet long, helped clear log jams and sweep bays for renegade logs. These pointers saw intense action in rapids, where they manoeuvered into tricky places for the equally tricky work of freeing jams. Imagine if your daily job involved rescuing pinned canoes, piled high during the river's spring run. Get the idea? The boats were controlled at the bow and stern with what a whitewater racer might call a power pry.

Larger pointers, 49 to 50 feet, were used in many ways. Blanket pointers, for example, carried bedrolls and supplies, and there were also cookery pointers. Portaging was heavy work. When portaged around the most difficult rapids, the boats were rolled on logs with many hands pushing and pulling. But to lead these 40-footers into the "V" of a large rapid certainly must have been one of the most exhilarating jobs of the river drive. Bill tells the story of one unfortunate logger who, in 1965, was swept overboard from the bow. The moment is caught on black and white film footage, but it took Bill twenty years to learn the identity of the logger – Isaac Toulousse. Interestingly, Isaac identified himself as Bill showed the video at the Massey Fair. The original pointer boats were made of pine and the larger 50-footers weighed more than half a ton, yet they could easily pivot with a tug on the oars and they had a remarkably shallow draw. At one time the Cockburn family advertised their famous pointer design with the slogan: "It's a boat that will float on a heavy dew."

The pointer was actually a combined initiative of Pembroke boat builder John Cockburn and the renowned logging entrepreneur, J.R. Booth. Booth asked Cockburn to design a boat especially for the spring drive. It had to carry lots of gear, have a shallow draw, be manoeuverable and able to work at levering logs from a high-flared bow and stern.

In the pointer's heyday in the 1880s, Cockburn turned out some 200 boats a year from his shop in downtown Pembroke. John's grandson, John Junior, was still making pointers until his retirement in 1969. In his last year of operation, he had 17 orders. In the previous 22 years during which records were kept, 1,700 pointers of various sizes were manufactured. The Cockburns were in business for 104 years – not a bad record. Today, detailed large-scale murals grace the side wall of buildings depicting this rich heritage of Pembroke history. There is also a pointer boat monument in the town's riverside park along the Ottawa River.

It was a shock for me to learn that while I was cutting my teeth on Algonquin waterways, men in pointers were still running the rapids north of me. As mentioned, the last drive on the Spanish was 1967. The last major log drive in Algonquin was in 1945 from the Nipissing River into the Petawawa River.

In all, we got what we had asked for – an experiential glimpse into a time when these quiet eastern rivers were brimming with human activity. Bill told us about men like Fred Commanda, Leo Restoule and Ernie Marion, all great men of the spring river drive. He pulled out his photo album of logging scenes from the 1950s, and painted graphic portraits of the nature of the work. In the logging era, for example, it is estimated that there were upwards of 10,000 horses in the Sudbury basin. Other days, he told us about the prisoner of war camp along the Spanish River and, when we needed to laugh, he recalled the practical jokes of the day.

Once, at the mouth of the Sable where it meets the Spanish, Bill recalled a spring day in the 1930s, when school was let out so the students could stand on the Sable River bridge to watch the spring drive pointers row by. All our varied travel stories from across Canada shared along the river that morning seemed to pale in comparison.

Shanty songs like "The Jam on Gerry's Rocks" and Wade Hemsworth's "Log Driver's Waltz" began to take on new meaning. Tom Thomson's 1916 painting, *Bateaux,* depicting a chain of pointers in Algonquin now seems alive in detail. And, as for the crew of Captain Blight's pointer boat I suppose we all agree with the words of Donald MacKay, who said that lumberjacks, like cowboys and sailors, did not simply do a job, "They spawned traditions and legends larger than life."

I'd still like to paddle – oops – row a York boat out of Fort Edmonton or down to York Factory. I'd like to try a coastal sailing ship too, like the kind George Vancouver used on the west coast or George Cartwright used on the Labrador coast. I'd love to travel in the Arctic with a fan-style dog harness' and komatics. Then there is travel by horseback or stagecoach in keeping with the Palliser and Hind expeditions

A York boat at Rocky Mountain House. York boats were used on the shallow western prairie rivers and routes out to James Bay.

of the 1850s in the prairies – the Cypress Hills of southern Saskatchewan and Alberta. These are all old ways, a far cry from the automobile and airplane. I'm grateful to folks like Gerry LeBlanc, Peter Labor and Bill Blight, and many others who have helped keep traditional practices alive. From them, we can learn to revive ways of seeing Canada's rivers, plains, forests and coastlines that expose our soul to the soul of the country still. How did folk-singer Murray McLaughlin put it in a haunting Canadian folk song "Out Past the Timberline?":

> *No Canada ain't some cabinet man*
> *In the Rideau club at election time*
> *Oh Canada is somewhere out there*
> *Out past the timberline.*[9]:

And there are so many ways to see and be out past the timberline. Old ways are particularly rewarding.

PART THREE

PEOPLE

*Alright, it's because I can't tell the difference between
me and this lake, these sounds, that moon. It's because
I don't know where I end and the wilderness begins.*
— WAYLAND DREW[1]

Dr. Foster Walker, a Philosophy professor whose thoughtful company I enjoyed in graduate school, once admonished me for using the expression, "Beauty is in the eye of the beholder." He clarified his opinion thus, "Wrong, Bob. Try this. Beauty is in the relationship between the beholder and the beheld." "Right! A fine distinction," I thought. More correctly, beauty is a matter of relationships.

This is similar to a story first told to me by the American educator Steve Van Matre. He tells the story of eastern philosopher Alan Watts walking with a friend. The friend says, "Alan, look at the beautiful flower

David Taylor with journal. Campsite contemplations often centre on where we are and who has been there.

growing in that field." To which Watts' reply, went something like this, "Okay, but perhaps it is wiser to think of it thus, – look at that beautiful field growing that flower." Again, the distinction concerns relationships and taking on a more ecological, broader or deeper view.

With these two ideas, I turn my attention to "People." It is the particular relationship between the person and the land that is most intriguing and sets most of the following people-based stories apart. Be it the hermit or loner (certainly a "character") quest, the woman pushing the conventions of her day, the artist and sketching site explorer seeking to capture a visual vision of the land, or the traveller exploring both the land and larger self-understanding within this new world of the Canadian bush, there is a matter of strong relationship for the beholder and the beheld, for the deeper connected view. The people brought forward here each have a compelling story of the land or a profound attention to deepening their relationship with the land. Many of them, in living "their way," have shifted into a new way of thinking. Many of the people within this section would, I believe, concur with the following sentiments of Elliott Merrick, Labrador traveller of the 1930s:

> "Through most of my stories weaves the thread that man is great but nature is greater and that the function of a highly developed civilization should be to lead men closer to the world not father away."[2]

13

JOURNAL WRITING AND EXPLORERS: STILL LOOKING FOR THE NEW WORLD

And they often turned to writing with an urgency, which suggests that it was a means of self-understanding, an essential way of shaping their lives after the facts. They seem too, to have been painfully aware of the many problems which language posed for people separated as they were from their own world.
— WAYNE FRANKLIN[1]

KEEPING A TRIP JOURNAL with your thoughts collected, along with the trips details and facts, is an act of great merit. Not only are you recording word images from the trail to revisit months or years later, you also play out a great Canadian tradition of trip recording as field notes. Being part of this tradition, with the likes of J.B. Tyrrell, Alexander MacKenzie, Anna Jameson, George Douglas and John Palliser, is rewarding – a sort of continuity you can bring to your experience on the land.[2] You are, in some small but not trivial way, a part of the great exploration of the Canadian North. And you are part of the great exploration of the self.

I love to read explorers' journals. Equally, I love to read about explorers. For understanding, both primary and secondary sources are necessary. The travellers write field notes often (they hope) as a means of self-understanding in a New World circumstance. Later the field notes are re-evaluated for their journals. Journals denote an audience. An audience, often an employer, must be taken into consideration. Journals become books, often receiving another rewrite by an old-world-schooled writer, but not well-travelled editor. The work may lose authenticity along the way, but it may be more amenable to the tastes of the far-off reader – perhaps a practice not so uncommon today. The final product for publication might be a far cry from the "in the field" encounter.[3]

The fur trade clerk, George Nelson, in the early 1800s was painfully aware of this tension between two worlds. He wrote with a notable honesty, seemingly in disregard for the judgmental audience of employer (fur trade), relatives (Montreal area) and populace at large. As a young fur trade clerk sent from the family farm to earn a wage, he wrote, "I merely write 'off hand' without any regard to elegance of language or 'purity of style' and all that sort of paraphernalia of which I know nothing. It is not to charm but to inform that I write, this, my Journal."[4] Good advice for us all. Nelson also understood the tension in his effort to "inform" on religious and mystical events. He wrote of a successful conjuring ceremony in his La Ronge, Saskatchewan, journal/letters in 1825:

> This is so strange, and so out of the way that I will ask no one to believe it. Those who will not believe the Gospel will still less credit this; yet I say it is true, believe who may. We had a Splendid fest at night, for they [the three bear revealing themselves to the conjurer for the hunt] were very fat.[5]

I wonder if other travellers in the New World left out observations they experienced of such events, or were they edited out by publishers. Nelson's reminiscences were published long after his death and appear to have been meant as a long untitled letter-journal to his father.

Reading primary and secondary sources help interpret a fuller story. The read is always an act of interpretation between field notes and book form and between their time and cultural viewpoint against our own. You must always ask yourself – who is this person who is writing? It is a richly complex affair in which, we, when on the land and recording our own field notes and journals, can feel a connection to something far greater than our own small travels. It is the greater enterprise of a cultural story and it will never be *the story* but always *a story*. Maritime novelist, Peter Such, put it this way, "We all need a sense of our past and how our present and indeed our future grow out, to see ourselves as part of that continuing tradition as it keeps evolving, and not separate from it."[6]

Given this introduction, which acknowledges the complexities in understanding the explorers' true personality and the events as they may genuinely unfold, I have a few favourites by way of explorers, and journals, who purposely or otherwise expose their struggles in "shaping their lives after the facts." Let's look briefly at George Vancouver, David Thompson, Gabriel Sagard, George Nelson and John McLean. Why this particular grouping? Well, they constitute a list of personal favourites. They all teach a lesson when thinking about our small explorations today, and they allow us to travel coast to coast with some time to touch down in the middle. In Canada, looking generally at explorers and their journal writings is a massive undertaking. "Touching down" here and there in different time periods with differing lessons is enough of a task here.

GEORGE VANCOUVER

It now seems a given that the mountains, the oceans' coastlines and the wild rivers that carve outrageous canyons are the landscapes for the "adventurer" – the serious traveller. How perceptions change! John Evelyn, on his 1645 tour of Europe, wrote, "I had been assur'd there was little more to be seen in the rest of the civil world, after Italy, France, Flanders and the Low-Country, but plains and prodigious Barbarisme." Similarly, in 1725, Daniel Defoe expressed the prevailing attitude of the time during his travels in Wales, "We were saluted with Monuchdenny Hill on our left, and the Black Mountain on the right, and all a ridge of horrid rocks and precipices between. And indeed we began to repent our curiosity, as not having met with anything worth the trouble."

Finally, that early English language lexicographer, Samuel Johnson, in 1775, said of his own "misguided" curiosity to see the Cairngorms of Scotland, that the destination could "afford very little amusement to the traveller," being the "wide extent of hopeless sterility."

Certainly the adventurers who came to Canada seeking wealth from the fur trade, or discovering a northwest passage, were influenced by the translucent cultural forms of thought about landscape that governed perceptions in the "Old World." Gardens and the pastoral were "in";

mountains and a "barren" grandeur were not. What would Evelyn make of the New World landscape where the mountains were gargantuan, the forests deeper and darker and the open "barrens" difficult to apprehend – sublime beyond any usual sublimate? What would the sophisticated Johnson or Defoe have written of the Canadian Shield or Pacific coastline? Barbarism, horrid and sterile in the extreme, no doubt.

One need not imagine a Johnson or Defoe exploring the New World. There is a rich collection of exploration and travel narratives concerning the still remote north woods and coastlines of Canada. Central among the "best places" for today's travels is the Pacific West Coast of Canada, and central among its early travellers is Captain George Vancouver (1791–95). Sea kayakers today will be amused at the "dreary prospect" Vancouver cast of the now superb wild beauty of the West Coast. Simply put, Vancouver was a man of this time. Credit him for naming "Desolation" Sound just north of Powell River. Among his many dreary descriptions are the following excerpts. At Desolation Sound he noted, "This afforded not a single prospect that was pleasing to the eye, the smallest recreation on shore, nor animal or vegetable food."[7] At Teakerne Arm of the inner passage between Vancouver Island and the mainland, Vancouver wrote, "...our residence here was truly forlorn. An awful silence pervaded the gloomy forests, whilst animated nature seemed to have deserted the neighbouring country...." North from Burrard Inlet, Vancouver bemuses about the landscape he was to survey, "stupendous snowy barrier, thinly wooded and rising from the sea abruptly to the clouds, from whose frigid summit, the dissolving snow in foaming torrents rushed down the sides and chasms of its rugged surface...." Beautiful we think, but for Vancouver as author, this was "...altogether a sublime, though gloomy spectacle." In Vancouver's defense we should remember that parts of this coast were known as the "graveyard of the Pacific." Cook, Vancouver's predecessor under whom Vancouver faithfully served, was in the habit of taking to the open sea during rough water rather than seeking shelter amidst the rocky coast. This is certainly not the inclination for today's explorers of shoreline. Vancouver did run aground at the northern tip of what is now Vancouver Island. Miraculously, once ballast was removed and the tide returned in their favour, the ship righted itself. Had a wind blown up during this wait, the dreary prospect that shrouded Vancouver's perspective would have reached unimaginable proportions.

One comical incident, of which there were many in the confused relations between the abundant Native inhabitants and the alien guests in big ships, is told here by Manby, one of Vancouver's crew at Nootka on the west coast of Vancouver Island. Thomas Manby writes:

> An Indian in one of the Canoes had with him a live Humming bird, of very beautiful plumage...tied by the leg with a single human hair. On seeing it, all on board became anxious to become the purchaser of this little curiosity, which enabled the owner to sell his little prisoner for something considerable. The Indians along side, eyed with peculiar attention, the avidity all on board express'd for this Bird, which apparently produced the greatest surprise. In an instant every Canoe left the Ship, and paddled with all their strength to the Shore...however, in two hours, the little Fleet of Canoes again made towards us, paddling with all their might, on gaining us, the object of their flight and return, evidently bespoke the pursuit of the whole, as every Man, Woman and Child, had three or four Living humming birds, to dispose of, which in a few Minutes so overstocked the Market, that a brass button was willingly received for two. Letters, 13 April.

It should be noted here that not all explorers of the time faced a dreary prospect in the New World landscape. David Thompson describes a moment from a view over the Bow River near Banff with excitement and curiosity rather than with the commitment to the surveyor's recording of detail and bleak reporting. Thompson writes of this November 30, 1800, view on the Bow River:

> Our View from the Heights to the Eastward was vast & unbounded the Eye had not Strength to discriminate its Termination: to the Eastward Hills & Rocks rose to our View covered with Snow, here rising, there subsiding, but their Tops nearly of an equal Height every where. Never before did I behold so just, so perfect a Resemblance to the Waves of the Ocean in the wintry Storm. When looking upon them and attentively considering their wild Order and Appearance, the Imagination is apt to say, these must once have been Liquid, and in that State when swelled to its greatest Agitation, suddenly congealed and made Solid by Power Omnipotent.[8]

Thompson's journal writing saw no style editor. I sense he is struggling to share what he thought of a world overly rich in superlatives, or what the Japanese might call *Yugen* – that which cannot be described. I imagine that for Thompson, many times he would arrive at New World places that slowed or even halted his writing, not for the gloom, but for the beauty.

Similar to Thompson's sighting of the Rockies is George Nelson's first sight of the open prairie on a hunting trip west of the Assiniboine River:

> My eyes were not big enough…all my faculties as it were, were arrested – I was lost in amazement and admiration! I stood riveted to my place and could [only] exclaim….Oh beautiful, beautiful! What art can ever come up to nature? My companion laughed at my foolishness.

Vancouver might not have enjoyed the scenery or grasped Thompson's imagination and Nelson's excitement, but he did do his job well. A diligent and largely unrecognized surveyor, Vancouver, over three seasons on the coast, surveyed over 100,000 kilometres (62,137 miles) with an estimated 16,000 (9,942 miles) more by hand-oar parties sent from the ship for detail work. One surveying party over a twenty-three day period by rowboat covered 11,000 kilometres (6,835 miles) and in so doing advanced the known shoreline north by a scant 100 kilometres (62 miles). Clearly a frustrating exercise, but someone had to do it. To compound Vancouver's "gloomy" mood, he suffered from a debilitating thyroid "complaint" and was detested by his men for his outbursts of rage. One officer wrote, "Our commander-in-chief is grown Haughty, Proud and Insolent, which has kept himself and officers in a continual state of wrangling during the whole of the voyage." One disgruntled midshipman, years later as a respected Baron, chased his former captain down in the London streets with the challenge of a duel. Great gossip was had of this incident by the London newspapers of the time.

Vancouver's payment, for his surveying of virtually the entire Canadian west coast and his proving that no northwest passage was to be found with inland access at these latitudes, took four years to arrive. He received little recognition for his efforts in this "miserable" land and died at age 40 within days of reading the proofs of his book.

All this is a sad story, particularly for today's wandering coastal sea kayaker who knows beauty where Vancouver saw gloom. But would we, the recreational traveller today, had we been with Vancouver, have seen the country differently from the cultural perception that dictated the context for seeing that framed Vancouver's view. Likely not. Translucent cultural assumptions are a powerful force. But it is intriguing to know that such places as the beautiful Pacific Coast were once not thought so beautiful. Perhaps with this knowledge we can understand that cultural perceptions change and, for the land's sake, the need to continue to evolve towards a reverence for preservation of beauty and an appreciation for a coastline that remains, in places, largely as it did at the time of Vancouver's "gloomy" exploration. Thankfully our explorations today of the coast by sea kayak are not so gloomy.

GABRIEL SAGARD AND DAVID THOMPSON

David Thompson's travels spanning decades, and the one and only trip of 1600s by the French missionary Gabriel Sagard, to my mind, were travels cut from another cloth than the more standard Old World viewpoint. David Thompson and Gabriel Sagard are two men who came to the north woods of the New World with a desire to record the facts. They travelled by canoe with Native Peoples. With curiosity and urgency, they challenged themselves to break their bonds with their own culture and landscape back home as they explored the newness of this new world. Thompson and Sagard were quite unusual for this openness of spirit to the differences of people and place. Others, such as Champlain, Mackenzie, Vancouver and Franklin, though noteworthy for their accomplishments, were bound by their fabricated vision of what the north woods should become, rather than what they were. Their vision was perhaps more blocked to any genuine meeting with indigenous peoples, lakes, rivers and forests. Thompson and Sagard, however, as a means to shaping their self-understanding, held in abeyance the presuppositions of their cultural world view. They did not automatically insist that their cultural baggage could fully account for all they were seeing for the first time. Their narratives are worth reading for the spiritual relationship they inspire and the cultural lessons they provide.

As canoeists today we seek wild lands more and more to break bonds with familiar urban ways. Perhaps we too, with curiosity and urgency, are still seeking the mysterious facts of the New World. We'd like to experience the Canadian bush and indigenous peoples as they really are, not through some pre-fab cultural lens that blocks the genuine meeting. For many the adventure in travel is "to fit in," not "to fill out." As we "fit in" we are learning the ways of the North – Bill Mason's "song of the paddle," Sigurd Olson's "ancient rhythms." We are making strides in self-understanding connecting us to the earth. As we "fill out," we are stuck in the groove of our own narrow thinking. We may be building an empire as Champlain believed or "discovering" new lands (not really) for a "landscape of commerce" as Mackenzie and perhaps Franklin believed, but we are not learning all that we might. We are not learning to genuinely meet the place and its people as they are. Thompson and Sagard offered a challenge to readers of their time in their thoughtful narratives. I'd say they were ahead of their time. The challenge remains with us today. Scottish writer Alistair McIntosh put the challenge this way, "Maybe a new song will emerge when ancient ways inform our times."[9]

Gabriel Sagard was a Franciscan missionary who, in the 1620s, had orders to travel to Huronia with the Huron by their means, the canoe. The community-minded Franciscan religious order wanted to "fit in" and understand as well as save souls. Civilization was, for them, a two-way street. Sagard wasn't keen on cornmeal mush and bugs and early morning paddling to beat the winds of the Ottawa River and Georgian Bay. The French River, however, had him in constant awe (unlike Mackenzie whose only recording of the river is "unsuitable for agriculture"). As for his hosts, the Huron, they offered him a new vision of humanity. Sagard saw "in man, in a natural state, uncorrupted virtues and qualities of humanness" he would rather emulate than corrupt to the French practice. Contrary to his culture's expectations, he did not see "utter darkness" along this canoeing highway of old. He did see beauty in the land and its people and judged the land and water to be responsible for the human qualities he admired.

Sagard wrote in *Le Grand Voyage* in the 1620s:

...and we shall find that their fervors surpass ours and that they have more love for one another in this life and after death than we who say we are wiser....[10]

Usually in a non-judgmental way, Sagard recorded what he saw. He was less a teaching missionary than a student of a life closer to nature. He wrote:

> They thought that the earth was pierced and that when the sun went down it entered this hole and remained hidden until the next morning when it came out the other end.

Certainly Sagard was influenced by Jean-Jacques Rousseau's 18th century philosophy. Rousseau had said, "The closer to his natural condition man has stayed, the smaller is the difference between his faculties and his desires and consequently the less removed he is from being happy." Still, to Huronia and back from New France (basically Montreal to Midland and back) is a tough introduction to canoeing. This he certainly noted as well. His well-documented hardships will boggle the mind of even the most austere tripper today.

The following list of instructions drawn up by Father Le Jeune in 1830, many of which were likely learned by Gabriel Sagard, showcases by way of an easy to read-between-the-lines style, the hardship of adjustments that Sagard would have had to endure. It is hoped he came to a realization of at least some of the suggestions from this list on his own accord:

Father Le Jeune's 1830s' instructions are often a reading shared at the beginning of the day's paddle during guiding trips.

➤ You must love these Huron's, ransomed by the blood of the Son of God, as brothers.

➤ You must never keep the Indians waiting at the time of embarking.

➤ Carry a tinder-box or a piece of burning-glass, or both, to make fire for them during the day for smoking, and in the evening when it is necessary to camp; these little services win their hearts.

➤ Try to eat the little food they offer you, and eat all you can, for you may not eat again for hours.

➤ Eat as soon as day breaks, for Indians when on the road, eat only at the rising and the setting of the sun.

➤ Be prompt in embarking and disembarking and do not carry any water or sand into the canoe.

➤ Be the least troublesome to the Indians.

➤ Do not ask may questions; silence is golden.

➤ Bear with their imperfections, and you must try always to appear cheerful.

➤ Carry with you a half-gross of awls, two or three dozen little folding knives (jambettes), and some plain and fancy beads with which to buy fish or other commodities from the nations you meet, in order to feast your Indian companions, and be sure to tell them from the outset that here is something with which to buy fish.

➤ Always carry something during the portages.

➤ Do not be ceremonious with the Indians.

➤ Do not begin to paddle unless you intend always to paddle.

➤ The Indians will keep later that opinion of you which they have formed during the trip.

➤ Always show any other Indians you meet on the way a cheerful face and show that you readily accept the fatigues of the journey.[11]

Sagard was crushed to learn of his orders for an early return to France. His narrative of 1623 and the secondary treatment of Jack Warwick in *The Long Journey: Literacy Themes of French Canada* help us understand our philosophical traditions for meeting peoples and place in the ever shrinking unknown that Sagard travelled.[12]

David Thompson, Mackenzie's junior but still a contemporary, offers a sharp contrast in spirit to Mackenzie's "landscape of commerce." Rather, in a landscape of wonder, Thompson, an unconventional hero, was already shaped by New World phenomena. He was unconventional because he quietly and humbly travelled and mapped most of northwestern Canada

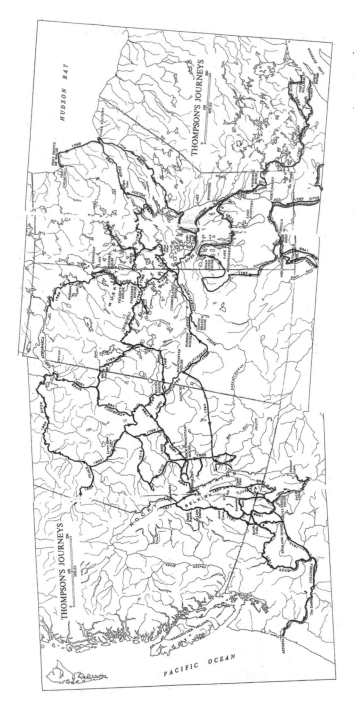

David Thompson's great map of the Canadian North West. It is estimated that Thompson travelled over an estimated 50,000 miles (80,468 kilometres). *Taken from Victor G. Hopwood (ed.),* David Thompson: Travels in Western North America 1784–1812 *(Toronto: Macmillan, 1971).*

including the Fond du Lac, the Columbia River, the North and South Saskatchewan rivers and, later at age 67, the Muskoka Lakes and a route to the Ottawa River via Algonquin Park. It is not one grand exploration of "discovery" but a lifetime of travels by canoe and horse.

Canadian travel literature scholar, I.S. MacLaren, writes of Thompson as "one of the first writers to evince an intense interest in the relation between the human mind and Canadian nature."[13] Like Sagard, Thompson's journal is an outstanding read for today's canoeist. He was without the seemingly overwhelming influence of Old World assumptions and practices that formed rigid patterns of thought for so many nineteenth-century travellers. He was free to grow in the New World, to assimilate the land and Native People on their own terms. In him, we see some balance between fitting in and filling out, between being shaped and shaping.

Thompson's sense of wonder, his unabashed imagination and moral conviction set him apart from the store of commerce-minded "superior" traders that Mackenzie represents so well. At the Painted Stones at the Hayes River headwaters, a standard canoe route of the time, Thompson states his great disdain for his European compatriots who had desecrated a Native site of worship. The painted stones mark the easy headwaters crossing of a mere canoe length of smooth exposed rock. Such a crossing is an oddity as geographer and mapmaker Thompson would appreciate all too well. Rather then pass off the European disrespect as comical, he noted the lack of wisdom and understanding that his countrymen brought to the landscape.

No better example of Thompson's openness to the tension between Old World deductive science and Native cosmology exists than his well-known "instinct" passage:

> Then applying themselves to me, they said, you that look at the Stars tell us the cause of the regular march of this herd of Deer. I replied, "Instinct." What do you mean by that word? Its meaning is "the free and voluntary actions of an animal for its self-preservation." Oh, Oh, then you think this herd of Deer rushed forward over deep swamps, in which some perished; the others ran over them, down steep banks to break their necks; swam across large Rivers, where the strong drowned the weak; went a long way through woods where they had nothing to eat, merely to take care of themselves. You white

people, you look like wise men, and talk like fools.. I had to give up my doctrine of Instinct, to that of their Manito. I have sometimes thought Instinct, to be a word invented by the learned to cover their ignorance of the ways and doings of animals for their self-preservation; it is a learned word and shuts up all the reasoning powers.

Here, Thompson casts the Indian as superior of intellect reminiscent of anthropologist Claude Levi-Strauss' experience with Australian aborigines. Levi-Strauss labelled the aborigines "intellectual snobs," for he (Levi-Strauss) knew so little about how the world worked and, in fact, how to see with a cosmological vision, which they told him in no uncertain terms. Thompson's lack of total devotion to the European turn of mind brought his awareness to a richer science and ethnography. Thompson's narrative offers a challenging unit of vision whereby the goal was to portray the inter-connectedness of geography, climate, animals and the people, both Native and European.

Thompson and Sagard are exemplary of a unity of vision we might seek today on our canoe trips. From their vision we learn to be open to what the north woods and the Native traditions might offer. And like these two travellers we might turn to writing in a tradition of shaping our lives after the facts as a means of self-understanding. Even though, like them, there is the problem of accurately conveying our feelings and thoughts in our ragged field journals. It is a worthy challenge of self-expression.

GEORGE NELSON

The fur trade clerk George Nelson is another Canadian traveller who similarly stands out for his openness to the New World view before him. Nelson left his Montreal family in 1802 at age 15 as the eldest son sent inland with the fur trade to draw a good wage. But, the boy learned more than how to make a living as an underling clerk in the fur trade. Nelson learned, and more surprisingly recorded, a cosmology that "rocked his world" – one that he hesitantly recorded, knowing it would more than rock the world of his Anglican roots. His parents, William and Jane Nelson, were United Empire Loyalists who settled in Sorel, Quebec. His father was a schoolmaster and sent his son into the "wilderness" with a Bible and prayer book.

Nelson observed conjuring ceremonies of the Midewiwin religious order and medicine society gatherings. He reported on their functionality and success as theological practices. He recorded myths and relations to animals, the importance of song and windigo dreams. Of his 1823 ethnographic account of Cree and northern Ojibwe religious practices in the Lac La Ronge area, he expressed a desire to form "a view of Indian life" as a "proper estimate of man in his Natural State." He was impressed with this "primitive" world view and thought of civilized life as "unpolished barbarisme" (particularly because of the well-defined class system). His Christian virtues, however, clouded any clear opinion providing an interpretative dilemma for him as a writer. For example, his letters home written nineteen years into his service among Native Peoples repeatedly affirm the truth of his assertions and a claim that he is not bound by superstition, but rather by analysis. There is a sense when reading Nelson's writings that though the recording of his experiences wasn't supposed to make sense to him, his observations did appear concrete to him, and the events and qualities they bespeak fit well in the Canadian bush. He wrote of a June 1823 conjuring ceremony at Lac La Ronge, "I have almost entirely converted myself from these foolish ideas of ghosts and hobgoblins, but I assure you in truth that I more than once felt very uneasy." Nelson saw conjuring work. What is a good Christian boy to do with that?

Nelson when "scarcely more than a boy" had many experiences that must have played on his memory, an arranged marriage among them. Twenty years later, he comments on an early encounter with song "delivered in Notes, impressed or drawn on bark, in the form of hieroglyphics." Note the self-mockery he now employs twenty years later towards himself and his fur trade colleagues in terms of their pretentious treatment of Native Peoples:

…I rem[em]ber throwing away the contents of one of these medecine bags in which there were several strips of Bark covered with these Notes. An Indian happened to be by – he took one up and with the Point of his knife placing it on one of these began to sing, moving the knife regularly as children do when they begin to learn their a, b, c. This surprised me a little at the time, for the Indian was a stranger and had but lately arrived from his own lands that were several hundred miles off. After laughing at and ridiculing him as is the custom with us, I asked how he could make them out?

"The same," said he, "as you do to reckon (i.e., read) your papers. See, this one is (meant for) the Thunder; that, the Earthy &c, &c; but I only know a few of these songs: the possessor of this bag knew a great deal – he was a great medecine man, i.e., Doctor."[14]

George Nelson provided in the 1820s what must now be regarded as early anthropological treatments, not vicariously, but working centrally as a keen observer engaged in a respectful serious inquiry. He noted the windigo (cannibalistic monster) phenomena as a "kind of disease or distemper rather, and of the mind I am fully persuaded..." Later anthropologist would come to many of Nelson's same conclusions. He studied dream guardians and vision fasts, medicines for hunting, healing and love, myths and legends, and especially sorcery.

We must remember too that the conditions for writing were often not easy. Nelson recorded of his 1811 Lake Winnipeg post conditions, "I have wrote this in a small room of 12 or 13 foot square, where we cook, eat, drink and sleep together besides the trouble of Indians and the noise of troublesome and unruly children."

Certainly under such conditions, Nelson, surely was compelled, and not casually, to relate his "off hand" observation. It was a matter of some importance to him, in part I sense, to resolve inner confusion towards conflicting beliefs. Nelson's ethnographic journal reads true and is a rare example of a narrative open and attentive to the "New World."

JOHN MCLEAN

John McLean, a lesser-known fur trader, wrote *Notes of a Twenty-Five Years' Service in the Hudson's Bay Territory* in 1849. Published first in 1932 and again in 1968, he offers a record of tales that spans the country coast to coast throughout the early 1800s. Like Sagard, Thompson and Nelson, but all for different reasons, McLean ended his working career in the New World, disgruntled. In a matter of fact year-end summary, McLean noted, "This is truly an eventful year for me. Within that space I became a husband, a father and a widower. I traversed the continent of America, performing a voyage of some 1,500 miles by sea, and journey by land of fully 1,200 miles on snowshoe."[15]

In this year, 1837, McLean left the Pacific "slope," the New Caledonia region of the Hudson's Bay Company, for York Factory on Hudson

Bay. He then travelled to Fort Chimo (now Kangiqsualuujuaq on Unvaga Bay, Quebec) with orders to traverse the interior from Ungava to Hamilton Inlet (currently Lake Melville/Goose Bay). Significant travel and upheaval in life's direction to say the least! On the Labrador Plateau overland journey, McLean, in a charmingly understated way, writes of his discovery of the Great Falls of Labrador on the then Hamilton River:

After one day's rest, we embarked in a canoe sufficiently large to contain several conveniences, to which I had been for some time a stranger – a tent to shelter us by night, and tea to cheer us by day; we fared, too, like princes, on the produce of "sea and land," procured by the net and the gun. We thus proceeded gaily on our downward course without meeting any interruption, or experiencing any difficulty in finding our way; when, one evening, the roar of a mighty cataract burst upon our ears, warning us that danger was at hand. We soon reached the spot, which presented to us one of the grandest spectacles in the world, but put an end to all hopes of success in our enterprise.

About six miles above the falls, the river suddenly contracts from a width of four hundred to six hundred yards to about one hundred yards; then rushing along in a continuous foaming rapid, finally contracts to a breadth of about fifty yards, Here it precipitates itself over the rock which forms the falls; when, still roaring and foaming, it continues its maddened course for about a distance of thirty miles, pent up between walls of rock that rise sometimes to the height of three hundred feet on either side. This stupendous fall exceeds in height the Falls of Niagara, but bears no comparison to that sublime object in any other respect, being nearly hidden from the view by the abrupt angle, which the rocks form immediately beneath it. If not seen, however, it is felt; such is the extraordinary force with which it tumbles into the abyss underneath, that we felt the solid rock shake under our feet, as we stood two hundred feet above the gulf. A dense cloud of vapour, which can be seen at a great distance in clear weather, hands over the spot. From the fall to the foot of the rapid – a distance of thirty miles – the zigzag course of the river presents such sharp angles, that you see nothing of it until within a few yards of its banks, Might not this circumstance lead the geologist to the conclusion that the fall had receded this distance? The

mind shrinks from the contemplation of a subject that carries it back
to a period of time so very remote: for it, the rock, syenite, always
possessed its present solidity and hardness, the action of the water
alone might require millions of years to produce such a result!

Quite a discovery! Quite a portage! He comically titles this section of
his narrative; "Impracticability of Expedition." In 1993, I looked down
a one-kilometre-plus canyon beginning with the 22-metre (72-foot)
drop on the Upper Notokwanon River in Labrador, north of McLean's
Great Falls but part of the same height of land which drops off of the
Labrador Plateau. I remember vividly staring at the white water, the
falls, the rock walls, and thinking what next. Have we arrived at a place
best not to travel by canoe, by walking…at all? Certainly this put an
end to our own proceeding gaily downstream. Even though the map
indicates "the interruption," we were not mentally prepared. What must
McLean, without benefit of maps, have been thinking that day in 1837?
Indeed as he suggests, the mind shrinks amidst the grandeur and greater
focus than oneself at work.

McLean's journal is full of stories – stories best carried for retelling
around evening campfires on the trail. Here is one such vignette from
a traveller's life:

> The descent of the Clearwater and Athabasca rivers [in Saskatchewan
> and Alberta] was effected without an accident, and we arrived at
> Athabasca on the 16th of September; whence I set out again, after
> a few days' delay, for Fort Resolution, on Great Slave Lake, where
> I was detained by stress of weather until the 29th.
>
> I left the post late in the evening, and intended to encamp on an
> island at a convenient distance; but the season being far advanced,
> I felt anxious to proceed, and inquired of my pilot whether he thought
> there would be any risk in travelling all night? "Not the least," was
> the reply and we rowed on accordingly till morning, when lo! the
> only objects to be seen were sea and sky. In vain we strained the
> organs of vision to discover land; there we were, as if in the midst
> of the ocean, surrounded on all sides by the unbroken circle of the
> horizon. I do not know that I ever felt more seriously alarmed than
> at this moment, thus to find myself exposed on an unknown sea, as
> it might well be termed, in an open boat and at such an advanced

period of the season without any means of ascertaining what course to steer for land. It would appear our steersman had been napping at the helm in the course of the night and thus allowed the boat to deviate from her course without noticing it; hence the awkwardness and even the danger of our present situation.

Likely, during this encounter with the open sea of Great Slave Lake, McLean remembered his learning of an Inuit family's crossing of Hudson Strait between Baffin Island and the Ungava mainland. He wrote of this, "…'and what if you had been overtaken by a storm?' said I. 'We should all have gone to the bottom,' was the cool reply."

Like his contemporary, George Nelson, McLean's journal reveals a tension between the pull to "go Native" as so many Canadians had and the push to retain the civility of the "Christian world."

John McLean remained true to his Isle of Mull birthplace, but remained true to the North country as well. He adopted a "new" Canadian sensibility informed by the Canadian wilds in his later life. In these latter years, living in Toronto, Montreal, Elora and, finally, with his

Like John McLean's "interruption" at the Great Falls, though on a much reduced scale, this 22-metre (72-foot) drop marked a significant change to our travels.

daughter in Victoria, British Columbia, where he died at age 90 in 1890, he had been a veracious "letter to the editor" writer under the pen name Viator. His theme was constant: "to awaken the people of Canada to the greatness of the heritage they had in the Northwest." Perhaps his written sermons even played a hand in the young Canada's acquisition of his former employer's territory in 1869. He would have supported this.

McLean's desire to awaken post-confederation Canadians to the greatness of the land's heritage is in sharp contrast to far-flung travellers like Alexander Mackenzie who, though much venerated for his travels, was not apart of this group of explorers readily valued for their openness to the New World. Mackenzie had commented, "[it is] unpardonable in any man to remain in this country who can afford to leave it."[16] Mackenzie returns us to Vancouver's "dreary prospect." Thompson, Sagard, Nelson and McLean remind us that, beyond the physical struggles on the land, there are metaphysical struggles to come to terms within the wild land of the New World. Today, I believe we are still looking for this New World. We still carry erroneous cultural baggage we would be wise to discard when heading into the bush. It is wise, too, to consider our time with the Canadian wilds to those of the likes of the traders and travellers touched on here. Our 10-to-50-day trips will always pale in comparison to those of the likes of John McLean. Reading the journals of these travellers helps the travellers of today put their ventures and life into a perspective suitable to the land as a whole and to the continuity of time, while adding a new perspective that can shape one's imaginative gaze over the country. One way to feel this connection is to share in the fine tradition of journal writing, to record both the facts and the lessons in self-understanding to be learned in looking still for the New World. Many people today at their trips' end are fond of saying, "Now back to reality." Thompson and others tried to capture a larger reality they experienced in the Canadian bush. There is a reality in the wilds, then and now, that is a quest to tap and record in our journals, like Thompson, Sagard, Nelson and McLean tried before us.

14

ROOTS AND WINGS: A PECULIAR COLLECTION OF WOMEN'S STORIES

We can starve as well as they; the muskeg will be no softer for us
than for them; the ground will be no harder to sleep upon;
the water no deeper to swim, nor the bath colder if we fall in.
— MARY T.S. SCHÄFFER[I]

IN THE SUMMERTIME at the south end of Smoke Lake in Algonquin Park you are likely to find Esther Keyser in her cabin or a note on the cabin door saying, "Gone canoe tripping." Esther has served as an anchor for me since I first heard her story and soon after met her casually at the lake's landing. I have visited Esther a few times and some of my children have gone down the lake to tell Esther about their recent canoe trips, as have I.

Once Esther had me promise that I would make a return visit following a spring river-poling trip in New Brunswick to give her all the details. Here was a paddling skill new to her. Then, at age 84, she was fascinated to hear how that trip went. I was in awe and remember vividly my excitement and hers as I recapped the trip. What a fine tradition we were revelling in that day!

I do not visit often. It is more that it is satisfying to know that Esther is there, a presence on the lake that, for me, serves as a strong reminder of the charm and grace involved in connecting one's soul or spirit, or is the right word love affair – having a love affair – with a place. In Esther's case, the place is Algonquin Park, where I hang

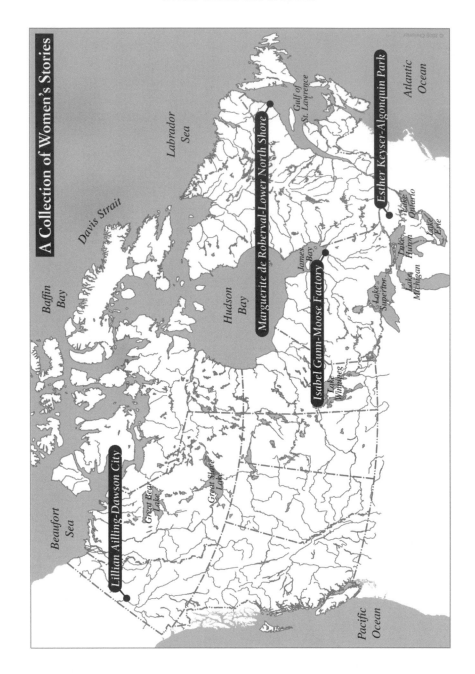

my hat for much of the summer. It's been 76 years and counting for Esther in Algonquin and almost 40 years of association with Algonquin for me.

But that's the rub. My association with Algonquin though similarly starting at a children's camp in Algonquin (Camp Ahmek for me in the mid-1960s and Northway Lodge for Esther in the 1920s) took me in a different direction. By age 19 Esther was establishing herself as an Algonquin Park canoe-tripping guide. She is commonly referred to as Algonquin's first female guide. I dare say, in 1934 she would be the first female guide in many parts of the country. By age 19 my camp experiences had inspired a gaze beyond Algonquin to the great spread of the woods to the north. Sigurd Olson's and Eric Morse's writings had a big hand in this for me also. My point is this. Esther's youthful love of Algonquin had made these lakes and forests the source of a lifelong passion. There is an intensity that connects a specific place with one's personality and a richness of knowledge and stories that allows words such as soul, spirit and love to be so easily used. I, rather, flirt about, exploring widely a range of places near and far. Building relationships yes, but relationships not at the same intensity. Compared to Esther, I feel a bit of a voyeur. If the first love truly is the deepest (I'm only talking about place-based relationships here) then I should stay put, follow Esther's example, and grow my roots deeper in Algonquin. But I know my gaze outward is too wide and now too well-established. I do wonder though how my personality would be different had I followed Esther's lead more – that is, more than I already have.

Esther, by the age of 19, was bringing her friends to Algonquin. Then came her husband Joe. Then came her family – kids, grandkids and now great-grandkids. She has canoe tripped in Algonquin with three generations of family. Under her and Joe's guidance all have learned to paddle, to fish, to bake over the fire and to be at home in Algonquin woods.[2] Esther can visit that first campsite on Big Trout Lake once out of the Otterslides, and recall clearing and establishing the site in the 1930s. Next time I visit that lake I plan to stop there in respect. Esther has stopped there over sixty years later to relive that memory. Incredible! She can point out sites of former fire ranger cabins on Opeongo, White Trout and more, and former fire towers, and can fill these cabins and towers with the intriguing characters of the bush who lived and

Esther Keyser, Algonquin Park's first female guide. In the 1930s, Esther, as a travel guide, continued to build on her summer camp foundation. *Above left*, A young Esther packing for a trip. *Above right*, Esther Keyser, still active. *Courtesy of Esther Keyser.*

patrolled in Algonquin. It is clear that Esther was not an outsider to these heydays (I'd suggest) of Algonquin peoples and early ranger camping and canoeing; she is a big part of this heritage of Algonquin.

I have had the privilege of meeting the senior Norwegian eco-activist and eco-philosopher, Sigmund Kvaloy Saetereng. Sigmund recently changed his name by adding Saetereng to it, the name of the family farm. He can boast eleven generations on the family farm. Amazing! Like Esther in Algonquin, such passionate and lasting association inspires me. I know it is not at the same intensity for me, but when I think of Sigmund and Esther, there is an anchor for me in the stormy sea of our culture's landlessness,[3] and I live a little bit more clearly when they are close to mind.

Esther recently published her life story in *Paddle Your Own Canoe*. Here she fills in the details of her life and those of her extended family. We also learn many of the old ways, the stories and the characters of Algonquin canoe tripping. The roots for Esther's family are deep in Algonquin and can help others ground themselves a bit more deeply and richly.

Another anchor for me that also helps me lay down roots on the land (a mixed metaphor I know) is Mary Schäffer's 1911 book, *Old Indian Trails*. I return to her writing and story often. I first lifted her book from the University of Alberta library bookshelf simply because I liked the title. It would become one of my favourite reads in the Canadian travel literature genre and a fine example of self-effacing, wise humility. Like Esther, Mary's love of the land compelled her to firmly establish herself with her place – the Canadian Rockies, her first love. For both Esther and Mary these were bold unconventional steps from women in their time. Certainly I am attracted to this "stepping out from the mainstream" prompted by a love affair with a place.

Mary was not alone as a source of root inspiration. Mina Hubbard in 1905 found a respect for travel and a love of the Labrador interior in retracing her dead husband's aborted earlier exploratory route. What a grand story this is.[4] Anna Jameson escaped the rigid social life of Toronto for her "summer rambles" by streamer, stagecoach and canoe, along the Lake Huron coastline in 1837. Canoeists will enjoy her travels along the northern shore of this lake. Jameson, I believe, can speak for Esther, Mary, Mina and many others from her time until now, with the following passage from *Winter Studies and Summer Rambles in Canada* written in 1837:

> The clinging affections of a warm heart, – the household devotion – the submissive wish to please…. the tender shrinking sensitiveness,…to cultivate these, to make them, by artificial means, the staple of the womanly character, is it not to cultivate a taste for sunshine and roses, in those we send to pass their lives in the Arctic zones.[5]

All the women mentioned above found their sunshine with pine and spruce trees on the trail. All broke with conventions to pursue a self-determined higher purpose. All wrote eloquently of a woman's struggles and rewards in seeking out her place in a part of the Canadian bush.

Today I teach travel-based courses to "mostly" young women of university age. Assigned course work encourages many to study and retell the life stories and travel accounts of women's adventures and wise dwellers of place. The stories continue to be inspirational in providing roots to the land and travel for both men and women.

When I first thought of writing about women in the Canadian bush, my thoughts first turned to roots, women who inspire grounding with the land. Quickly though, I can also add the wings that come from stories that set the imagination reeling. I have three favourites, peculiar stories I might add, that span the country: two of which are studied and told each year as part of a story-telling assignment for a university travel course, and the third is an exciting new story for me, to be added to this list of stories with wings.

Isabel Gunn, an Orkney woman, was also John Fubbister who lived in Canada from 1806 to 1809 with the Hudson's Bay Company fur trade centred out of Fort Albany. Let me explain. The young Isabel arrived on the company ship in June 1806 as a recruit. She arrived as John Fubbister for a three-year term as a company labourer. Her circumstances are unknown. We do know that in order to join the trade she would have to practise the seemingly incomprehensible subterfuge of role-playing as a man.

Did she follow a lover? Was she bent on escaping impoverished conditions back home? Was she expelled by her family? The Canadian folk singer Eileen McGann, in song, has Isabel following a lover:

> *My love was signed by the Hudson's Bay for to be*
> *   a voyageur*
> *To paddle and explore the northern ways, to trade*
> *   and transport fur*
> *And if you think I would be left behind, it's little that*
> *   you understand*
> *For on the very next line I signed for to do the work*
> *   of a man.*
>
> *And oh how I loved the life we led, though my love*
> *   and I worked apart*
> *But adventure delighted my very soul and the forest*
> *   land healed my heart*
> *My heart, the forestland healed my heart....*

In the historical fiction, *Isobel Gunn*, novelist Audrey Thomas suggests that Isabel was escaping the expected dreary prospects of home for the adventures of the Canadian fur trade. We'll never know. We do know that she worked well within the ranks, travelling upriver to Henley House and in the following year from his/her Albany post, travelling 1,500 kilometres (932 miles) to winter at the Pembina Post on the Red River (near present-day Winnipeg). Fubbister was well-received by fellow workers and superiors. All seemed well until the Christmas celebrations hosted at the rival North West Company post were to come to an end. Fubbister, complaining of ill health, asked to stay behind. The chief factor, Alexander Henry, granted permission but soon was called to the lad/lass' bed and later records the moment thus:

> Accordingly I stepped down to him, and was much surprised to find him extended out upon the hearth, uttering most dreadful lamentations. He stretched out his hand toward me and in a pitiful tone of voice begg'd my assistance, and requested I would take pity upon a poor, helpless abandoned wretch, who was not of the sex I had every reason to suppose. But was an unfortunate Orkney girl, pregnant and in childbirth. In saying this she opened her jacket and display'd to my view a pair of beautiful round white breasts.[6]

John soon became "Mary" Fubbister and was put in a sleigh and returned to the Hudson's Bay Company post the same day of her child's birth. In the spring of 1808 back at Fort Albany, Mary becomes Isabel Gunn. She completes here three-year term at a labourer's wage now as a washerwoman and perhaps as a nurse at the fur trade post's school. In 1809, she was discharged and returned to the Orkney Islands to a fate unknown to her then and still to us now. It is believed she returned without her child preferring he have a life in Canada.

A fellow labourer, John Scarth, who was also on her outbound voyage in 1806 is presumed to be the child's father. A question remains, had Isabel been raped or not? Filmmaker Anne Wheeler tells the story as one of a rape to turn the concealed identity. Novelist Audrey Thomas does not. Again we'll never know. But we should all know this story for the audacity, courage and subterfuge played out on northern fur trade posts and waterways. Who knows? Perhaps you have been on a canoe trip with a woman in the role of a man, an expedition meant only for men. Perhaps or perhaps not.

Lillian Ailling landed in New York City in the spring of 1927 from Belorussia, Russia. Soon after arriving and while working as a house-maid, for whatever reason, she decided to return home. She couldn't

The rugged Lillian Ailling during her cross-country (literally) and northwest walk. *Taken from C. Pybus,* The Woman Who Walked to Russia, *the visual credited to the Atlin Historical Society.*

afford the conventional Atlantic steamer, so she set off, refusing all offers for a lift, walking across North America with an iron rod strapped to her leg concealed under her pants. She had studied maps in the New York City library and had planned out a route that would involve the overland telegraph route north into the Yukon. The route "home" would culminate with a crossing of the Bering Sea between Alaska and Siberia. I have yet to look up how far northern Siberia is from Belorussia.

Likely with a combination of riding the rails and walking, she arrived in British Columbia on the Yukon telegraph trail in late September 1927. In Hazelton, B.C., she was charged with vagrancy – certainly for her own protection from the upcoming winter. She was tried in court and fined $25.00 and $1.75 in court costs or she could spend two months in a Vancouver jail. I think the Hazelton authorities knew she had less than $20.00 in her possession. She spent the time in jail likely regaining her strength and determination to travel.

By June of 1928 she was again travelling on the telegraph trail with her main contact being the linesmen who operated the various stations. The linesmen knew to look out for her and help as circumstances demanded, but to let her continue. As the story goes, she arrived in Whitehorse on August 31, 1928. We can follow her story because she caught the attention of the local newspapers along the way. Apparently, she turned down an offer for a car ride from Carcross to Whitehorse, and passed through Carmacks, over 160 kilometres north of Whitehorse by September 14. Lillian arrived in Dawson City on October 5, having slept out each night without a sleeping bag or tent, living mostly off the land. In Dawson, Lillian worked as a waitress and repaired an old boat for a spring paddle down the Yukon River to the Bering Sea. There is a report out of Providenirja, Russia, of a strange woman in "American" dress having arrived in the fall of 1930 with three Inuit.

In 2002, a curious book, titled *The Woman Who Walked to Russia,* from a Tasmanian English professor and writer Cassandra Pybus, was released. Cassandra became intrigued by the bare-bones story. She began a search of genealogy records and municipal archives and spent time by car retracing Lillian's route through British Columbia and the Yukon. She did find a Lillian Smith (1897–1979), who died in Skagway south of Dawson City. She did flush out the story among the telegraph linesmen, but basically she returned home to Tasmania discouraged.

On her trip home, she retrieved from her notes a fax of a letter to the editor written by Greenfield, a retired Mountie, responding to a British Columbia newspaper's telling of a Lillian Ailling story. Out of the blue it seemed he wished to set the story straight.

Greenfield reported that he had been on duty when Lillian spent time in Hazelton charged with vagrancy. At that time she had told him that she had left New York City for North Dakota to marry. However, her love was gone by the time she arrived. Lillian was presumably following him north to the Yukon. Greenfield reported receiving a letter from Lillian thanking the police for detaining her because, while she hadn't met the North Dakota man, she had met and married a trapper named Smith in Telegraph Creek. Together they homesteaded in the Dawson area.

Lillian Ailling's travel down the Yukon River in no way mirrored my own idyllic float. *Courtesy of Kathleen Henderson.*

So now we have two Lillian Ailling stories. Both are peculiar. Why the staunch independence? Why the secrecy from so many would-be helpers along the trail? The two stories leave us still bemused and captivated by the events in Lillian Ailling's life from the spring of 1927 to 1930. Did she go to Russia as was one theory for her vision or did she follow a love west and then north, only to find another and homestead in the Yukon? For me, it matters not which. This is a story with wings, one that stays with you as it did for Cassandra Pybus to whom we should be grateful. I like the fact that each winter season I hear a new interpretation of these stories told by a budding student storyteller to our small class as a course assignment. Isabel's and Lillian's stories likely inspire a quicker steady tempo to one's stride when fatigue begins to set in on our winter trail together.

Marguerite de Roberval, the exiled demoiselle of the 1542 Roberval colonizing scheme, with her story set on the Lower North Shore of the St. Lawrence, has been called, "the most romantic 'true' story of the sixteenth century"[7] The story about the story is equally as interesting as the events themselves. First, the story closest to the historic truth account will be shared, along with inserts from less "authentic" versions. Then there is the story of the story.

Marguerite, the niece of the captain and colonizing leader Roberval, was marooned, likely on one of the Harrington Islands of the St. Lawrence Lower North Shore, as punishment for a clandestine love affair while on board the ship. Roberval must have felt his name disgraced by the couple's actions. Left ashore with guns, ammunition, some food and clothing, and perhaps her maid, she saw her lover leap from the ship at the last moment to join the desolate pair. Soon after the maid and lover die, Marguerite survives the year and is rescued by a French ship and returns to France. She was much influenced by the ordeal, fearing demons and close to death herself.[8] Not much of a romance I'd say. Yet this simple tale, first told in print less than fifteen years after the events, has received much attention over four centuries from 1558 to now. Three literary versions in the sixteenth century lay the foundations. One author, the Queen of Navarre, has Marguerite faithfully joining her exiled husband in the first telling. She tells a true romance story of a strong faithful partner. Andre Thevet in 1575 has Marguerite exiled first for, "their [lovers'] wanton and shameless passions, this illegitimate and libidinous union." He claims to have interviewed Marguerite, which is possible, claiming she stayed on the island for over two years before being rescued. She gives birth to a child that soon died in his version. Both versions mention the demonic forces that were "entertained by the couple." Marguerite Roberval's researcher, Arthur Stabler, speculates that the Queen of Navarre's version is careful to tell an exile story without damaging the name of Roberval. Thirty years later, Thevet is free to tell the more authentic account. Four centuries later, Douglas Glover has a field day with the bare-bones story in a fun and intriguing fiction. Glover's 2003 *Elle* is visited not so much by demonic forces, but by indigenous travellers and sorcerers who struggled to fit "Elle" into their world as much as "Elle" struggles with the same. The out-of-body state of Elle is a challenging read, but once a reader is informed by Stabler's historical detective work, Glover's novel takes on a greater intrigue and credibility. Glover certainly picks up the lustful demoiselle part of the tale.

Over the years, there has been a long poem, (*Marguerite: or the Isle of Demons*, George Martin, 1887), a drama (*De Roberval*, John Hunter-Duvar 1888), and novels (*Marguerite de Roberval*, Thomas G. Marquis, 1899; *Isle of Demons*, John Clarke Bowman, 1953), and finally *Elle* (Douglas Glover, 2003).

Why such attention to such a sparse historical event? Stabler reminds us that, "the number of literary and historical treatments of her story over the centuries is probably unequalled by any other legend of its period, thus bearing witness to the universality of its appeal." Is it the cruelty of Captain Roberval, the love interest, the haunting setting of a remote offshore island on the exposed Lower North Shore or is it that because we know so little we are free to dream into and dream up so much of the story on our own? In short, it is a good story to dream into. And, if you have paddled somewhere between the Mingan Islands and Blanc Sablon you have a feel for the country in question that adds a visual impact.

The forces of nature are omnipresent and aggressive on this shoreline. I remember standing in the wind facing east on the exposed south side of one of the Mingan Islands. I felt a touch of fear and pull to keep heading east towards the Harrington Islands to Blanc Sablon. I didn't know about the Marguerite de Roberval story then. The pull to keep heading east remained strong (as has that touch of fear) and today the image of Marguerite/Elle adds to the intrigue. My July 2004

Marguerite de Roberval's story of abandonment has captured the imagination through many retellings over four centuries. *Taken from Denis and Chauvin*, Les Vrais Robinsons.

trip allowed me to seek new dimensions to Marguerite's story. I paddled by her island en route to Blanc Sablon.

Arthur P. Stabler, in 1972, suggested a memorial stone be erected, possibly at Harrington Harbour where the town has laid claim to the specific locale of Marguerite's exile, or a spot between Old Fort and Blanc Sablon might also fit the bill as municipalities debate the possible exact site. Stabler is keen on the Harrington site. I suggest we should tell and retell this story to bring it back into a collective consciousness as it was in the 1500s and late 1880s, when Canadians began to write their historical stories.

Let your imagination run wild with Marguerite. As with Isabel Gunn and Lillian Ailling, these are tales with wings. These peculiar stories, mostly unknown to Canadians, show a side of our history that drives home the point, crystal clear – Canadian history is not boring. But these peculiar stories need roots, roots like Esther Keyser, Mary Schäffer and Anna Jameson to, in effect, ground the women's experience in a "landful" way in the Canadian bush. We need both kinds of stories. The specific location is secondary though fine material for speculation.

While generally not as well-known as male travellers' and settlers' stories, Canada has women discoverers (Mina Hubbard and Marguerite de Roberval), explorers (Mary Schäffer and Isabel Gunn), and settlers (Lillian Ailling and Anne Jameson) who embody the full spirit of discovery/exploration and settling. Esther Keyser, for me, with her life in Algonquin captures some of all of these three spirits of enterprise. All these women, against greater odds than their male counterparts, made their mark on the Canadian storied landscape. Their particular stories should be told – often.

15

CAPTURING THE ARTIST'S EYE

I come to you by brush and paddle
Through the lingering mist of a northern lake
There that's my canvas – my canoe
Can you see me clearly now?
— IAN TAMBLYN[1]

BEFORE US WAS the view we were seeking – A.Y. Jackson's view, *Nellie Lake,* 1938. It was white rock, glacial-smoothed but scarred. It was reddish with underbrush of an advanced autumn season. The small pond (end of the lake really) was offset by the mounding of mixed forested hills beyond. One dominant feature of this vista was a clear saddle, a significant dip in the land between two protruding hills. From our location on the northern ridge, this saddle was central and most obvious. After some debate, my friend, Leona Amann, and I agreed it was likely this formation that had caught the artist's fancy, although the shape of Carmichael Bay at the western foot of Nellie Lake in Ontario's Killarney Park also commands attention.

Jackson's sketch had brought the view closer to the mind. His colours were more vivid, his rocks more alive, like a whale's back when surfacing, his hill forms more pronounced. His exaggerated saddle seemed almost comical compared to the actual landscape. On canvas the saddle rocks appear more like towering bastions dividing a gorge, than a subtle yet obvious saddle. Yet with time on site the apparently tame landscape took on a "Jackson look" as our perceptual focus broadened. Our experience had been complete, right down to the weather. We enjoyed the same wispy cloud cover and marvelled at all our good fortune.

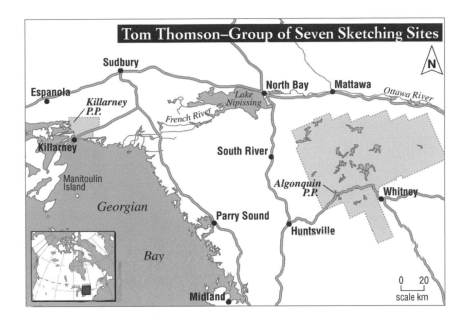

There is no better way to learn the Canadian landscape artist's style, to ponder the vision, imagery and love for the land, than by our activity of matching land with art, natural beauty with creative flair and imagination. The relationship of the unique character of artist and landscape was there for our interpretation. Our task was to capture the artist's eye, to feel this involvement exposed.

If you want to understand the voyageurs of the fur trade, you must sweat and cuss on a portage while bent over by the load. You must dig into a headwind with paddle and delight in the next day when you would hoist a sail. You must relax by the evening with stories. You must wonder if you'll ever make it home again. Then you start a song in rhythm with your paddle, savouring both as a celebration of life and as a prayer for life.

It is the same for the Group of Seven, those Canadian artists of the early 1900s. If you want to understand the Group and their "primary precursor and catalyst," Tom Thomson, as Robert Stacey described him, then you must walk not only among the galleries, but you must walk *their* Canada. You must visit their sketching sites to feel their interpretations of land, water and sky put to canvas.

How hard could it be to find the sketching site of A.Y. Jackson's 1938 painting *Nellie Lake*? It is somewhere on the shores of Nellie Lake!

Encouraged, perhaps by Jackson's vision, Leona drifted off over the open ridge to seek her own sketching site. I remained at the lookout, switching modes to take up the detective's eye. This revealed a fallen tree, charred and rotting, but in the likely location to suggest it was once the weather-beaten, twisted trunk in Jackson's foreground. Perhaps an area fire had also changed the vegetation type of the distant hills, explaining Jackson's deciduous colourful forest, compared to the mixed forest of today. Perhaps Jackson simply wanted it that way.

Later that trip, we portaged over that Jackson saddle into what we thought of as a Carmichael's lake, Grace Lake. Franklin Carmichael, another of the Group of Seven, was obviously intrigued by the grand vista. He liked height – the horizon and looking out – the space between land and sky. We hoped to discover the sketching site for *Mirror Lake*, a classic Carmichael La Cloche painting. The search was less satisfying. The group of islands and hills didn't match well. All the pieces were there but the puzzle didn't fit. I remember wondering, "Why would anyone feel the need to alter this view." Back to this later.

My first impetus to seek out Group of Seven sketching sites came from Sue and Jim Waddington, friends from Hamilton, Ontario. Sue had decided to take an advanced rug hooking course and selected Jackson's *Nellie Lake* as her subject. It was 1977. Jim suggested that given the painting was named, how hard could it be to visit the site and, with the time it would take to rug hook such a painting, they would be quite familiar with the visual image. Anyway, they found the site and framed the lovely wool fabric image. It hangs in their living room. They were truly hooked. And they told me about their adventure in Killarney Provincial Park soon after and I too became hooked.

Today, Sue and Jim have found about forty sketching sites of the Group, mostly in the Killarney/La Cloche region.[2] But they also have found a white house painting by A.J. Casson in old Waterdown. The painting is called *First Snow*. Better still, they have ongoing research or rather ideas as to the sketching locations of about another thirty sites, again mostly in the La Coche area. They are back there each summer. In 2003, they carried a pole mount (a modified sail mast) of three metres to elevate the camera for those times when they needed to get above an annoying built-up treeline blocking their view. A lot will have changed on those ridgetops from the 1930s until now.

With twenty-five years of being a Sherlock Holmes of the La Cloche sites of the Group, Jim tells me you learn something about the habits of the artists. Jackson, for example, was a walker. Expect to travel beyond the first ridge. Wander a bit. Casson and Carmichael tend to stay closer to home base – on the first ridge. All seemed to interpret the terrain the way *they* wished. Remembering my frustrations on the north ridge over Grace Lake seeking out the *Mirror Lake* canvas, I listen. Jim tells me that it all starts to make sense when you simply reverse the mountains but not the islands. I'd thought at the time, I just didn't have the staying power for such inquiry, though Jim said it took him years of returning to Grace Lake to finally have this "eureka" moment unfold.

I'd also hunted in vain for Carmichael's *Bay of Islands* image. Jim figures the sketch was painted from the fire tower (now gone) on Tower Hill outside Willisville on the western edge of Killarney Park. A general rule is to look first to the foreground details for clues and then shift to the background. With *Bay of Islands*, the background sweep of the horizon islands and water match well between land and painting, but the details of the foreground do not since, in this case, Carmichael added the church and village.

Sue and Jim enthusiastically share highlights from over their years of ridge walking. Again overlooking Grace Lake, there is a photograph of Carmichael sketching, seated on a rock on a cliff's edge. In 1995, the Waddington family came upon the exact rock perch. The rock sadly is gone now, kicked over the edge perhaps. Recently, Jim had another "eureka" moment turn highlight. He loves Jackson's painting *Bent Pine*

Jim and Sue Waddington look over their presentation of
research on the Group of Seven sketching sites.

(one I do not know) and loves Table Rock Island, the rocky feature on
Grace Lake. One day after many visits to the island, it dawned on him
when browsing through his La Cloche photographs that these loves
were one and the same.

For me, the first love is the sweetest. Visiting Nellie Lake remains
a highlight, but I also had a fine time hunting, unsuccessfully, for
Lismer's *Bright Lands* painting around the tarn lakes found north of
the OSA and Killarney lakes. Very delightful wanders as I recall. Jim
tells me, with a wink, to try Topaz Lake, also in Killarney Park. I
will soon.

I have highlights from Algonquin Park as well. Tom Thomson's *Jack
Pine* was sketched in 1916 at Grand Lake in the eastern end of Algonquin, when Thomson worked for a summer as a fire ranger. In the mid-
1980s, informed with this knowledge and assuming the painting's shoreline image might be near the still-standing ranger's cabin, I gazed out
for clues in an effort to match the profile line of hills across the lake.
I assumed the 1916 tree would be long gone. Sure enough, you can do
this. Today a new jack pine has sprouted up and the site is much revered
with a new historic plaque. The plaque begins: "You are standing at
one of the most famous sites in Canadian art history." Admittedly it
was fun to have come to this same conclusion long before the interpretive sign was posted. Great to have the site commemorated though.

In 2002, I followed up on a lead from Algonquin friends, George

Garland and John Ridpath.[3] Thomson's *Northern River* has long been a personal favourite painting from the overall collection of all these artists. Why? It is a generic sort of image. You can imagine coming to the end of many a portage throughout the northern forest and there it is – Northern River. This doesn't exactly make for confident sketching site hunting.

I heard the theory that this sketch was made on an early Thomson trip on the South River, west of the Park. The 2002 National Gallery Thomson exhibit suggests *Northern River* is "likely an amalgam of experience rather than a view of a specific site." Far be it for me to challenge a more researched view – so I'll let George Garland's research do the talking.

Garland and Ridpath write that Thomson's actual name for this painting was "my swamp picture." It would have been sketched in the summer of 1914, a summer Tom spent almost entirely on Canoe Lake, Algonquin. So a swamp near Canoe Lake makes sense, perhaps a bend in the Oxtongue River? This hardly narrows the search. But we learn (thanks to Garland and Ridpath) that Tom had a favourite sketching site along the now long forgotten set of trails to Drummer Lake (then Gill Lake) north of the current portage. Thomson was known to be headed to Gill Lake on the last day he was seen alive. In the search for him, his good friend and park ranger, Mark Robinson, choose to retrace

Tom Thomson's *Jack Pine* sketching site near the Grand Lake campground, Algonquin Park.

Linda Leekie and Don Standfield comparing the terrain in this swamp
with the general lay of the land in Tom Thomson's *Northern River.*

this route along the current portage trails of that day. Oddly, it seems
today, Robinson reports in his diary that he spent a good part of a day
on a detour to search by a "large beaver pond," surely a known popular sketching site for Tom or why bother with such a detour.

Old maps make the appropriate pond stand out amongst the old trail
systems. Today it is a bushwack north from the current Drummer Lake
portage. With a reprint of the original field sketch and the final painting in hand, I walked around this large pond with my curious friends.
It was 88 years later but the possibility of black spruce, marsh and an
apparent bend in a river (or pond) was feasible, and this theory was
better than any other I'd heard. It was a fine way to spend a day in Algonquin. Another friend, David Standfield, thinks *Northern River* is
painted in a quiet bay on Canoe Lake's west shore near Thomson's home
base of Mowat. Dave's view is based on the look of the land now and
the certain frequency of Thomson's wandering on that bay. I'll have to
wander that way myself for a serious look. Another friend, Dave Hod-
getts, believes he has located Thomson's *The Pointers* sketching site as
Windy Point on the west shoreline of Smoke Lake. He uses the distinct
profile of the imposing background hill as his main evidence. It is exciting to enter your friend's imaginative gaze along with the artists. Fun
theories all – and all useful for exploring land and artist. I can't help
wonder what Thomson would make of all this. I hope he'd be proud.
I'm certain that the Waddingtons and Carmichael (a central La Cloche

artist) would be mutually inspired with a face-to-face meeting.

Thomson's painting *Northern Lights* has also received a sleuth's attention. Astronomy columnist, Ivan Semeniuk, using the location of the star constellation Cassiopeia in Thomson's 1917 painting, along with the profile of the hills and Thomson's general whereabouts in 1917, has determined Thomson was facing north by northeast on an April evening soon after arriving to Algonquin for a new year. The sketching site is the north shoreline of Mowat by the Mowat Lodge ruins.[4]

Apparently this same astronomical dating techniques, involving computerized simulations, has dated Van Gogh's painting *Moonrise* to 9:08 p.m. on July 13, 1899 – give or take a minute. Needless to say, I sent this recent information off to the Waddingtons.

Thomson allegedly drew 128 sketches in the spring/summer of 1915 alone. That could represent many a fine day's wandering in Algonquin. Jim and Sue Waddington were back in the La Cloche area in the summer of 2003, picking away at another thirty or so sketching sites there. But I'm confident they are also using this search as a bonus to the compelling pull they feel each summer to canoe trip this familiar terrain. Jim and Sue might be a Sherlock Holmes of the Group of Seven in Killarney, and I a very poor fumbling Dr. Watson there and in Algonquin, but mostly what we share together (and we also share with Tom Thomson and the Group to follow him) is a love of these particular northern landscapes and the bonus of a creative way of seeing. As I watched Jim and Sue describe their interpretations and insights involving the land and the paintings, I saw another kind of creative flair, not that of a painter certainly, but an imaginative rewarding quality all the same. From them I have learned both to capture the artist's eye and the interpreter's eye: a specialist in the art/land critic realm you might say. The Waddington's way of studying the Group of Seven is one that captures the true spirit of these artists I think. I am thrilled to have been part of their quest.

16

HERMITS I'D LOVE
TO HAVE MET

I had to work for a living. The hours were long and the wages
small but I learned four trades – barbering, painting, carpentering
and mason work. At 33 I checked up and found I wasn't
getting along fast enough so, like the poet, I said,
"What care I?" and took to the woods.
– NOAH JOHN RONDEAU[1]

I'VE ALWAYS BEEN intrigued by hermits. There are specific hermit characters of course, but also there is the whole general idea of reclusiveness. Perhaps solitude intrigues because when on solo canoe trips I've found myself going a bit squirrelly after the delight of the first few days. But, then again, like growing a beard, I settle into the experience after about day six.[2] Perhaps there is a balance to solitude and community that all people seek, though at different points along the continuum of life. Certain monastic orders would come out of solitude and engage in weeks of community service, then retreat back into solitude. The Adirondack hermit, Noah John Rodeau, left his very remote cabin for a few years to be Santa Claus in New York City and appeared to people at the time (the 1930s) that he shifted between the dramatically different settings effortlessly. Ragnar Jonsson is known to have dogsledded over 300 kilometres (186 miles) from the Nueltin Lake area to Churchill, Manitoba, for groceries and return the same day. Eskimo Charlie, (also known as Farmer Charlie and Charlie Plenanshek) a contemporary of Jonsson's, perhaps his closest neighbour in the 1940s, wishing to see the

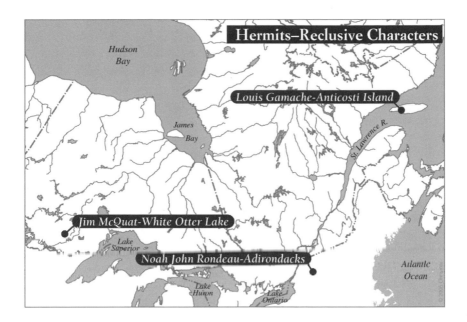

world, abandoned his Pelican Narrows homestead in 1929 to travel south by canoe. Charlie, with his two sons age six and eight and a friend, Frank O'Grady, eventually travelled down the Mississippi, having his sons do shoreline dances to earn money for food along the way. Once the epic trip was complete, he returned via the Atlantic coast to Montreal and headed back to his more reclusive life in the Canadian bush to Putahow Lake near the Manitoba/Nunavut border.

Elliott Merrick wrote of Labrador trappers as living an existence in a "long round of contrasts." In the 1931 essay, "Snow Shoe Trail" for *Scribner's Magazine* (and later in his book *The Long Crossing and Other Labrador Stories*) Merrick wrote:

> Toward the end of the summer, living with their families in their snug houses by the shore of the bay, they begin to grow restless for the absolute freedom of their solitary fur paths way off in the country. In the silence and the snow there will be no one to consider but themselves. There will be no one to get hungry or sick or cold, no one to slow them up, no one to make concessions to or expect help from. A hunter works alone, supreme and free, sufficient unto himself in the life he knows and understands.

But by the time the winter is over each man is tired of the silence, hating the smell of the balsam bed, sick to the soul of walking and hauling, mending snowshoes, skinning fur, partridge stew, the dirt, the hardship. He starts on the long haul home "drivin' 'er," and he keeps it up to unbelievable limits of endurance.[3]

I think this contrast of seeking solitude and community is not uncommon to travellers generally.

Most of us though, lean towards the community end of the continuum. Generally, it is fair to say we are a gregarious species by choice. But some thrive more on the solitude end of the continuum and some need intensive flashes of each. Hermits, and generally reclusives, can intrigue us for the lesson they can teach or simply for the difference they represent. Either way, the Canadian bush had, and still has, a wealth of them – people and stories to fill many a solo night reading in the tent, with additional wondering about the many unrecorded stories. Trouble is, the book on this topic is not written yet. So I'll start the process here with attention to two stories: firstly, a place of reclusives, Anticosti Island at the mouth of the St. Lawrence and secondly, my favourite hermit, Jimmy McQuat of Northwestern Ontario's White Otter Lake.

I shouldn't say there is no book to read. Isabel Colegate's book, *A Pelican in the Wilderness: Hermits, Solitaries and Recluses,* is a good general start on this topic, but much to my chagrin there is not a Canadian story to be had. You can read about Chinese hermits, often former royal officials who were exiled to remote corners of the kingdom. With a change in regime, the outcast upon his or her call back might refuse the invitation. As Colegate reports, one such poet Li Bai wrote, in 701:

> *They ask my why I live in the green mountains,*
> *I smile and don't reply; my heart's at ease,*
> *Peach blossoms flow downstream, leaving no trace,*
> *And there are other earths and skies than these.*[4]

You can read about Czar Alexander I who, in the early 1800s, cancelled his true identity for a new life as a poor pilgrim. There are Christian mystics, cave dwellers in Northern Africa, Irish monks in stone huts, stylites who lived atop of pillars such as St. Simeon between 476 and

491, and dendrites who lived atop of trees. Yes, they had names for these people. Recently, Julia Butterfly Hill lived for two years 180 feet up a giant redwood tree in California to attract attention to the threat to these trees from logging interests. She succeeded and, like St. Simeon 1,500 years earlier, she mixed solitude with evangelist purpose. There are "fools for Christ" who wandered the Syrian desert weighed down in chains, transcendentalists like Henry David Thoreau who was really a social hermit,[5] and the hired hermits of the 1700s who were meant to inhabit English gentlemen's hermitage gardens where they might entertain picnic guests. One such hermit even advertised his services.[6]

Colegate's overview includes reclusives who are exiles, disenchanted leaders, holy individuals or members of sects. Common to most through time was a closeness to nature (Peach blossoms flow downstream, leaving no trace) and a life of study and contemplation (and there are other earths and skies than these). The need for solitude may be occasional, frequent or in perpetuity. Today, I'd say that solitude is undervalued and for all too many only a lingering nostalgia for us gregarious types. As one friend put it, in considering the long solo canoe trip, "I don't know if I like myself well enough." For the Canadian examples to follow, all of them I think, liked themselves enough, and craved a closeness to nature and/or life of study and contemplation on a hermit's end of the solitude/community continuum. Each seems to fall in nicely with the opening epigram of Colgate's book: "A man [or woman] that studies happiness must sit alone like a sparrow upon the house top, and like a pelican in the wilderness." (Thomas Traherne, 1637–74).

I have seen pelicans facing the wind, solo and motionless both times I've entered Nipew Lake on the Churchill River. It is a most noble image to consider deeply. As you would expect, despite Colegate's complete Canadian omission, we have a wealth of characters, those "pelicans in the wilderness" to consider.

First, Hermits Island, a namesake among many for Anticosti Island, a monstrous island out where the St. Lawrence has long since become the open ocean. Here is an 8,000-square-kilometre (3,089-square-mile) area of dangerous reef, high cape bluffs and occasional beaches with few harbours. Given its location, as a gateway to the St. Lawrence, the island was also known as the "graveyard of the gulf." In the mid-1800s, upwards of 2,000 ships would pass, mostly carrying white pine back to Europe, many having brought emigrants to Canada. Shipwreck

Lobster Bay, Anticosti Island, has a wealth of secluded bays between its limestone reefs and capes that have served the recluse well.

accounts tend to lead to stories of epic rescue, cannibalism and…hermits.

One story tells of a Native woman at Sanvagesse Cove near Cape Nord who would help shipwrecked victims. She lived alone in the remote cove and nurtured victims back to health and safe passage onward. Legend has it that many men enchanted by her would return later to ask for her hand in marriage, but she was always gone. She would reappear with each shipwreck, as her services were needed. The catch is, she, or someone, served in this role over two full centuries, the sixteenth and seventeenth.

Another Anticosti hermit story concerns Nova Scotia fisherman, Peter MacDonald, who lived with his wife for twenty years in MacDonald Bay, also on the north shore of Anticosti, some 40 miles (64 kilometres) from his nearest neighbour. As the story goes, eventually his wife asked the much dreaded relationship question, "It's either me or this place." MacDonald now into his 80s, chose the place. The island, the whole island, was purchased in 1895 by Henri Menier, the King of Chocolate in France. Menier's rules included no hermits living peacefully or otherwise on his shores, so MacDonald was first encountered about his removal when in his late 80s. The enforcer, Martin Zédé, befriended Peter and coaxed him into the village hospital at Baie-Sainte-Claire on the western tip of the island, 100 kilometres (62 miles) away. Peter grew anxious to return home, so one January day he started out on foot to his remote bay. He was 89 years old. In March, he was found sitting in a chair in his cabin with his feet in a bucket of ice. MacDonald is buried in his garden by his beautiful bay.

The most famous Anticosti recluse is Louis Oliver Gamache. How I would have liked to have met this fellow. Gamache lived in Ellis Bay, later Port Menier, where the town is currently located. All other town sites on the island, with time, have been abandoned. From the 1820s to 1857 (and long after that in folklore) Gamache was a larger-than-life figure who pulled pranks and told tall tales to bolster his own reputation as a person to fear. Correspondingly, Ellis Bay, one of the island's best harbours, became a homestead and a harbour to fear. And it also follows that with few visitors here, Gamache and family lived a relatively peaceful farming outpost lifestyle. In one story, he tricked an innkeeper in Rimouski, a town on the south shore of the St. Lawrence, into believing his dinner partner was with the devil. "A table for two," he would request, as the story goes, "and a private room for my special guest and I." He would then eat for two and practise some clever, likely amateurish, ventriloquism to appear in heated conversation. Apparently he even rigged a hidden cord-and-stick device to open and slam the door for his guest the devil himself.

Gamache had run away to sea at age eleven on a British ship. At 20, he married and opened a store in Rimouski. When this burned down, he left with his young family to establish a farm and run the government's emergency supply depot for shipwreck victims. There was good fishing and trapping. And while he would save victims of shipwrecks along the south coast of Anticosti, he would also salvage supplies for his own use, a common practice, but for someone of his expanded reputation, it won him the horrid title of a shipwrecker. This is someone who purposely misleads ships into the dangerous reef to reap the bounty. There is no evidence Gamache practised such a devious act, but he likely only mildly defended himself on this point. His mahogany staircase would have been a sight to see. He raised many children, though both his wives died young, one of smallpox, while his second wife fell dead on the first day of what was supposed to be a three-day outing for her husband. Eight days later in November, Gamache returned to starving and cold children and his wife still lying on the kitchen floor.

Gamache died at the age of 70, "while taking his breakfast, a mug of undiluted navy rum," as author Donald MacKay writes.[7] From the Lower North Shore to the Baie de Gaspé, Gamache was known as a local bogeyman, a sorcerer, but really he was a clever man who saw the benefits of few visitors to his island outpost.

Madame Gitony, another clever island survivor on the south shore, was often alone while her husband was fishing or trapping. Once she survived for weeks during the winter when her cabin burnt down. She built a lean-to shelter, hunted for food, and maintained a fire. Born of a well-to-do Quebec City family, she travelled north in the St. Lawrence area originally for the health of the open sea air. When her husband, a cooper from St. Malo, France, was off trapping, she had her Newfoundland dog as her only companion. Another time, while her husband was away, she saw a crew of American sailors land on the shore of the beach. Quickly she cropped off her long hair, dressed in her husband's clothes, dusted soot on her chin and practised an elegant subterfuge. Communicating in sign language given that the Americans spoke no French, she entertained the crew, playing cards and drinking all night. Her deception had been complete.

In the case of Anticosti, "Hermits Island," the stories, as I hope to suggest, go on and on. Neighbours were usually about 40 kilometres (25 miles) apart. Here, before settlements started in the 1860s, solitude was a way of life. In 2003, I paddled a section of the northern shore. Each pebble beach cove seemed removed from the next, each

Louis Gamache's grave at Port Menier, Anticosti, can be the touchstone to remind travellers of the once extreme remoteness here. Most think Anticosti Island is remote enough.

distinctive, each beautifully lonely and set apart. The wind would blow up in the afternoon, but the coves afforded us a quiet stare out to sea or a pensive beach walk. This is a haunting beautiful shore, with a heritage of fiercely independent cove dwellers. Today, some coves have road access thanks to the Trans-Anticosti highway (a dirt road). Most coves, though, remain approachable only by sea. It is a tricky and rewarding place to sea kayak. Exposure to winds means that progress will likely be slow (and I mean both meanings of progress here), but the mind can be racing with the island's wealth of stories.

It is odd to have a place of hermits like Anticosti. Rather, a hermit and his place form a deep association as a solo act. My favourite hermit story is one I will tell in full, rather than telling snapshots of stories as I did for Anticosti.

Jimmy McQuat (pronounced McKewitt) will always be the "Hermit of White Otter Lake" on the Turtle River system between Ignace and Atikokan in Northwestern Ontario. In Scotland, Jimmy McQuat might have built a stone fortress on a lonely loch. It would have been the kind of place that inspired Shakespeare as a setting for Hamlet. In the American South, he might have built a mansion suited to the likes of Scarlet O'Hara. But it was to be south of Ignace, in classic Canadian Shield canoe country, that Jimmy built a log structure of three storeys, two porches, twenty-six windows and, to top it all off, complete with a four-story tower overlooking the lake.

Jimmy set his mind on building the antithesis of a log cabin, trapper's hut or shack. As the story goes, he had been scolded as a child in the Ottawa Valley – "Jimmy McQuat, you'll never do no good, you'll die in a shack." When it seemed that this prophecy had validity, Jimmy rose to the occasion, so to speak, and he rose alone. He undoubtedly was proud when he said, in 1918, the year he died, "and I put it up without any help whatever." He was also reported to have said, "...all the time I lived in a shack, I kept thinking – I must build me a house. And so I have. Ye couldn't call this a shack, could ye?"[8]

Mile after mile of rugged shoreline drops behind and then about 2:30 p.m., "Old Jimmy's Place" quite suddenly slips into view. A hundred yards back from the lake it stands, on the edge of a small clearing. In the background are dark pine woods. No one speaks but with one accord the paddles pause here. Eyes strain. Heartbeats quicken. In the very air is mystery. Almost, we fear to approach this retreat of the wild man. We are intruders – trespassers. Then, slowly, the paddles dip. The bow grates on a strip of sandy beach. Gingerly we step ashore and approach the hermitage.

That's how C.L. Hodson first approached "Old Jimmy's Place" in the summer of 1914. Many others and I have felt these same feelings throughout this century – a mystery, a careful approach, a pause to stare. The only real difference to Hodson's story and mine (first in 1988 and then again in 1997) is that they had the exciting potential of finding Jimmy actually at home, working about the garden perhaps, or laying down a new roll of tar paper on the roof.

Hodson, an American tourist keen to see the "wildest country of all" off the rail line, had little idea about the castle, or Jimmy, other than that it was to be a highlight and a destination. He had no picture. He wrote of the mysterious hermitage at that time of arrival:

> ...three stories high, a massive structure of heavy logs, at one corner raises the tower log upon log. Yes, it must be all of forty feet high, but tell us not that its building was accomplished by the unaided strength of one old man!"

Obviously he had heard stories to fuel his intrigue. Hodson's party camped by the castle and met Jimmy the next day. Jimmy had made a canoe trip into Ignace that day for supplies. Together, they enjoyed iced lemonade:

> In the bush – thirty miles from anywhere – with the Hermit of White Otter Lake!! Beat it if you can!

Well no, this cannot be beat. Now, this sort of meeting is one for dreams. But, with my two visits to the castle I must say the castle alone was enough – plenty, in fact – almost more than one can handle. Hence, a strange irrational feeling, like an intruder, can come even now, even an odd calm when you stand in the presence of some unusual isolated greatness of human spirit.

Although perhaps a hermit, Jimmy still welcomed guests, supplied area loggers from his garden, travelled to Ignace or further afield to Fort

The view approaching the White Otter Lake Castle today. In Jimmy McQuat's time, the surroundings would have been much more open since Jimmy used trees from the immediate area for the castle's construction.

Frances for supplies and maintained a subscription to the *Fort Frances Times* and a Montreal paper. Jimmy died having completed, alone, quietly and peacefully, what must be considered a latter life project of the century. These sentiments I take from the chief White Otter Lake Castle historian, Elinor Barr, whose studies have prompted her to suggest that Jimmy had been a most contented man. My own experiences with the castle allow me to concur. Sitting out on the restored front upper porch, the evening view over White Otter Lake was all it took to feel something of the spirit of this man. Contentment was easy to find.

As for the castle, it was built of red pine from the immediate site. Trees were felled, winched from the woods, squared and, with what must have been an elaborate block and tackle and pulley arrangement, he raised the logs, some 1,000 pounds (454 kilograms) in weight, slowly and steadily.

The logs varied in diameter from 10 to 18 inches, some being as large as 24 inches, laid in with dovetail joints no less. The twenty-six windows arrived by canoe over fifteen portages from Ignace (borne on what is still a standard canoe in the area). The windows were set in with a taper to offer more visibility to the outside with more protection. Dimensions are also confusingly outstanding. The 28 feet × 38 feet structure has three storeys in the main, with a two-storey kitchen and the infamous four-storey tower. But these impressive numbers are not the castle. The castle must be seen. Don't be surprised if you stop, stare, and wish somehow to ask for permission to enter.

I first visited White Otter Lake as part of a summer rendezvous initiative organized by the energetic Dennis Smyk from Ignace. It was a very welcoming, spirited journey by canoe into the castle for the fifty or so travellers. The castle then was in trouble. Rotting foundation logs had raised concerns amongst a small but dedicated local group. It was felt that the much-vandalized castle was only still standing due to the excellent ventilation afforded by the many windows and doors. At that time (1988), there was delight in seeing the castle, as nature would have it run its course. (It had had a first round of restoration work completed in 1954 by the Ontario Department of Lands and Forests). There was also regret for the seeming inevitability of seeing the castle's last days.

How I would love to show my own children this site and share with them the mystery of its story. Happily, I can report here, that shortly after 1988, a Friends of White Otter Lake Castle group was formed, monies were raised and matched by Ontario Heritage (before the days of cutbacks) and from 1992 to 1994 a major restoration initiative was undertaken. In 1997, I revisited the shore of the magnificent White Otter Lake with my four-year-old son and told him the whole story. Quinn listened, played amongst the array of stairs, sat with me on the porch, ran about and departed for the shoreline to skip rocks. Many days later when reunited with his sister, he told her the whole story, hardly pausing to breathe. You'd think he'd met a Mats Sundin or Todd Bertuzzi, (hockey players for those unfamiliar with the mind of a typical Canadian boy). I was a swell of emotion, proud to be a Canadian in a land of such northern stories, proud and excited by the youthful energy of my son and the perpetuation of storytelling, grateful to the likes of Dennis Smyk, Elinor Barr, Tony Tolar (the chief engineer for the 1990s' restoration) and many others among the "Friends" group. Overall, I was and remain captivated by the spirit of this place and joyful to be a small part of what Hodson called in 1914, "Old Jimmy's Place," a hermit's castle forever on the shores of White Otter Lake. I think it is fair to say that Jimmy found his own balance between solitude and community. He was a true "pelican in the wilderness." And, whether through nobility or madness, this hermit in his own quiet way has become a standout in Canadian bush lore.

The White Otter Lake Castle, *top*, before restoration
work in 1988 and, *bottom*, as it stands today.

With Jimmy's Castle in mind, I easily consider future trip destinations. I have been curious to visit Best Island on Whitewater Lake, northeast of White Otter Lake, ever since my tripping group selected a route just east of Wendell Beckwith's cabins there in 1977. Wendell died a few years later. I missed my chance to meet him, but, like Jimmy McQuat, his story can be explored through what he left behind. A master at inventory, cosmologist and carpenter extraordinaire, Beckwith pursued a quiet life of study. This involved theories of the earth's energy patterns and peculiar cabin designs to maximize natural insulating warmth – castles of another sort I think.

Each time I pass an Arctic esker, I think of John Hornby and James Critchell-Bullock spending a six-month winter in a hollowed-out cave in the side of an esker (a sand and gravel mound), "to live like the animals do," to quote Hornby. Hornby finally revealed his plan to the shocked and ill-informed Critchell-Bullock, but only once they had arrived at the Arctic interior east of Pike's Portage from Great Slave Lake. Hornby had elegant reclusive qualities. Critchell-Bullock had none. Theirs was a strained relationship, both spending much of their time alone: Hornby out of the esker cave, Critchell-Bullock in it. After a tough winter (for C-B), they travelled down the Thelon to Baker Lake. Hornby's cabin (shared with Harold Adlard and Edgar Christian) on the Thelon River is another trip destination for the future. This 1920s' cabin was meant to be Hornby's castle (better than the esker). The three died there when the life-giving caribou didn't pass through as expected.[9]

There is no lack of choice stories of hermits and reclusives in the Canadian bush. With each story explored and site visited, there is a gaining of insight as an accumulating knowledge of a quiet and humble way to go about life in the remote reaches of Canada. These Canadian bush characters provide small meaningful portholes into the psyche of dwelling in an, at times, overwhelming Canadian bush.

References

PREFACE

Notes

1 Bertrand Russell, "How to Read and Understand History," in *Understanding History and Other Essays* (New York: Philosophical Library, 1957) 9.
2 Sigurd F. Olson *The Lonely Land* (New York: Alfred A Knopf, 1961) 112.
3 J. Wreford Watson, "A Note on the Geography of North American Settlement," in *Canadian Geographer*, Vol. 13, 1969, 10–27.
4 Wallace Stevens, *The Necessary Angel: Essays on Reality and the Imagination* (New York: Vintage Books, 1942) 150.

INTRODUCTION

Notes

1 For more information, see Bruce Chatwin, *The Songlines* (New York: Penguin, 1988).
2 Kenko Yoshida, *Essays in Idleness: The Tsurezuregusa of Kenko*, translated by Donald Keene (Tokyo: Charles E. Tuttle, 1984) 12.
3 From a talk given by Stewart Coffin at the Wilderness Canoeing Association Symposium in Toronto, 1990.
4 David James Duncan, *The River Why* (New York: Bantam, 1985) 53–54.
5 Bertrand Russell, "How to Read and Understand History," 54–56.

Additional References

Grey Owl (Archie Belaney), *The Men of the Last Frontier* (Toronto: MacMillan, 1976) 25–26. The book was originally published in 1931.

PART ONE – PLACES

Notes

1 Barry Lopez, as quoted in Kent C. Ryden, *Mapping the Invisible Landscape: Folklore, Writing, and the Sense of Place* (Iowa City: University of Iowa Press, 1993) 207.
2 A fuller treatment of Goethe's passage as quoted, is in Theodore Roszak, *Where the Wasteland Ends: Politics and Transcendence in Post Industrial Societ* (New York: Anchor Book 1972) 306, is as follows: "…because mystery is truth's dancing

partner...because a respect for mystery may go deeper than our knowledge ever can...and because our knowledge, where it pretends to replace mystery, may only be an arrogant caricature of truth."

3   See Chapter 8 of Alfred North Whitehead's *Adventure of Ideas* (New York: The Free Press 1967) beginning page 279. Of particular interest to the resurfacing of the importance of "place" in our lives is Whitehead's discussion of adventure in modern society, "But given the vigour of adventure, sooner or later the leap of imagination reaches beyond the safe limits of the epoch, and beyond the safe limits of learned rules of taste. It then produces the dislocations and confusions marking the advent of new ideals for civilized effort. A race preserves its vigour so long as it harbours a real contrast between what has been and what may be; and so long as it is nerved by the vigour to adventure beyond the safeties of the past. Without adventure civilization is in full decay." Reconnecting with place is a powerful redirection, "marking the advent of new ideals for civilized effort."

4   For more on canoe tripping in Quebec/Labrador, see Max Finkelstein and James Stone, *Paddling the Boreal Forest, Rediscovering A.P. Low* (Toronto: Natural Heritage Books, 2004).

5   Stan Rowe, *Home Place: Essay on Ecology* (Edmonton: NeWest, 1990) 30–31. The essay "Wilderness as Home Place" is highly recommended. Here you will find the "should be" famous quote of the irrepressible former member of Parliament John Crosby: "ten years ago we didn't know about environment, but now it's all around us."

6   Ibid.

1 – SPECIAL INVISIBLE PLACES

Notes

1   Barry Lopez, *Arctic Dreams: Imagination and Desire in a Northern Landscape* (New York: Charles Scribner & Sons, 1986).

2   The Birney passage quoted here is from Cynthia Sugars, "Haunted by (a Lack of) Postcolonial Ghosts: Settler Nationalism in Jane Urquhart's *Away,*" in *Essays on Canadian Writing*, No. 79, Spring 2003. This essay elaborates on the themes of postcolonial identity and the "settler-invader."

3   Ibid. McGee appeared to be reflecting a common "settler" viewpoint. More than thirty years earlier Catharine Parr Traill said, "as to ghosts or spirits they appear totally banished from Canada. This is too matter-of-fact country for such super naturals to visit. Here there are no historical associations, no legendary tales of those that came before us."

4   See R. Edward Grumbine "Going to Bashō's Pine: Wilderness Education for the Twenty-First Century," in *Teaching in the Field: Working with Students in the Outdoor Classroom* (Hal Crimmel, ed.) (Salt Lake City: University of Utah Press, 2003) 49.

5   Exploring Canadian history by automobile is the theme of two excellent books: Barbara Huck, *Exploring the Fur Trade Routes of North American: Discover the Highways That Opened a Continent* (Winnipeg, MB: Heartland, 2000) and Joyce and Peter McCart, *On the Road with David Thompson* (Calgary: Fifth House,

2000). See also Barbara Huck and Doug Whiteway, *In Search of Ancient Alberta* (Winnipeg, MB: Heartland, 1988), a highway-oriented guide to the geological and archaeological past of Alberta.

6 Sigurd F. Olson, *The Singing Wilderness* (New York: Alfred A. Knopf, 1987) 45.

7 For a fascinating interpretation of Ojibwe language connected to visions, rock art, spiritual sites, see Louise Erdrich, *Books and Islands in Ojibwe Country* (Washington, DC: National Geographic, 2003) 81–89.

8 See Paul Shepard, *The Tender Carnivore and the Sacred Game* (New York: Scribner's, 1972), for an intriguing study of hunter-gatherer societies.

9 See Marion Robertson, *Rock Drawings of the Mic Mac Indians* (Halifax: The Nova Scotia Museum, 1973).

10 See J.F. Dormaar, *Sweetgrass Hills: A Natural and Cultural History* (Lethbridge, AB: Lethbridge Historical Society, 2003). Also see J.F. Dormaar, "The Sweetgrass Intrusive in the Milk River Area," in *Alberta Archaeological Review*, No. 30, Spring, 1999.

11 For more on James Evans and the Cree alphabet, see Roger Burford Mason, *Travels in the Shining Island: The Story of James Evans and the Invention of the Cree Syllabary Alphabet* (Toronto: Natural Heritage Books, 1996).

12 Ogam script is, rightly so, a contentious idea in the Milk River Valley. Given that there is at least one "Ogam Pillar" place name to my knowledge, a mention of this is deserved for story value if nothing more. See Barry Fell, *America BC: Ancient Settlers in the New World* (New York: Demeter Press, 1976). John Dormaar tells me that the "Ogam Pillar" is close to eroding away, given its tenuous vertical position just separated from the riverbank and the main sandstone bank.

13 Most of the quotes concerning voyageur baptizing have come from Carolyn Podruchny, "Baptizing Novices: Ritual Moments among French Canadian Voyageurs in the Montreal Fur Trade, 1780–1821," in *The Canadian Historical Review*, 83, June 2, 2002.

14 Ibid.

15 Douglas Hunter, "The Mystery of Champlain's Astrolabe, " in *The Beaver*, Dec. 2004/Jan. 2005, 14–23.

16 Podruchny, "Baptizing Novices..."

17 Ibid.

18 See W.O. Kupsch, "A Valley View in Verdant Prose: The Clearwater Valley from Portage La Loche" in *Musk-Ox*, 20, 1977. This article contains all the known historic written passages concerning this portage trail.

19 Ibid.

20 For two very different treatments on the Methye, see S.C. Ells, "La Loche Portage," in *Canadian Geographic Journal,* Vol. 12, 1936 and W.O. Kupsch, "A Valley View in Verdant Prose: The Clearwater Valley from Portage La Loche." The former offers rich romantic prose. The latter provides a comprehensive gathering of historical travel passages concerning this significant height of land portage. My travel over this portage can be found in "Clearwater: Gateway to the North," *Wildwaters: Canoeing Canada's Wilderness Rivers* (James Raffan, ed.) (Toronto: Key Porter Books, 1986).

21 For the quotes by Ross Cox, George Simpson and David Thompson, see William C. Wonders, "The Toast at the Punch Bowl," in *Alberta Historical Review,* Vol. 22, No. 4, Autumn 1974.

22 See Robert W. Newbury, "The Painted Stone: Where Two Rivers Touch," in *Nature Canada,* Vol. 3, No. 1, January/March 1974.

23 For a treatment of Arctic-Canadian Shield prominent rock sites, see the photo essay by Norman Hallendy, "Places of Power," in *Canadian Geographic,* March/April 1997.

2 – THE LABRADOR

Notes

1 John Steffler, *The Afterlife of George Cartwright* (Toronto: McClelland & Stewart, 1992), historical fiction.

2 John McLean, *Notes of a Twenty-Five Year's Service in the Hudson's Bay Territory, 1849* (New York: Greenwood Press, 1968), facsimile editon.

3 For both the Hubbards' stories and Herman Koehler's two trips in Labrador, see the references provided in the Additional References for this chapter. For the Hubbard/Wallace/Elson 1903 trip, also see the short story by Margaret Atwood, *The Labrador Fiasco* (London: Bloomsbury, 1996) and Elliott Merrick, "The Long Crossing" in *The Long Crossing and Other Labrador Stories* (Orono, ME: University of Maine Press, 1992).

  For the Herman Koehler story, see also Lynne D. Fitzhugh, *The Labradorians: Voices from the Land of Cain* (St. John's, NL: Breakwater Books, 1999). Both the Merrick account (1933) and Fitzhugh record testimonies of local Innu and settlers who heard these stories of "American tourist adventurers" first-hand.

4 See Herb Pohl, "On the Notakwanon," in *Nastawagan: The Quarterly Journal of the Wilderness Canoe Association*, Vol. 12, Numbers 2 and 3, 1985; "Ugjoktok River," Vol. 3, 1987; "Journey to the Fraser River," Vol. 16, No. 4, 1989; "Labrador," Vol. 9, No. 3, 1982.

5 For a fuller version of the Koehler story, see Bob Henderson, "The Travels of Herman J. Koehler: Another Labrador Story," in *Kanawa*, Fall 1995.

6 For the quote attributed to Jacques Cartier, see Lynne D. Fitzhugh, *The Labradorians*, 15.

7 Jennie Barron, "Innu support and the Myth of Wilderness," in *Nastawgan: The Quarterly Journal of the Wilderness Canoe Association*, Spring 2002. Jennie writes: " As for wilderness, it's a very tricky subject. William Cronon, in his edited volume *Uncommon Ground,* has written a seminal essay titled "The Trouble with Wilderness; or Getting Back to the Wrong Nature." In it he argues that wilderness, "far from being the one place on earth that stands apart from humanity…is quite profoundly a human creation – indeed, the creation of very particular human cultures at very particular moments in human history." I'm of that culture and within that moment in human history. I, like many, seek wilderness, but at a time when this cultural creation is being probed for its illusory qualities. There are too many insidious interventions in the way of airborne toxins and low-level flyers. But also, we are beginning to acknowledge that most so-called wilderness areas

were, and are peopled places. Wilderness is an awkward term. I avoid it. It separates people from nature and makes nature devoid of history. Indeed wilderness planners try to "delete" human history."

Additional References

William Brooks Cabot, *In Northern Labrador* (Boston: Gorham Press, 1912).

George Cartwright, *A Journal of Transactions and Events During a Residence of Nearly Sixteen Years on the Coast of Labrador* (3 volumes) (Newark: Allin & Ridge, 1872); facsimile edition (Ann Arbor, MI: University Microfilms International, 1981).

James West Davidson and John Rugge, *Great Heart: the History of a Labrador Adventure* (New York: Viking Penguin, 1988).

Bob Henderson, "The Travels and Final Struggles of Herman J. Koehler," in *Nastawgan: The Quarterly Journal of the Wilderness Canoe Association*, Vol. 20, No.3. 1993.

Mina Hubbard, *A Woman's Way Through Unknown Labrador* (St. John's, NL: Breakwater Books, 1983).

_____, "My Explorations in Unknown Labrador," in *Harper's Monthly Magazine*, May 1906.

Judy McGrath (guest editor), "Life in Voisey"s Bay," Theme issue of *Them Days: Stories of Early Labrador*, Vol. 12, No. 2, Winter 1997.

Elliott Merrick, "A Memory from Merrick: A Letter from March 1997 to those attending the Annual Wilderness Paddlers Gathering at the Hulbert Outdoor Center, Fairlee, VT" in *Che-Mun: The Journal of Canadian Wilderness Canoeing*, Outfit 88, Spring 1997. Merrick was 92 years of age in 1997.

_____, *True North* (New York: Charles Scribner's & Sons, 1942; Lincoln: University of Nebraska Press, 1989).

H.H. Prichard, *Through Trackless Labrador* (New York: Sturgis and Walton, 1911).

John Steffler, *The Afterlife of George Cartwright* (Toronto: McClelland & Stewart, 1992).

Dillon Wallace, *The Lure of Labrador* (London: Fleming H. Revell Co., 1905). Reprinted by Breakwater Books, St. John's, NL, 1983.

3 – THE YUKON: A BIG SPACE TURNED BIG PLACE

Notes

1 Yi-Fu Tuan, *Space and Place: The Perspective of Experience* (Minneapolis: University of Minnesota Press, 1977) 6.

2 Barbara Hodgson, *Hippolyte's Island* (Vancouver: Raincoast Books, 2001) 5. This historical fiction concerns a modern day adventure in search of the, as yet rumoured but undiscovered islands, the Auroras, in the South Atlantic.

3 "Tracing one thin line" originally comes from a well-known Canadian folk song, "North-West Passage" by Stan Rogers – "Tracing one thin line through a land so wide and savage. And make a North West Passage to the Sea." It may also appropriately be referenced here to I.S. MacLaren "Tracing one discontinuous line through the poetry of the Northwest Passage," in *Canadian Poetry: Studies, Documents, Reviews*, No. 39, Fall/Winter 1996.

4 Barbara Hodgson, *Hippolyte's Island*, 17.

5   See the excellent final essay on travel writing in Tim Cahill, *Jaeger Ripped My Flesh* (Penguin, 1989).

6   See Ian McCulloch, "The Yukon Field Force," in *The Beaver,* October/November 1997.

7   Ibid.

8   Gus Karpes has written a number of local guidebooks for the Yukon Territory rich in heritage stories. See A.C. (Gus) Karpes, *The Teslin River* (Whitehorse, YT: Kugh Enterprises, 1995). He tells the stories of Jonas (John) Hagstrom, the Boswells and others.

9   See Allan Ingelson *et al., Chilkoot: An Adventure in Ecotourism* (Calgary: University of Calgary Press, 2001) and Dianne Newell, "The Importance of Information and Misinformation in the Making of the Klondike Gold Rush" in *Journal of Canadian Studies,* Vol. 21, No. 4, Winter 1986–87.

10 For a variety of historical passages and a collection of photo images of the tent "cities" thrown up along the trail, see Graham Wilson, *The Klondike Gold Rush: Photographs from 1896–1899* (Whitehorse, YT: Wolf Creek Books, 1997).

11 For an account of "The Lost Patrol," see Dick North, *The Lost Patrol: The Mounties, Yukon Tragedy* (Vancouver: Raincoast Books, 1995). For one travel account of the Rat-Bell-Porcupine route into the interior, see Clara Vyvyan, *The Ladies, The Gwich'in and the Rat* (I.S. McLaren and Lisa N. Framboise, eds.) (Edmonton: University of Alberta Press, 1998). For the "Mad Trapper" story, see Rudy Wiebe, "On Being Motionless," in *Playing Dead: A Contemplation concerning the Arctic* (Edmonton: NeWest, 1989) and Frank Anderson, *The Death of Albert Johnson: Mad Trapper of Rat River* (Vancouver: Heritage House, 1986).

Additional References

Robert Koretsch, *The Man from the Creeks* (Toronto: Vintage Canada, 1998)

Catharine McClellan, *Part of the Land, Part of the Water: A History of the Yukon Indians* (Vancouver: Douglas and McIntyre, 1987).

4 – FILLING CABINS WITH STORIES
(NORTHERN MANITOBA)

Notes

1   Hap Wilson in Cliff Jacobson, *Expedition Canoeing: A Guide to Canoeing Wild Rivers in North America*, 3rd edition (Guilford, CT: The Globe Pequot Press, 2001) 236.

2   Sigurd F. Olson, *The Singing Wilderness* (New York: Alfred A. Knopf) 99.

3   University of New Brunswick English professor R.H. Cockburn has studied the life of P.G. Downes and the southeast Keewatin area of northern Manitoba/ Nunavut.

    See R.H. Cockburn, "Voyage to Nutheltin," in *The Beaver*, January/February 1986; "Revillon Man," in *The Beaver*, February/March 1990; "The Past in Colour: P.G. Downes travels north with a camera, 1939–40," in *The Beaver*, April/May 1993. See also P.G. Downes, "Distant Summer: P.G. Downes' 1937 Inland Journal" (R.H. Cockburn, ed.), in *Fram (2)*, 1985; "North of Reindeer: The 1940 Trip

Journal of Prentice G. Downes" (R.H. Cockburn, ed.), in *The Beaver*, Spring 1983.

See also Robert H. Cockburn, "After-Images of Rupert's Land from the Journals of Ernest Oberholtzer" (1912) and P.G. Downes, (1939) *In Rupert's Land: A Cultural Tapestry* (Richard C. Davis, ed.) (Waterloo, ON: Wilfrid Laurier University Press, 1988), and Ernest Carl Oberholtzer, *Toward Magnetic North: The Oberholtzer-Magee 1912 Canoe Journey to Hudson Bay* (Marshall, MN: The Oberholtzer Foundation, 2000). Like P.G. Downes, Oberholtzer was an early traveller through this region following Native trails. His 1912 trip with Ojibwe guide Billy Magee is a little-known landmark in northern travel. Oberholtzer returned to Nueltin in 1963, 51 years later. Many of the finest images in print of this region can be found in *Toward Magnetic North*.

4   P.G. Downes, *Sleeping Island* (Saskatoon, SK: Western Producer Prairie Books, 1998), originally published in 1943.

5   Ibid.

6   "P.G. Downes Distant Summer: P.G. Downes' 193/ Inland Journal" (R.M. Cockburn, ed.) in *Fram* (2), 1985.

7   Sydney Augustus Keighley, *Trader, Tripper, Trapper: The Life of a Bay Man* (Winnipeg, MB: Watson and Dwyer, 1989) 145.

8   Ibid, 98.

9   R.H. Cockburn, ed., "North of Reindeer: The 1940 Trip Journal of Prentice G. Downes," in *The Beaver*, Spring 1983.

10 Ibid.

11 Sydney Augustus Keighley, *Trader, Tripper, Trapper: The Life of a Bay Man* (Winnipeg, MB: Watson and Dwyer, 1989).

12 Ibid.

13 Islae Carol Johnson, *The Hugh Mattila Story: Mush On* (Howard Mattilla and Islae C. Johnson, 1976) 88.

14 The Inuit trapper Kakut (or Kakoot), is the subject of a chapter, "My Friend Kakoot" in Captain Thierry Mallet, *Glimpses of the Barren Lands* (New York: Revillon Frères, 1930) 83–104. Mallet writes of Kakoot, "While the other natives never go to the sea, and live entirely on the caribou between the edge of the trees on Nueltin Lake and Baker Lake farther north, he has travelled extensively. He knows three hundred miles of the western shores of Hudson Bay, has been as far as Bothnia to the north and the Great Slave Lake to the west, and has picked up a lot of knowledge and experience through dealing with other tribes and meeting, occasionally, white men...When there was nothing of special interest to show, Kakoot would describe in gestures the country ahead of us, the lakes, the winding of the river, the rapids, and the portages. He had discovered that I had a notebook and a pencil. At regular intervals he would borrow them and draw for me maps of the surroundings over and over again. First he would draw one starting from where we were at the time and going northward. Then, another time, he would draw the same one starting from where we were going to for instance, backward to where we were at the time. The maps, made perhaps half a day apart, would always coincide exactly.

He would always add information about the country by little crude drawings on the side – reindeer, musk-ox, willows if there was a certain quantity, fish, topeks with people around them. At first it was somewhat confusing, but in a very short time one could understand them perfectly. The only thing he could not do was to decrease the scale of his map. He was used to a certain scale, and when he had to draw two hundred miles he needed sheets and sheets of paper, which was very expensive."

15   Grey Owl, *The Men of the Last Frontier* (Toronto: Macmillan, 1976) 25–26.

16   Graham Guest, "The Packet: Letters, Notes and Opinion – A Ghost in the Wilderness" in *The Beaver*, October/November 1999, 57–59.

17   Ibid.

18   See William C. Taylor, *Tracks Across My Trail: Donald "Curly" Phillips, Guide and Outfitter* (Jasper, AB: The Jasper-Yellowhead Historical Society, 1984) 24.

19   E.O. Engstrom, *Clearwater Winter* (Edmonton: Lone Pine, 1984) 5.

20   Bob Lowrey, "Wilderness Master Ragnar Jonsson Dead at 88," in *Opasquiatimes*, Vol. II, No. 30, June 29, 1988.

21   Gerald Malaher, *The North I Love* (Winnipeg, MB: Hyperion Press, 1984) 165.

22   Bob Lowrey, "Wilderness Master Ragner Jonsson Dead at Age 88."

23   Hugh Brody, *Maps and Dreams* (Vancouver: Douglas and McIntrye, 1982), see Chapter One.

24   For the Dene and Inuit connections to the white trappers and traders stories I shared here, see Father Jean Mégret, O.M.I., *Benasni, Mémento, Memento: Forty Years with the Dene* (Lynda Holland, ed.) (La Ronge, SK: Holland-Dalby Educational Consulting, 1996); J.A. Rodgers, "Lac Du Brochet" in *The Beaver*, March 1945; and Lynda Holland and Lois Dalby, eds., *The Wollaston Interviews* (La Ronge, SK: Holland-Dalby Educational Consulting, 2001). The missionary Father Jean Mégret writes of spending four-fifths of his time in the late 1940s and early 1950s on the trail and one-fifth at the Mission in Brochet. He writes in *Forty Years with the Dene*, "I remember my longest trip in March/April 1952 – from Brochet, to Nueltin Lake to Duck Lake, and back to Nueltin. Then I went on to Fort Hall, Stony Rapids and Wollaston. I spent Easter there and around the lake, returning to Brochet on the ice. There was no snow and very long portages between Wollaston and Brochet. When there was open water spring and fall, the people as a group came sometimes to *Shai dare* (North of Lac Brochet) from Charcoal Lake, Sunrise Lake and further north. Some of them also came to Brochet towards the end of June and at Christmas. I tried to spend a month in each camp and after 1953 I spent freeze up and break up at one place or another – in my tent, with my dogs." See page 34.

     It is exciting following such travels of Mégret and other missionaries travelling among the Dene. Their experience "on the land," day-to-day, and week-to-week, is the stuff of my year-long planning for a "big" trip north into "their" country. Mégret's reminiscence are full of casually mentioned route descriptions that would constitute "expeditions" to my "southern" mindscape. For example, he writes so matter-of-factly, "an Inuit accompanied us one day. He had gone to Churchill and was returning home by way of Ennadai Lake." Hmm, the Kazan River to Churchill and return via dog team in March. A big "WOW" for me! It is best to pause when reading of such, understated travels with a map in hand.

Additional References

Gerry Dunning, *When the Foxes Run* (Churchill, MB: Churchill Museum, nd).

Francis Harper, "In Caribou Land" in *Natural History*, May 1949.

Jack London, *Jack London's Stories* (New York: Platt and Munk, 1960).

Farley Mowat, *The Desperate People* (Toronto: McClelland & Stewart, 1980).

Virginia Petch, *The Life Story of Charlie H. Schweder: Whose Heart and Soul Knew No Boundaries* (Winnipeg, MB: Manitoba Hydro, 1996).

W. Gillies Ross, "On the Barrens 1934," in *The Beaver*, Fall 1968.

5 – STORIES OUT THE BACKDOOR

Notes

1   Sylvia Bowerbank, "Telling Stories About Places: Local Knowledge and Narratives can Improve Decisions about the Environment," in *Alternatives Journal* 23:1, Winter 1997.

2   John Terpstra, *In Falling into Place* (Kentville, NS: Gaspereau Press, 2002). Terpstra offers a beautifully written study of an engagement to a place with geographic and historic themes at the centre. It is worthy of special attention here because the subject matter is the Head of the Lake with particular attention to the Iroquois Bar of Burlington Bay. From Carroll's Point, a good resting spot on a Hamilton Harbour canoe outing, he writes, "It's intimate and broad, this landscape; embracing and open. Debased and persisting. Glaciated countrysides are often more subtle than they are dramatic, as though tamed by the long-term crushing violence of waves of ice. They have a low-key, inviting energy that draws you into their features, folds and cleavages, their rolling roundnesses, into their meetings of land and water. And here, at Head of the Lake, it's all land meeting water." See page 37.

Here he provides a geological – deep time – view of the Dundas Valley. "The Niagara Escarpment provides a backdrop to the view. Dundas Valley breaches the escarpment's rock wall with a wide canyon, a gorge that the hills fall over and through as though they were the earthbound version of the Niagara River below the Falls, the water rolling through the high walls. The Dundas Valley hills are, in fact, the memory of a river – a frozen river. They were shaped by the various ice-age glaciers that advanced through the gorge." See page 34.

3   I am indebted to Peter Carruthers for this ability to provide me, the amateur, with a clear big picture analysis for this time period. Peter Carruthers' notes on Quinaouatova (Tinawatawa, etc.) and the historical canoe portage between the western end of Lake Ontario and the Grand River. His unpublished notes were invaluable for the sense of the big picture. Notes were prepared for the Ministry of Tourism, Culture and Recreation, Toronto, 2001.

4   For the Galinée quote, see James H. Coyne, "The Dollier-Galinée Expedition, 1669–70," Ontario Historical Society Papers and Records, Vol. 20, 75–81.

5   Ibid.

6   We enjoy clear descriptions of the Toronto Carrying Place from the 1700s. Here is but one example from fur trader Alexander Henry (1764): "The next day was calm, and we arrived at the entrance of the navigation which leads to Lake Aux Claies [Lake Simcoe]. We presently passed two short carrying-places, at each of which were several lodges of Indians containing only women and children, the men being gone to the council at Niagara. On the 18th of June we crossed Lake Au Claies, which appeared to be upward of twenty miles in length. At its further end we came to the carrying-place of Toronto. Here the Indians obliged me to carry a burden of more than a hundred pounds' weight. The day was very hot, and the woods and marshes abounded with mosquitoes; but the Indians walked at a quick pace, and I could by no means see myself left behind. The whole country was a thick forest, through which our only road was a foot-path, or such as, in America, is exclusively termed an Indian path." Quote taken from Peter Carruthers.

7   Laura Peers and Theresa Schenck, eds., *My First Years in the Fur Trade: The Journals of 1802–1804, George Nelson* (Montreal and Kingston: McGill-Queen's University Press, 2002) 48–49.

8   William Pope, albeit in relative obscurity, offered attractive illustrations of the bird life in Upper Canada. Of special note is his illustration of the now extinct passenger pigeon so common in his day. He was also a master of the cynical journal entry. After one month and a half in Canada, it is clear he had his fair share of trials. Here he rivals Susanne Moodie for the sour journal entry: "Beginning to get tired of living in the backwoods. Tales of the woods may read well in Cooper's novels or at a distance; in theory they may appear all charming and delightful – dwelling in the forest – in a log house – free and undisturbed by the cars and vanities of this deceitful busy world. What a happy life !!! How full of bliss!! Who so void of sense as not to try? And who on trying so full of idiotry as not to embrace the opportunity? That man must be a fool indeed who would not swell beneath a beautiful American forest – full of bogs and swamps – breeding-places and nurseries of fever, ague, rheumatism evils and mosquitoes – who would not look upon blackened stumps and trees and rotten unsightly logs and think them the most fascinating objects on the earth – who would not have a log house ten feet square – furniture in the most sumptuous and splendid manner – 1 – bed-stead, 2 – wooden chairs, a frying pan, and tables – and in short who would not live in the most luxurious and epicurean style on-salt-pork, sour-bread, rye-whiskey, maple-sugar and pumpkin 'sace'."

"Very hot. Busy packing up some clothes, etc. intending to set off tomorrow for the States – writing letters for England – and home. A wretched affair is a back-wood life – seasoned however with plenty of salt and chopping." In Harry B. Barrett, *The 19th Century Journals and Paintings of William Pope* (Toronto: M.F. Feheley, 1976) 26.

For more information on William Pope, see also William C. Bermingham, "Talk About the History of Otterburn: To the Mountain," Historical Society of Hamilton, Ontario, January 20, 1999; Edwin C. Guillet, *Pioneer Travel in Upper Canada* (Toronto: University of Toronto Press, 1933); *Historical Sketches of the County of Elgin* (St. Thomas, ON: The Elgin Historical and Science Institute, St. Thomas, 1895).

9   Harry B. Barrett, *The 19th Century Journals and Paintings of William Pope*, 22.
10 Ibid.
11 John Terpstra, *Falling Into Place* (Kentville, NS: Gaspereau Press, 2002) 19.

PART TWO – PRACTICES
Notes

1   David Strong, *Crazy Mountain: Learning From Wilderness to Weight Technology* (Albany, NY: State University of New York, 1995) 155–156.

2   Rocky Mountain traveller and author A.O. Wheeler wrote, "The diamond hitch, or rather series of hitches the shape of a diamond, is the combination of rope twists by which a load is kept in position on the back of a pack animal. I am not aware who invented it – he should have been knighted." See E.J. Hart, *Diamond Hitch: The Early Outfitters and Guides of Banff and Jasper* (Banff, AB: Summerthought, 1979) inside cover. This remains *the* book to learn about this very particular breed of Canadian traveller, their lifestyles and their techniques.

3   For a treatment of the Beothuk story, see Bernard Assiniwi, *The Beothuk Saga* (Toronto: McClelland & Stewart, 2000). See also Michael Crummey, *River Thieves* (Toronto: Doubleday Canada, 2001) and Edwin Tappan Adney and Howard I. Chapelle, *The Bark Canoes and Skin Boats of North America* (Washington, DC: Museum of History and Technology, Smithsonian Institution, 1964) 94–98, for a study of the unique Beothuk canoe.

4   Among the best photographs you will see of the York boat in action can be found in Ernest Carl Obertholzer, *Toward Magnetic North: The Oberholtzer-Magee 1912 Canoe Journey to Hudson Bay* (Marshall, MN: The Oberholtzer Foundation, 2000). Fort Edmonton, along the North Saskatchewan River in Edmonton, Alberta, has a number of York boat replicas. In the 1980s, one of their boats was used in a recreated trip from Rocky Mountain House to Edmonton.

5   Prince Henry Sinclair's (1345–1404), (Earl of Orkney and Envoy of the King of Norway) story is among my favourite Canadian accounts. His controversial travels in North America centre in Nova Scotia where he allegedly made his historical landfall at Guysborough in 1398. His travels and geographical descriptions match well with today's landforms. The Mi'kmaw legends of Glooscap even record a strange visitor from the east wintering over in the Bay of Fundy area. To travel the east coast in a Sinclair or Cabot or Cartier replica ship is a dream to explore in the future. For the Sinclair story, see Frederick J. Pohl, *Prince Henry Sinclair: His Expedition to the New World in 1398* (Halifax: Nimbus, 1995) and Mark Finnan, *The Sinclair Saga* (Halifax: Formac, 1999). A group *did* build a John Cabot replica ship for an Atlantic crossing and tour of Maritime, North America. For this story, see Brian Cuthbertson, *John Cabot and the Voyage of the Matthew* (Halifax: Formac, 1997).

6 – SURFACE ARCHAEOLOGY
Notes

1   Rainer Maria Rilke, *Letters to a Young Poet*.
2   See John H. Brumley, *Medicine Wheels on the Northern Plains: A Summary and*

Appraisal Archaeological Survey of Alberta (Government of Alberta, Manuscript Series No. 12, 1988). See also Geoffrey Ian Brace for his Master's Thesis from the University of Alberta 1987, titled, "Boulder Monuments of Saskatchewan" (non-published), based on archaeological examination of 33 sites. He noted, for Saskatchewan, the greatest concentration of surface stone structures was at the Big Muddy River and at the junction of Moose Mountain Creek with the Souris River, both found at the Saskatchewan-Montana border. See also Andrew Nikiforuk, "Sacred Circles," in *Canadian Geographic Journal*, July/August 1992, and Barbara Huck and Doug Whiteway, *In Search of Ancient Alberta* (Winnipeg, MB: Heartland, 1998).

3   For a detailed paper on buffalo stones, see Brian Reeves, "Iniskim: A Sacred Nitsitapii Religious Tradition," in *Kunaitupii: Coming Together of Native Sacred Sites: Their Sacredness, Conservation and Interpretation: A Native and Non-Native Forum: Proceedings of the First Joint Meeting of the Archaeological Society of Alberta and the Montana Archaeological Society, May 2–6, 1990, Waterton Lakes National Park, Alberta, Canada*, edited by Brain O.K. Reeves and Margaret A. Kennedy (Calgary: Archaeological Society of Alberta, 1993).

4   See J.H. Carpenter, "Oka-Katzi (Sundial Butte): A Report on Two Projects," No. 13 and No. 24, published by the Archaeological Society of Alberta, 1995.

5   The Many Spotted Horses site is constructed on flat ground. It is a circle of stones with four radiating lines of stone along the cardinal points. At the end of each radiating line is a slightly elevated cluster of stones. This structure known to be of recent origin and is meant to commemorate the victories in battle of the Blackfoot Chief, Many Spotted Horses. The site is on Indian Reserve land south of Calgary.

6   Geological Survey of Canada's George Dawson's story in the Queen Charlotte Islands is well told in Kathleen E. Dalzell, *The Queen Charlotte Islands, 1774–1968* (Terrace, BC: C.M. Adam, 1968).

7   Ibid.

8   For a comprehensive Haida history, see Kathleen E. Dalzell, *The Queen Charlotte Islands, Book 2: Place and Names* (Prince Rupert, BC: Cove Press, 1973).

9   For a history of the settlement patterns along the Nova Scotia Eastern Shore, see Philip L. Hartling, *Where Broad Atlantic Surges Roll* (Antigonish, NS: Formac Publishing, 1979).

10   To compare the theories of Farley Mowat and Gavin Menzies regarding the large stone dwelling houses and villages on the Bache Peninsula, Ellesmere Island and the west shore of the Kane Basin, Greenland, see Farley Mowat, *The Farfarers: Before the Norse* (Toronto: Seal Books, 1998) and Gavin Menzies, *1421: The Year China Discovered the Worlds* (London: Bantam Press, 2002) 299–313. Menzies, in particular, turns the story of exploration around the globe from 1400 to 1600 upside down with his well-researched account of the Chinese mass exploration in 1421.

11   Stephen Hume, *Ghost Camps: Memories and Myths on Canada's Frontiers* (Edmonton: NeWest, 1989).

12   Wallace Stevens, *The Necessary Angel: Essays on Reality and the Imagination* (New York: Vantage Books, 1942) 150.

Additional References

Emily Carr, *Klee Wyck* (Toronto: Oxford University Press, 1941).

Farley Mowat, S*ea of Slaughter* (Boston: Atlantic Monthly Press, 1984).

7 – CANADIAN ROCKY MOUNTAIN HIGH: BACK COUNTRY SKI HERITAGE

Notes

1   Sepp Renner, operator of Mt. Assiniboine Lodge since 1983, talking about Mt. Assiniboine and Skoki, March 2003.

2   European mountain guides had a significant role to play in promoting and teaching cross-country ski touring in Western Canada. The Duke of the Albizzi (Marquis Nicolas Albizzi) brought the first professional mountain guides to be employed to North America. They were Italian. The Vaux brothers, regular Banff tourists, suggested that the CPR hire Swiss guides to serve the tourist patrons in the mountains. One guide, Edward Feuz Jr. (1884–1981) moved permanently to Canada in 1912. He retired from guiding in 1953. For more information, see Andrew Kaufmann and William Putnam, *The Guiding Spirit* (Revelstoke, BC: Footprint, 1986).

3   Another interesting story in Canada's ski heritage involves the Norwegian Franz Wilhelmsen. Franz had turned to Alta Lake, close to Whistler Mountain of the British Columbia coastal range, to escape the busier winter slopes near Vancouver in the 1950s. He and other ski touring enthusiasts travelled here by rail. Eventually he realized that the region's mountains could easily rival European ski destinations. Soon Franz was leading a group interested in a downhill ski lift development in the early 1960s. A highway project commenced in 1964 and lifts opened at Whistler Mountain in 1965. And the rest is history. It is interesting that what began for Franz Wilhelmsen as a desire to get away for tranquil remote ski touring soon became a dream to create a crowded ski resort like those in his native Europe. For another early ski heritage story that includes the first promotion of competitive skiing in Eastern Canada, see Jon and Frankie O'Rear, *The Mont Tremblant Story* (Mont Tremblant, QC: Les Éditions Altitude, 1988).

4   "Code of the Mountains" and "A Night in the Cascade Bar" in Jim Deegan, *Timberline Tales* (Canmore, AB: Coyote Books, 1994).

5   Lorne Tetarenko and Kim Tetarenko, *Ken Jones: Mountain Man* (Calgary: Rocky Mountain Books, 1996) 13.

Additional References

Beyond evening conversations with long returning guests such as Marg and Neil Walker from Victoria and the Gormans and Harrops from Calgary, along with those from lodge operators, the following books were used as sources for this ski heritage story:

Jim Deegan, *Hotter than a Bandit's Shotgun and other Stories* (Canmore, AB: Coyote Books, 1996).

Kathryn Manry, *Skoki: Beyond the Passes* (Calgary: Rocky Mountain Books, 2001).

Ruth Oltmann, *Lizzie Rummel: Baroness of the Canadian Rockies* (Exshaw, AB: Ribbon Creek, 1983).

Erling Strom, *Pioneers on Skis* (Central Valley, NY: Smith Clove Press, 1977).

8 – ON THE HORSEBACK OUTFITTER
TRAIL WITH MARY SCHÄFFER

Notes

1   Mary T.S. Schäffer, *Old Indian Trails in the Canadian Rockies* (New York: G.P. Putnam & Sons, 1911).

2   Pearl Ann Reichwein, a colleague from the University of Alberta, wrote to me in response to an early draft of this chapter, "What you wrote about being born in to the outfitter's life reminded me of one summer night when I was at the Stoney Creek Warden Cabin in BNP [Banff National Park]. A bunch of outfitters and packers from a nearby group camp rode in to socialize. They just showed up out of the darkness outside the cabin window, wearing their hats pulled down low. Pulling out nearly drained whiskey bottles, they began outfitter and horse banter, deriding each other like you've never heard or imagined, slinging shots about gelded horses and debating who was more unfortunate, the guy originating from BC or the one from Alberta – a hot topic near the Divide. They entertained the cabin for about an hour before getting on their feet again. The leader's parting line was understated, "Sorry about the cowboys." It was half performance and half real. We couldn't stop laughing. A masterful show of storytelling bordering on the surreal." Pearl Ann eloquently captures one aspect, and only one aspect, of this distinctive culture well. Thanks, Pearl Ann.

3   Mary T.S. Schäffer, *A Hunter of Peace* (Banff, AB: Whyte Museum of the Canadian Rockies, 1980). *A Hunter of Peace* is a reprint of *Old Indian Trail* with the addition of Schäffer's heretofore unpublished account of her 1911 expedition to Maligne Lake. Quotes from Schäffer's book that follow are taken from *A Hunter of Peace.*

4   Rudyard Kipling quote from *A Hunter of Peace.*

5   British Columbia playwright Sharon Stearns has written a play about Mary and Billy Warrens' 1907 trip along with actual and fictional companions. The play, as one might expect, centres on a budding romance between Mary and Billy. Billy is twenty years her junior. The play, called "Hunter of Peace," was performed at the Alberta Theatre Project's Play Rites Festival in 1993.

6   Ralph Edwards, *The Trail to the Charmed Land* (Victoria, BC: Herbert R. Larson, 1950) v. For a long distance western horse-packing trip, see Cliff Kopas, *Packhorses to the Pacific* (Sidney, BC: Gray's Publishing, 1976).

7   Mary Schäffer Warren's letter is housed in the Whyte Museum of the Canadian Rockies. The words are taken from *A Hunter of Peace*, inside front cover.

8   For details of packhorse outfitters and guides, see E.J. Hart, *Diamond Hitch: The Early Outfitters and Guides of Banff and Jasper* (Banff, AB: Summerthought, 1979).

Additional References

Ralph Edwards, *The Trail to the Charmed Land* (Victoria, BC: Herbert R. Larson, 1950).

Jill Foran, *Mary Schaffer: An Adventurous Woman's Exploits in the Canadian Rockies* (Canmore, AB: Altitude Publishing, 2003).

J. Beck Sanford, *No Ordinary Woman: The Story of Mary* Schäffer *Warren* (Calgary, AB: Rocky Mountain Books, 2001).

Mary T.S. Schäffer, *Old Indian Trails of the Canadian Rockies: Incidents of Camp and Trail Life, Covering Two Year's Exploration through the Rocky Mountains of Canada* (Toronto: William Briggs, 1911).

9 – DOGSLEDDING: OLD CANADA AMBIENCE

Notes

1 Edward Hoagland as quoted in Wendy Bush, *Ascent of Dog: Working Dogs in the West* (Calgary: Detselig, 1998) 183.

2 For an excellent account of the Arctic travels of Knud Rasmussen, see "Knud: Champion of the Eskimos," in Frank Rasky, *The North Pole or Bust: Explorers of the North* (Toronto: McGraw-Hill Ryerson, 1977).

3 There are many exciting mentions of caribou migrations witnessed first-hand by northern travellers. My favourite is the following by the French fur trader, Captain Thierry Mallet, in the 1920s, in his excellent read about Kazan River country north and west of the Seal headwaters:

> when we saw across the river, on the horizon, a small yellow streak which seemed to be moving toward us. It looked exactly like a huge caterpillar creeping on the ground. We watched it intently. The yellow streak, little by little, grew in length and width until suddenly, in a second, it spread into a large spot, which, widening and widening on either side, still kept moving in our direction.
>
> ...on and on the horde came, straight for the narrows of the river where we were camped. While the flanks of the herd stretched irregularly a mile or so on each side of the head, the latter remained plainly pointed in the same direction. One felt instinctively the unswerving leadership which governed that immense multitude. For two hours we sat there, looking and looking, until the caribou were only a few yards from the water's edge, right across the river from where we were.
>
> ...little by little, right and left, thousands of animals lined the bank for over a mile. Behind them thousands more, which could not make their way through the closed ranks in front of them, stopped. Then all their heads went up, bucks, does, yearlings, fawns, and motionless, they looked at the Kazan River. Not a sound could be heard. My eyes ached under the strain. Beside me I could feel one of my Indian's trembling like a leaf in his excitement. I started counting and reached three thousand. Then I gave it up. There were too many.
>
> After what seemed to us an interminable pause, the leading doe and the big bucks moved forward. Unhesitatingly they walked slowly down the bank, took to the water, and started to swim across, straight for our little sandy cove.
>
> We were standing up, then, behind our fire. The first ones saw us from the water, but they never changed their direction until they touched bottom. Then they scattered slightly on either side, giving us room. The next ones followed suit. And for what seemed to us an eternity we were surrounded by a sea of caribou galloping madly inland.

See Captain Thierry Mallet, *Glimpses of the Barren Lands* (New York: Revillon Frères, 1930), 20–23.

4 The great Arctic traveller, John Rae, used the term "raise the road" to describe the task of walking in advance of the dogs. In January 1845, Rae and three companions set out from Red River for Sault Ste. Marie as part of preparations for northern survey work – four men, one dog team, 1,200 miles. When I read such matter-of-fact details in travel accounts, I usually pause and contemplate what I have just read. Amazing! See Ken McGoogan, *Fatal Passage: The Untold Story of John Rae, the Arctic Adventures Who Discovered the Fate of Franklin* (Toronto: HarperFlamingo, 2001).

5 Wendy Bush, *Ascent of Dog: Working Dogs in the West* (Calgary: Detselig Enterprises, 1998) 78.

6 See "The Journal of the Reverend J.A. Mackay," in *Saskatchewan History,* Autumn 1963, 98–9.

7 Dick North, *The Lost Patrol: The Mounties Yukon Tragedy* (Vancouver: Raincoast Books, 1995).

8 Fitzgerald's journal entry as recorded in Dick North, *The Lost Patrol.*

9 For more details about the lost patrol, see Ann Chandler, "The Lost Patrol," in *The Beaver,* Vol. 83:1, December/January 2003–04.

10 – ROCK ART: A LIFELONG
QUEST AND MYSTERY

Notes

1 Louise Erdich, *Books and Islands in Ojibwe Country* (National Geographic Press, 2002) 10.

2 John Fowles as quoted in Wayland Drew, *The Haunted Shore* (Toronto: Gage Publishing, 1983) 69.

3 Louise Erdrich suggests that the Lake of the Woods pictographs, in any case, were drawn in recent memory by Ojibwe ancestors back one generation. The ancient symbols were recognizable to them. There is some controversy here. In other circles, the suggestion is that the meanings to a region's pictographs have been lost with time.

4 Don Godwin quote taken from Luann LaSalle, "Native Spirituality Preserved in Stone," a Canadian Press story in the *Globe & Mail.*

5 In the main, I have used Grace Rajnovich's book *Reading Rock Art* as my interpretive guide for Canadian Shield images. She presents a compelling order of logic, but I realize it is still her "best guess." George Nelson's 1820 journals speaks of a distinct miniature race of cliff/cave dwellers also known as underwater man (sea man and mermaid) in the Lac La Ronge area – *Mimikwisiwak* in Nelson's 1820s Cree spelling and *Maymaygwayshi* in Dewdney's contemporary Ojibwe spelling. Travellers in canoes or human-like figures might, given fur trader George Nelson's 1820 recording, also be *O-May-Me-Thay-Day-Ace-Cae-Wuck,* or hairy-heart beings. They are the ancients, who preceded human beings in the world. They presumably are different again from "underwater men" or shamans. See Jennifer S.H. Brown and Robert Brightman, *The "Orders of the Dreamed": George Nelson on Cree and Northern Ojibwa Religion and Myth, 1823* (Winnipeg, MB: University of Manitoba Press, 1988).

Additional References

J. Conway, and T. Conway, *Spirits on Stone: The Agawa Pictographs* (San Luis Obispo, CA: Heritage Discoveries, 1990).

S. Dewdney and K.E. Kidd, *Indian Rock Paintings of the Great Lakes* (Toronto: University of Toronto Press, 1973).

M. Furtman, *Magic on the Rocks: Canoe Country Pictographs* (Duluth, MN: Birch Portage Press, 2000).

T.E.H. Jones, *The Aboriginal Rock Paintings of the Churchill River* (Saskatchewan Department of Culture and Youth, Anthropological Series 4, 1981).

J.D. Keyser, and M.A. Klassen, *Plains Indian Rock Art* (Vancouver: UBC Press, 2001).

Grace Rajnovich, *Reading Rock Art: Interpreting the Indian Rock Paintings of the Canadian Shield* (Toronto: Natural Heritage Books, 1994).

11 – TRADITIONAL WARM WINTER CAMPING: FOLLOWING EXAMPLES

Notes

1   Elliott Merrick, *True North* (New York: Charles Scribner, 1942) 256.

2   Craig Macdonald of Dwight, Ontario, has written detailed notes on the techniques for setting up a wall tent camp and hand-hauling instructions. Craig also manufacturers and sells quality winter camping gear through his company, Odawban. Contact Craig via R.R.#1, Dwight, Ontario P0A 1H0. See also Alexandra and Garrett Conover, *A Snow Walker's Companion* (Camden, MN: Ragged Mountain Press, 1995).

3   For more information on *Aki-a-Gun* see Arthur C. Twomey, *Needle to the North* (Ottawa: Oberon Press, 1982) 192. He witnesses the receiving of news from the "death-news tree, felled, and then buried upside down with the bushy end in the snow." Also see Craig Macdonald's "Aki-a-Gun" in *Nastawgan: The Quarterly Journal of the Wilderness Canoe Association*, No. 3, 1985.

4   Elliott Merrick, *True North*.

5   For a thorough treatment concerning engaging versus "disburdening" technologies, see, "The Technological Subversion of Environmental Ethics" in David Strong's *Crazy Mountain: Learning From Wilderness to Weigh Technology* (Albany, NY: State University of New York, 1995) 80–87.

6   Personal correspondence with Craig Macdonald of Dwight, Ontario.

7   Elliott Merrick, "Snowshoe Trail" in *The Long Crossing and Other Labrador Stories* (Orono, ME: University of Maine Press, 1992) 49–50.

8   To acquire a copy of the "Historical Map of Temagami 1985," contact Craig Macdonald, R.R.#1, Dwight, Ontario, P0A 1H0.

9   For the Samuel Hearne story, see Samuel Hearne, *A Journey From Prince of Wales' Fort in Hudson's Bay to the Northern Ocean* (New York: Greenwood Press, 1968). Also see Ken McGoogan, *Ancient Mariner* (Toronto: HarperPerennial Canada, 2003). This book tells the full story of Hearne's life, but errs on the side of hero worship as noted by Christopher Moore, "The Fictions of Biography" in *The Beaver*, Dec. 2004/Jan. 2005.

For the Lagimodière/Prichard story, see Jean Morrison, *Superior Rendezvous-Place: Fort William in the Canadian Fur Trade* (Toronto: Natural Heritage Books, 2001) 87. For this Peter Frenchen story, see *Arctic Adventure: My Life in the Frozen North* (New York: Farrar and Rhinehart, 1935) 448.

10 John Rae was never to receive the reward money of 10,000 English pounds for his discovery of the fate of Franklin's men. Rather he and his Inuit informants were discredited. Rae had written in *The London Times* on October 23, 1854, "our wretched countrymen had been driven to the last resource...." Rae was clear in his report that cannibalism, "as a means of prolonging existence" was employed. Charles Dickens, a staunch supporter of Franklin responded in *The Times* that Rae was not careful with his claims, and that Eskimo witnesses were "covetous, treacherous and cruel," though he'd never met one. In Dickens' opinion, the character of Franklin and his men would not succumb to such behaviour. *The Times* refused to accept Rae's report. One editorial even suggested that, "If Eskimos could live through starving times, it would be strange indeed that the white men should not have been able to accomplish the same feat." This Rae/Dickens conflict had a hand in the 1857 dramatic play by Collins and Dickens, *The Frozen Deep*, a play based on "the mighty original notion" of "the noble heart of the hero." For more on this interesting story, see Robert Louis Bannan, *Under the Management of Mr. Charles Dickens: His Production of the Frozen Deep* (Ithaca, NY: Cornell University Press, 1966). Also see "The Discovery of Truth" in Ken McGoogan, *Fatal Passage: The Untold Story of John Rae, the Arctic Adventurer Who Discovered the Fate of Franklin* (Toronto: HarperFlamingo, 2001) 201–289.

Additional References

Paul Provencher, *I Live in the Woods: A Book of Personal Recollections and Woodland Lore* (Fredericton, NB: Brunswick Press, 1953).

Calvin Rustrum, *Paradise Below Zero* (New York: Collier Books, 1968).

12 – OLD WAYS: NEW PERCEPTIONS

Notes

1 I.S. MacLaren, "Slendor Sine Occasu: Salvaging Boat Encampment" in *Canadian Literature*, 170–171, Autumn/Winter 2001, 179.

2 An exciting destination on my trip was a big river bend that looks like many others, called Popple Depot on the Nepisquit River. Appearances don't tell the story here though. From Popple Depot one can head north via Portage Brook to the Upsalquitch River to the Restigouche, then perhaps if intentions demand, up the Matapedia River to Quebec City to deliver news or mail between Saint John and Quebec City. Or, via the south branch of the Nepisquit, one could head south to a branch of the Miramichi. Popple Depot was a hub. I was on the standard east-west run. The Tobique was also used for such cross-watershed wizardry, as was the Gordon Meadow Brook (a major tributary on the Lower Nepisquit River) to the Miramichi towards the south. Get the point. In fact there are nine drainage basins in New Brunswick, a land mass so well connectable (once you settle into the upstream poling mentality) that's when the locals say, "Ah, you're in God's

country now" – which they often do – the canoeist knows God must love a good river run. This connectable nature was well-noted by many. In 1793, John Allan, a British garrison officier, reported of Native travel, "The very easy conveyance by lakes, rivers and streams so interspersed in this country, they can easy take their women, children and baggage, wherever their interest, curiosity, or caprice may lead them, and their natural propensity for roving is such that you will see families in the course of a year go through the greatest part of this extent." In a more poetic way, fisher Frederic Irland wrote of New Brunswick in 1904, "The face of that good old wilderness is seamed with 100s of wrinkles. Every wrinkle is a stream and some of them are so crooked you can scarcely tell which way they run." See Mike Parker, ed., *Rivers of Yesterday: A New Brunswick Hunting and Fishing Journal* (Halifax: Nimbus, 1997).

3   For an excellent instructional article, see Alexandra Brown Conover, "The Art of Poling a Canoe: Stand tall and carry a big stick," in *Canoeing and Kayaking Magazine*, August/Sept. 1980. She states, "as recently as 40 years ago, we could find a generation of people here on the Northeast's rivers skilled in the art of poling...roads were not as prolific as today, and rivers often were the best travel route between two points." Garret Conover has produced a fine book with poling instructions and shoulder season canoe travel operations. See *Beyond the Paddle: A Canoeist Guide to Expedition Skills* (Gardner, MN: Tilbury House, 1991).

4   See Mike Parker, *Rivers of Yesterday*....

5   Canot du maître, hybrid "express canoes, "were employed for express trips over great distances. The fastest recorded trip – from the mouth of the Columbia River at the Pacific Ocean to Hudson Bay at York Factory – is sixty-seven days." I.S. MacLaren, " 'I came to Rite Thare Portraits' ": Paul Kane's Journal of his western travels, 1846–1848" in *The American Art Journal*, Vol. xxi, No. 2, 1989, 19.

6   American writer Bil Gilbert has written a delightful essay titled, "After Franklin" in which he comes to realize that the exploration account is usually written by the explorer who is not doing the physical work of the voyageur. "We are in trouble," said Terry, a friend and travel companion, who is a pragmatist and had begun to appreciate that Franklin (the Arctic explorer) was inclined to treat portage problems casually because he did so little work on them. "We are the men he is talking about," said Terry, getting to the heart of the matter. Bil and company might have preferred to have voyageurs along with them too, but given their situation they were the workhorses whose voice isn't recorded. Later Bil noted, "We had then been out three weeks, Franklin had covered the same 120 miles in thirteen days." Really, Franklin's voyageurs had done the lion's share of this "covering!" See Bil Gilbert, "After Franklin" in *Our Nature* (Lincoln, NB: University of Nebraska Press, 1986) 3–30.

7   The first York boats were built in 1749 by Orkney Island men recruited by the Hudson's Bay Company for this reason. These first boats were used on the Albany River in competition with the North West Company. See "York Boat" in the *Canadian Encyclopedia* Vol. III (Edmonton: Hurtig, 1985).

8   Donald MacKay, *The Lumberjacks* (Toronto: McGraw-Hill Ryerson, 1978) 8. Reprinted 1986, 1998, 2002 by Natural Heritage Books, Toronto.

9   Murray McLaughlin, "Out Past the Timberline," Timberline Gullwing Music, True North Records, CAPAC, 1983: used with permission.

PART III – PEOPLE

Notes

1   Wayland Drew, *Halfway Man* (Ottawa: Oberon Press, 1989) 164.
2   Elliott Merrick, *The Long Crossing and Other Labrador Stories* (Orono, ME: University of Maine Press, 1992) xx.

13 – JOURNAL WRITING AND EXPLORERS

Notes

1   Wayne Franklin, Discovers, *Explorers, Settlers: The Diligent Writers of Early America* (Chicago: Univesity of Chicago Press, 1979) 2.
2   There are so many names I could have placed on this small list of journal writing explorers and travellers. I will showcase just one here. In 1911–12, George Douglas, from Lakefield, Ontario, travelled north exploring the region between Great Bear Lake and the Coppermine River. He was seeking the surface copper deposits that had, in part, sent Samuel Hearne travelling from Fort Prince of Wales (at the mouth of Churchill River) in 1771. Douglas' last northern trip was in 1938. Here was a well-organized, sound and wise adventurer, who certainly lived by Arctic traveller Vilhjalmur Steffanson's adage, (I paraphrase) if I had an adventure, I'd be too embarrassed to tell you about it and I quote, "A polar adventure is a sign of incompetence."

Recently I sat through an "inspirational" presentation meant for a corporate group on the Antarctic adventures and misadventures of Ernest Shackleton. Famous for returning, "eventually" from the harrowing trip without a loss of any men, he certainly delivered on his also famous recruiting notice (to which 5,000 men responded):

Men wanted for hazardous journey. Small wages. Bitter cold. Long months of complete darkness. Constant danger. Safe return doubtful.

At this Canadian presentation, Shackleton was celebrated for his leadership and elevated to hero status, a model for a corporate trainer to use now as an example to emulate. I couldn't help think (and said so, perhaps unwisely, during the Shackleton talk) that we might want to celebrate a total success story like George Douglas. Here we have a well-conceived and well-conducted expedition. No loss of lives and safe return likely. Nothing against Shackleton, but I'd suggest Douglas' efficient, calculated ways are more suited to a corporate example. I'd invest stock in a Douglas "inspired" outfit over a Shackleton one. Why do we, Canadians, not know more about George Douglas? Simple: nothing went terribly wrong. See George Douglas, *Lands Forlorn* (New York: Knickerbocker, 1914) and Enid Mallory, *Coppermine: The Far North of George M. Douglas* (Peterborough, ON: Broadview Press, 1989).
3   For some of I.S. MacLaren's work on the discrepancy between a travellers' field notes and their final book form, see I.S. MacLaren, "Writing the Wilderness Experience: A discussion of field notes, journals and books concerning Samuel Hearne's

account of the massacre at Bloody Fall," in *Nastawgan: Quarterly Journal of the Wilderness Canoe Association*, Vol. 19, No. 1, Spring 1992. See also I.S. MacLaren, " 'I came to rite thare portraits': Paul Kane's Journal of his Western Travels, 1846–1848" in *The American Art Journal*, Vol. Xxi, No. 2, 1989.

Following a winter dogsledding trip in northern Manitoba, I was interviewed for a magazine article. I was shocked to read the account in print quite different from the account I had presented. My quest to be part of the "Ways of the North" was refashioned into a high winter survival story. Thinking of MacLaren's work revealing the altering of travellers' field notes to suit the European reader of the day, I wonder how much had changed. I was more a part of a historical tradition more than I wanted to be on this occasion. See Bob Henderson "Thoughts on the idea of adventure" in Cass Adams, ed., *The Soul Unearthed: Celebrating Wildness and Spiritual Renewal Through Nature* (Boulder, CO: Sentient, 2002) 134–138.

4 This short quote is the conclusion to a much longer passage that begins, "Why then do I write?" Nelson provides three reasons: 1) "to while away some moment...a thought that oppress me," 2) "to retrace many incidents...of my past and checkered life" and 3) to share with my relatives and others "how people fared"...and "to preserve a few traits of Indian character that deserve a more conspicuous place." In Laura Peer and Theresa Schenck, eds., *My First Years in the Fur Trade: The Journals of 1802–1804 – George Nelson* (Montreal and Kingston: McGill-Queen's University Press, 2002) 31–32.

5 In Jennifer S.H. Brown and Robert Brightman, eds., *The Orders of the Dreamed: George Nelson on Cree and Northern Ojibwa Religion and Myth, 1823* (Winnipeg, MB: University of Manitoba Press, 1988) 9.

6 Peter Such, *River Run* (Toronto: Clark, Irwin, 1973).

7 See George Vancouver (W. Kaye Lamb, ed.), *The Voyage of George Vancouver, 1791–1795* (London: Hakluyt Society, 1984). For an easy read of Vancouver and others, see Steve Short and Rosemary Neering, *In the Path of the Explorers: Tracing the Expeditions of Vancouver, Cook, Mackenzie, Fraser and Thompson* (Vancouver: Whitecap Books, 1992). For a modern account of travels on the Northwest coast with attentions to Vancouver's travels, see Jonathon Raban, *Passage to Juneau: A Sea and its Meanings* (New York: Vintage Books, 1999). Raban describes an interesting moment in journal writing. Vancouver recalled (back in England) that the influence of tide and wind left him feeling, "...driven about as it were blindfolded in this labyrinth." Raban points out that at the time of writing this passage or polishing it for publication, Vancouver was lodging within six kilometres from the famous labyrinth at Hampton Court, England. This hedge-maze was originally planted in 1690. By the 1790s it was a tourist attraction, then known, in the language as a "wilderness" or, in Raban's words, "an allegory of the operations of chance and choice in human life." I wonder how Vancouver thought of his deadly coastal labyrinth in comparison to those wishing "to lose themselves, on sunny afternoons for fun." After all, he made the comparison. See Raban, 176–177.

8 Quote from David Thompson in Barbara Belyea, ed., *Columbia Journals* (Montreal and Kingston: McGill-Queen's University Press, 1994) 19.

9   Alastair McIntosh, *Soil and Soul: People versus Corporate Power* (London: Aurum Press, 2001) 2.

10. See Father Gabriel Sagard (B.M. Wrong, ed.) *The Long Journey to the Country of Hurons* (Toronto: The Champlain Society, 1939). Also see Jack Warwick, *The Long Journey: Literary Themes of French Canada* (Toronto: University of Toronto, 1973).

11   Thanks to Allan Crawford for first introducing me to this circulated e-mail message. For the full reference, see Sigurd F. Olson, *Reflections from the North Country* (Minneapolis: University of Minnesota Press, 1998) 93.

12   Jack Warwick, *The Long Journey: Literary Themes of French Canada*, 73–74.

13   I.S. MacLaren, "David Thompson on the Canadian Northwest" in *Ariel: A Review of International English Literature*, April 1984. Concerning David Thompson, also see Jack Nisbet, *Sources of the River: Tracking David Thompson Across Western North America* (Seattle, WA: Sasquatch Books, 1994).

14   See Notes #4 and #5. *My First Years in the Fur Trade...* concerns two years of George Nelson's travels. *The Orders of the Dreamed*, written twenty years later, concerns Nelson's recording of spiritual practices of Cree and Northern Ojibwe peoples. Beyond the main references for Nelson provided in Note 4, also see Sylvia Van Kirk, "This Basically and Ungrateful Country: George Nelson's Response to Rupert's Land" in Richard Davis, ed., *Rupert's Land: A Cultural Tapestry* (Waterloo, ON: Wilfrid Laurier University Press, 1988).

15   All passages concerning John McLean are from John McLean, *Notes of a Twenty Five Year's Service in the Hudson's Bay Territory* (New York: Greenwood Press, 1968) facsimile edition. The book was originally published in 1894.

16   See I.S. MacLaren, "Alexander Mackenzie and the Landscape of Commerce" in *Studies in Canadian Literature*, Vol. 7, No. 2, 1982. Mackenzie believed that the "original barbarity" of the Canadian bush and "any progress" in the conversion of indigenous peoples he encountered in exploration was hopeless. Also see Michael Bliss, "Conducted Tour" in *The Beaver*, Vol. 69:2, April/May 1986, 16–24.

14 – ROOTS AND WINGS: A PECULIAR
COLLECTION OF WOMEN'S STORIES

Notes

1   Mary T.S. Schäfer, *Old Indian Trails in the Canadian Rockies* (New York: G.P. Putnam's Sons, 1911).

2   Esther S. Keyser with Jon S. Keyser, *Paddle Your Own Canoe: The Story Of Algonquin Park's First Female Guide* (Whitney, ON: The Friends of Algonquin Park, 2003).

3   Aldo Leopold, in 1953, wrote eloquently about our North American Cultures drift to landlessness, "The problem, then, is how to bring about a striving for harmony with land among a people many of whom have forgotten their is any such thing as land, among whom education and culture have become synonymous with landlessness," in *A Sand County Almanac with essays on conservation from Round River* (New York: Oxford University Press, 1966). Molly Ames Baker from Colgate University in Hamilton, New York, coined the phrase "landfall expe-

riences" in reaction to Leopold's landlessness anxiety. She teaches a heritage-based education to support student travel experiences in her "place" of travel with students, the Adirondacks of New York State. I try to do the same work in and for the Canadian Shield.

4   Mina Hubbard's story can be found in her travel account, *A Woman's Way Through Unknown Labrador*. For the full Hubbards'/Wallace/Elson story, see James West Davidson and John Rugge, *Great Heart: The History of a Labrador Adventure* (New York: Viking, 1988).

5   In *The Embroidered Tent* by Marian Fowler. For collections of women's outdoor travel stories see Judith Niemi and Barbara Wieser, *Rivers Running Free: Stories of Adventurous Women* (Minneapolis: Bergamot Books, 1987); Cyndi Smith, *Off the Beaten Track: Women Adventures and Mountaineers in Western Canada* (Jasper, AB: Coyote Books, 1989); Marian Fowler, *The Embroidered Tent: Five Gentle Women in Early Canada* (Toronto: Anansi, 1982); Jean Johnson, *Wilderness Women: Canada's Forgotten History* (Toronto: Peter Martin Associates, 1973); Gwyneth Hoyle, "Women of Determination: Northern Journeys by Women Before 1940" in *Nastawgan: The Canadian North by Canoe and Snowshoe – A Collection of Historical Essays* (Bruce W. Hodgins and Margaret Hobbs, eds.) (Toronto: Betelgeuse Books, 1985); Les Harding, *The Journeys of Remarkable Women: Their Travels on the Canadian Frontier* (Waterloo, ON: Escart Press, University of Waterloo, 1994).

6   Alexander Henry in Les Harding, ed., *The Journeys of Remarkable Women: Their Travels on the Canadian Frontier*, 58.

7   Arthur P. Stabler, *The Legend of Marguerite de Roberval* (Pullman, WA: Washington State University Press, 1972).

8   See page 31 of *The Legend of Marguerite de Roberval* for an important synthesis of the sixteenth century accounts from the scholar of this story. One can also read the Marguerite de Roberval story in *Wilderness Women: Canada's Forgotten History*, see Note 5. Of particular interest is *Elle* by Douglas Glover (Fredericton, NB: Goose Lane Editions, 2003). *Elle* won the Governor General's Award for Canadian Fiction in 2003. The legend lives on in fine style.

15 – CAPTURING THE ARTIST'S EYE

Notes

1   Ian Tamblyn, from "Brush and Paddle" concerning Tom Thomson, *Angel's Share*, Sea Lynx Music, Socan, North Track Records. NT25, 2004).

2   Jim Waddington, "The Group of Seven in Killarney Park," in *Paddles'n Trails; Friends of Killarney Park Newsletter*, Summer 2003.

3   Jenny Cressman, "Celebrating Tom Thomson," in *The Muskokan*, July 2002, with "Northern River Revisited" by George Garland and John Ridpath within the same article.

4   Stephen Strauss, "Thomson painting's location is written in the stars," *Globe and Mail*, Ideas/Science F7, Saturday, October 18, 2003.

Additional References

Roger Boulet, *The Canadian Earth: Landscape Paintings by the Group of Seven* (Thornhill, ON: Cerebrus/Prentice-Hall, 1982).

Joan Murray, *The Best of the Group of Seven* (Edmonton: Hurtig Publishers, 1984).

Dennis Reid, ed., *Thomson* (Art Gallery of Ontario, National Gallery of Canada, Douglas and McIntyre, 2002).

Harold Town and David P. Silcox, *Tom Thomson: The Silence and The Storm* (Toronto: McClelland & Stewart, 1977).

16 – HERMITS I'D LOVE TO HAVE MET

Notes

1 Noah John Rondeau (1941) in Maitland C. De Sormo, *Noah John Rondeau: Adironack Hermit* (Utica, NY: North Country Books, 1960) 52.

2 My solo outings pale in comparison with many. Here is what veteran solo tripper Herb Pohl said about his extensive solo trips through the 1970s into the present – mainly in Labrador, the Richmond Gulf area of western Ungava and the country north of Great Slave Lake, "There is an overture, musically speaking. It takes a few days to get into the first act, to become attuned. It is not an instant process. I don't feel like I am really on a canoe trip until the end of the second or beginning of the third week. Then you are truly out there. Before that, you are still carrying the baggage of civilization. But that doesn't mean that you don't have intense experiences right from the start. It just takes a while to get in sync with everything." "Herb Pohl: A Wild and Glorious Land," an interview by Rod MacIver, in *Nastawgan: The Quarterly Journal of the Wilderness Canoe Association*, Autumn Vol. 29, No. 3, 2002, 9–12. For the solo canoe tripper side of reclusiveness, see Robert Perkins, *Against Straight Line: Alone in Labrador* (Boston: Little, Brown, 1983) and *Into the Great Solitude: An Arctic Journey* (New York: Henry Holt and Co., 1991). See also *Lonely Voyage by Kayak* to *Adventure and Discovery* by Kamil Pecher (Saskatoon, SK: Western Producer Prairie Books, 1978). Kamil paddled 1,000 kilometres (621 miles) solo along the Churchill River. He concludes his book with differing sentiments to Herb Pohl, and serves as a useful foil to keep a balanced view on the solo/loner travel experience:

> Should some of my readers cherish the idea of travelling alone in the wilderness, I have three words of advice – don't do it. It's stupid and hazardous. I know there will always be lonely trappers and prospectors, but probably they are unusual individuals. It's not worth it to go alone, just to find out that you are not that kind, that you are as vulnerable to loneliness as I was. I don't mean to imply that you would end up with ulcers. I'm probably just the type to get them, and the Churchill trip was the last drop in my cup. Actually I was lucky; your fate might be worse. And what could be better than to paddle with friends and experience the river together? *Lonely Voyages*, 182.

Read about Herb Pohl's trips in various back issues of *Nastawgan: The Quarterly Journal of the Wilderness Canoe Association*. For example, see "On the Notakwanon,"

Autumn 1985, Vol. 12, No. 3, and "Richmond Gulf Revisited," Autumn 1991, Vol. 18, No. 3.

3 Elliott Merrick, *The Long Crossing and Other Labrador Stories* (Orono, ME: University of Maine Press, 1992) 48–49.

4 Li Bai in Isabel Colegate, *A Pelican in the Wilderness: Hermits, Solitaries and Recluses* (London: HarperCollins, 2003) 5.

5 Henry David Thoreau was known to have three chairs in his cabin at Walden Pond, "one for solitude, two for friendship, three for society." In Isabel Colegate's *A Pelican in the Wilderness*, 217.

6 Isabel Colegate quotes an advertisement in an 1810 English newspaper: "A young man, who wishes to retire from the world and live as a hermit in some convenient spot in England is willing to engage with any nobleman or gentleman who maybe desirous of having one." In another ad, this time from the landowner, the terms of the ad necessitated that the hermit would receive a fee of 700 guineas if he lasted the full seven years. Apparently the hired hermit in this case lasted three weeks. He was fired after he was noticed sneaking off the grounds for the local pub, see page 187.

7 See Donald MacKay, *Anticosti: The Untamed Island* (Toronto: McGraw-Hill Ryerson, 1979).

8 There is another story about a would-be-bride who demanded a proper house, then later refused outright to call White Otter Lake home. This story is the more popular telling in poetry and song but has lost favour overall. Certainly it is a proper house like no other. See Elinor Barr, *White Otter Castle: The Legacy of Jimmy McQuat* (Thunder Bay, ON: Singing Shield Productions, 1984, revised 2003). The quotes that follow in this section are found in Elinor Barr's passionate and thorough treatment of Jimmy's life.

9 For an account of the esker wintering-over, see Guy Blanchet, "The Letter," in *The Beaver*, Spring, 1963. For an account of the story centred around the Hornby cabin on the Thelon River, see Clive Powell-Williams, *Cold Burial: A True Story of Endurance and Disaster* (New York: St. Martin's Press, 2002).

Index

About the Author

Bob Henderson teaches Outdoor Education at McMaster University, Hamilton, Ontario. Starting as a camper and canoe-tripping staff member at Camp Ahmek in Algonquin Park, he has developed a lifelong interest in Canadian travel heritage and travel guiding. Beginning in 1994, he continues to write a regular heritage travel feature for *Kanawa Magazine*. In 1995, Bob completed his Ph.D concerning approaches to travel guiding from the University of Alberta. He takes pride in baking a golden brown bannock and leading a spirited campfire singsong.